WILLIAM SHAKESPEARE

Romeo and Juliet

Edited with a Commentary by
T. J. B. SPENCER
and with an Introduction by
ADRIAN POOLE

PENGUIN BOOKS

PENGUIN CLASSICS

UK | USA | Canada | Ireland | Australia
India | New Zealand | South Africa

Penguin Books is part of the Penguin Random House group of companies
whose addresses can be found at global.penguinrandomhouse.com.

This edition first published in Penguin Books 1967
Reprinted with revised Further Reading 1996
Reissued in the Penguin Shakespeare series 2005
Reissued in Penguin Classics 2015

001

Set in PostScript Monotype Fournier
Typeset by Palimpsest Book Production Limited, Falkirk, Stirlingshire
Printed in Great Britain by Clays Ltd, St Ives plc

ISBN: 978-0-141-39647-7

www.greenpenguin.co.uk

ROMEO AND JULIET

T. J. B. SPENCER, sometime Director of the Shakespeare Institute of the University of Birmingham, was the founding editor of the New Penguin Shakespeare, for which he edited both *Romeo and Juliet* and *Hamlet*.

STANLEY WELLS is Honorary President of the Shakespeare Birthplace Trust, Emeritus Professor of Shakespeare Studies at the University of Birmingham, and General Editor of the Oxford Shakespeare. His many books include *Shakespeare: For All Time*, *Shakespeare & Co.*, *Shakespeare, Sex, and Love* and *Great Shakespeare Actors*.

ADRIAN POOLE is Professor of English Literature and a Fellow of Trinity College, Cambridge. His publications include *Shakespeare and the Victorians* and *Tragedy: Shakespeare and the Greek Example*.

C016166688

Contents

General Introduction

Every play by Shakespeare is unique. This is part of his greatness. A restless and indefatigable experimenter, he moved with a rare amalgamation of artistic integrity and dedicated professionalism from one kind of drama to another. Never shackled by convention, he offered his actors the alternation between serious and comic modes from play to play, and often also within the plays themselves, that the repertory system within which he worked demanded, and which provided an invaluable stimulus to his imagination. Introductions to individual works in this series attempt to define their individuality. But there are common factors that underpin Shakespeare's career.

Nothing in his heredity offers clues to the origins of his genius. His upbringing in Stratford-upon-Avon, where he was born in 1564, was unexceptional. His mother, born Mary Arden, came from a prosperous farming family. Her father chose her as his executor over her eight sisters and his four stepchildren when she was only in her late teens, which suggests that she was of more than average practical ability. Her husband John, a glover, apparently unable to write, was nevertheless a capable businessman and loyal townsfellow, who seems to have fallen on relatively hard times in later life. He would have been brought up as a Catholic, and may have retained

Catholic sympathies, but his son subscribed publicly to Anglicanism throughout his life.

The most important formative influence on Shakespeare was his school. As the son of an alderman who became bailiff (or mayor) in 1568, he had the right to attend the town's grammar school. Here he would have received an education grounded in classical rhetoric and oratory, studying authors such as Ovid, Cicero and Quintilian, and would have been required to read, speak, write and even think in Latin from his early years. This classical education permeates Shakespeare's work from the beginning to the end of his career. It is apparent in the self-conscious classicism of plays of the early 1590s such as the tragedy of *Titus Andronicus*, *The Comedy of Errors*, and the narrative poems *Venus and Adonis* (1592–3) and *The Rape of Lucrece* (1593–4), and is still evident in his latest plays, informing the dream visions of *Pericles* and *Cymbeline* and the masque in *The Tempest*, written between 1607 and 1611. It inflects his literary style throughout his career. In his earliest writings the verse, based on the ten-syllabled, five-beat iambic pentameter, is highly patterned. Rhetorical devices deriving from classical literature, such as alliteration and antithesis, extended similes and elaborate wordplay, abound. Often, as in *Love's Labour's Lost* and *A Midsummer Night's Dream*, he uses rhyming patterns associated with lyric poetry, each line self-contained in sense, the prose as well as the verse employing elaborate figures of speech. Writing at a time of linguistic ferment, Shakespeare frequently imports Latinisms into English, coining words such as abstemious, addiction, incarnadine and adjunct. He was also heavily influenced by the eloquent translations of the Bible in both the Bishops' and the Geneva versions. As his experience grows, his verse and prose become more supple,

the patterning less apparent, more ready to accommo-
date the rhythms of ordinary speech, more colloquial in
diction, as in the speeches of the Nurse in *Romeo and
Juliet*, the characterful prose of Falstaff and Hamlet's
soliloquies. The effect is of increasing psychological
realism, reaching its greatest heights in *Hamlet*, *Othello*,
King Lear, *Macbeth* and *Antony and Cleopatra*. Gradually
he discovered ways of adapting the regular beat of the
pentameter to make it an infinitely flexible instrument for
matching thought with feeling. Towards the end of his
career, in plays such as *The Winter's Tale*, *Cymbeline* and
The Tempest, he adopts a more highly mannered style,
in keeping with the more overtly symbolical and emblem-
atical mode in which he is writing.

So far as we know, Shakespeare lived in Stratford till
after his marriage to Anne Hathaway, eight years his
senior, in 1582. They had three children: a daughter,
Susanna, born in 1583 within six months of their marriage,
and twins, Hamnet and Judith, born in 1585. The next
seven years of Shakespeare's life are virtually a blank.
Theories that he may have been, for instance, a school-
master, or a lawyer, or a soldier, or a sailor, lack evidence
to support them. The first reference to him in print, in
Robert Greene's pamphlet *Greene's Groatsworth of Wit*
of 1592, parodies a line from *Henry VI, Part III*, implying
that Shakespeare was already an established playwright.
It seems likely that at some unknown point after the birth
of his twins he joined a theatre company and gained
experience as both actor and writer in the provinces and
London. The London theatres closed because of plague
in 1593 and 1594; and during these years, perhaps recog-
nizing the need for an alternative career, he wrote and
published the narrative poems *Venus and Adonis* and *The
Rape of Lucrece*. These are the only works we can be

certain that Shakespeare himself was responsible for
putting into print. Each bears the author's dedication to
Henry Wriothesley, Earl of Southampton (1573–1624),
the second in warmer terms than the first. Southampton,
younger than Shakespeare by ten years, is the only person
to whom he personally dedicated works. The Earl may
have been a close friend, perhaps even the beautiful and
adored young man whom Shakespeare celebrates in his
Sonnets.

The resumption of playing after the plague years saw
the founding of the Lord Chamberlain's Men, a company
to which Shakespeare was to belong for the rest of his
career, as actor, shareholder and playwright. No other
dramatist of the period had so stable a relationship with a
single company. Shakespeare knew the actors for whom
he was writing and the conditions in which they performed.
The permanent company was made up of around twelve
to fourteen players, but one actor often played more than
one role in a play and additional actors were hired as
needed. Led by the tragedian Richard Burbage (1568–1619)
and, initially, the comic actor Will Kemp (d. 1603), they
rapidly achieved a high reputation, and when King James
I succeeded Queen Elizabeth I in 1603 they were renamed
as the King's Men. All the women's parts were played by
boys; there is no evidence that any female role was ever
played by a male actor over the age of about eighteen.
Shakespeare had enough confidence in his boys to write
for them long and demanding roles such as Rosalind (who,
like other heroines of the romantic comedies, is disguised
as a boy for much of the action) in *As You Like It*, Lady
Macbeth and Cleopatra. But there are far more fathers
than mothers, sons than daughters, in his plays, few if any
of which require more than the company's normal complement of three or four boys.

The company played primarily in London's public playhouses – there were almost none that we know of in the rest of the country – initially in the Theatre, built in Shoreditch in 1576, and from 1599 in the Globe, on Bankside. These were wooden, more or less circular structures, open to the air, with a thrust stage surmounted by a canopy and jutting into the area where spectators who paid one penny stood, and surrounded by galleries where it was possible to be seated on payment of an additional penny. Though properties such as cauldrons, stocks, artificial trees or beds could indicate locality, there was no representational scenery. Sound effects such as flourishes of trumpets, music both martial and amorous, and accompaniments to songs were provided by the company's musicians. Actors entered through doors in the back wall of the stage. Above it was a balconied area that could represent the walls of a town (as in *King John*), or a castle (as in *Richard II*), and indeed a balcony (as in *Romeo and Juliet*). In 1609 the company also acquired the use of the Blackfriars, a smaller, indoor theatre to which admission was more expensive, and which permitted the use of more spectacular stage effects such as the descent of Jupiter on an eagle in *Cymbeline* and of goddesses in *The Tempest*. And they would frequently perform before the court in royal residences and, on their regular tours into the provinces, in non-theatrical spaces such as inns, guildhalls and the great halls of country houses.

Early in his career Shakespeare may have worked in collaboration, perhaps with Thomas Nashe (1567–c. 1601) in *Henry VI, Part I* and with George Peele (1556–96) in *Titus Andronicus*. And towards the end he collaborated with George Wilkins (*fl.* 1604–8) in *Pericles*, and with his younger colleagues Thomas Middleton (1580–1627), in *Timon of Athens*, and John Fletcher (1579–1625), in *Henry*

VIII, *The Two Noble Kinsmen* and the lost play *Cardenio*. Shakespeare's output dwindled in his last years, and he died in 1616 in Stratford, where he owned a fine house, New Place, and much land. His only son had died at the age of eleven, in 1596, and his last descendant died in 1670. New Place was destroyed in the eighteenth century but the other Stratford houses associated with his life are maintained and displayed to the public by the Shakespeare Birthplace Trust.

One of the most remarkable features of Shakespeare's plays is their intellectual and emotional scope. They span a great range from the lightest of comedies, such as *The Two Gentlemen of Verona* and *The Comedy of Errors*, to the profoundest of tragedies, such as *King Lear* and *Macbeth*. He maintained an output of around two plays a year, ringing the changes between comic and serious. All his comedies have serious elements: Shylock, in *The Merchant of Venice*, almost reaches tragic dimensions, and *Measure for Measure* is profoundly serious in its examination of moral problems. Equally, none of his tragedies is without humour: Hamlet is as witty as any of his comic heroes, *Macbeth* has its Porter, and *King Lear* its Fool. His greatest comic character, Falstaff, inhabits the history plays and *Henry V* ends with a marriage, while *Henry VI, Part III*, *Richard II* and *Richard III* culminate in the tragic deaths of their protagonists.

Although in performance Shakespeare's characters can give the impression of a superabundant reality, he is not a naturalistic dramatist. None of his plays is explicitly set in his own time. The action of few of them (except for the English histories) is set even partly in England (exceptions are *The Merry Wives of Windsor* and the Induction to *The Taming of the Shrew*). Italy is his favoured location. Most of his principal story-lines derive from printed writings; but the structuring and translation of these narratives into dramatic terms is Shakespeare's own, and he invents much additional material. Most of the plays contain elements of myth and legend, and many derive from ancient or more recent history or from romantic tales of ancient times and faraway places. All reflect his reading, often in close detail. Holinshed's *Chronicles* (1577, revised 1587), a great compendium of English, Scottish and Irish history, provided material for his English history plays. The *Lives of the Noble Grecians and Romans* by the Greek writer Plutarch, finely translated into English from the French by Sir Thomas North in 1579, provided much of the narrative material, and also a mass of verbal detail, for his plays about Roman history. Some plays are closely based on shorter individual works: *As You Like It*, for instance, on the novel *Rosalynde* (1590) by his near-contemporary Thomas Lodge (1558–1625), *The Winter's Tale* on *Pandosto* (1588) by his old rival Robert Greene (1558–92) and *Othello* on a story by the Italian Giraldi Cinthio (1504–73). And the language of his plays is permeated by the Bible, the Book of Common Prayer and the proverbial sayings of his day.

Shakespeare was popular with his contemporaries, but his commitment to the theatre and to the plays in performance is demonstrated by the fact that only about half of his plays appeared in print in his lifetime, in slim paperback volumes known as quartos, so called because they were made from printers' sheets folded twice to form four leaves (eight pages). None of them shows any sign that he was involved in their publication. For him, performance was the primary means of publication. The most frequently reprinted of his works were the nondramatic poems – the erotic *Venus and Adonis* and the more moralistic *The Rape of Lucrece*. The *Sonnets*, which appeared in 1609, under his name but possibly without his consent, were less successful, perhaps because the vogue for sonnet sequences, which peaked in the 1590s, had passed by then. They were not reprinted until 1640, and then only in garbled form along with poems by other writers. Happily, in 1623, seven years after he died, his colleagues John Heminges (1556–1630) and Henry Condell (d. 1627) published his collected plays, including eighteen that had not previously appeared in print, in the first Folio, whose name derives from the fact that the printers' sheets were folded only once to produce two leaves (four pages). Some of the quarto editions are badly printed, and the fact that some plays exist in two, or even three, early versions creates problems for editors. These are discussed in the Account of the Text in each volume of this series.

Shakespeare's plays continued in the repertoire until the Puritans closed the theatres in 1642. When performances resumed after the Restoration of the monarchy in 1660 many of the plays were not to the taste of the times, especially because their mingling of genres and failure to meet the requirements of poetic justice offended against the dictates of neoclassicism. Some, such as *The Tempest* (changed by John Dryden and William Davenant in 1667 to suit contemporary taste), *King Lear* (to which Nahum Tate gave a happy ending in 1681) and *Richard III* (heavily adapted by Colley Cibber in 1700 as a vehicle for his own talents), were extensively rewritten; others fell into neglect. Slowly they regained their place in the repertoire, and they continued to be reprinted, but it was not until the great actor David Garrick (1717–79) organized a spectacular jubilee in Stratford in 1769 that Shakespeare began to be regarded as a transcendental genius. Garrick's idolatry prefigured the enthusiasm of critics such as Samuel Taylor Coleridge (1772–1834) and William Hazlitt (1778–1830). Gradually Shakespeare's reputation spread abroad, to Germany, America, France and to other European countries.

During the nineteenth century, though the plays were generally still performed in heavily adapted or abbreviated versions, a large body of scholarship and criticism began to amass. Partly as a result of a general swing in education away from the teaching of Greek and Roman texts and towards literature written in English, Shakespeare became the object of intensive study in schools and universities. In the theatre, important turning points were the work in England of two theatre directors, William Poel (1852–1934) and his disciple Harley Granville-Barker (1877–1946), who showed that the application of knowledge, some of it newly acquired, of early staging conditions to performance of the plays could render the original texts viable in terms of the modern theatre. During the twentieth century appreciation of Shakespeare's work, encouraged by the availability of audio, film and video versions of the plays, spread around the world to such an extent that he can now be claimed as a global author.

The influence of Shakespeare's works permeates the English language. Phrases from his plays and poems – 'a tower of strength', 'green-eyed jealousy', 'a foregone conclusion' – are on the lips of people who may never have read him. They have inspired composers of songs, orchestral music and operas; painters and sculptors; poets, novelists and film-makers. Allusions to him appear in pop songs, in advertisements and in television shows. Some of his characters – Romeo and Juliet, Falstaff, Shylock and Hamlet – have acquired mythic status. He is valued for his humanity, his psychological insight, his wit and humour, his lyricism, his mastery of language, his ability to excite, surprise, move and, in the widest sense of the word, entertain audiences. He is the greatest of poets, but he is essentially a dramatic poet. Though his plays have much to offer to readers, they exist fully only in performance. In these volumes we offer individual introductions, notes on language and on specific points of the text, suggestions for further reading and information about how each work has been edited. In addition we include accounts of the ways in which successive generations of interpreters and audiences have responded to challenges and rewards offered by the plays. The Penguin Shakespeare series aspires to remove obstacles to understanding and to make pleasurable the reading of the work of the man who has done more than most to make us understand what it is to be human.

Stanley Wells

The Chronology of
Shakespeare's Works

A few of Shakespeare's writings can be fairly precisely dated. An allusion to the Earl of Essex in the chorus to Act V of *Henry V*, for instance, could only have been written in 1599. But for many of the plays we have only vague information, such as the date of publication, which may have occurred long after composition, the date of a performance, which may not have been the first, or a list in Francis Meres's book *Palladis Tamia*, published in 1598, which tells us only that the plays listed there must have been written by that year. The chronology of the early plays is particularly difficult to establish. Not everyone would agree that the first part of *Henry VI* was written after the third, for instance, or *Romeo and Juliet* before *A Midsummer Night's Dream*. The following table is based on the 'Canon and Chronology' section in *William Shakespeare: A Textual Companion*, by Stanley Wells and Gary Taylor, with John Jowett and William Montgomery (1987), where more detailed information and discussion may be found.

The Two Gentlemen of Verona	1590–91
The Taming of the Shrew	1590–91
Henry VI, Part II	1591
Henry VI, Part III	1591

Introduction

TOO SWIFT, TOO SLOW

Live fast, die young. Or so an influential motto from the later decades of the twentieth century has it, inspired by the life and early death of the film star James Dean. But what does it mean? You can take it as encapsulating a great Romantic myth, to which too many celebrities in the rich First World – and nonentities in their wake – have sacrificed their lives. At its most dignified it expresses a belief in heroism, that it's best to go out in a blaze of glory at the height of your powers or at least on the brink of attaining them. The horror, the tragedy even, would be to grow old, ordinary and boring, like your parents. But there's another way of understanding this motto. Suppose it is the parents speaking: '*If* you live fast, . . .' Then it sounds like the kind of sensible, hopeless advice that grown-ups give the young about the risk of living so fast they'll burn up or crash.

You can hear it either way. *Romeo and Juliet* is a hymn to youth, to passion, to speed, to danger. It is also a warning, a memento mori. It is scarcely the only play of Shakespeare's to pose such a challenge to the audience, at once inviting and frustrating the impulses to sympathy and judgement, insisting we hear the conflicting voices and see the contrary points of view. But it boasts a profusion of collisions at many levels, as if at some point in the mid 1590s Shakespeare determined to write a play characterized by the convergence of mighty opposites, in its subject matter (love and death), in its characters (youth and age), in the verbal medium in which they move (the formal and the colloquial), in the genres with which the play associates itself (comedy and tragedy), in the explanations it offers for its culminating catastrophe (fate and accident). The play reverberates with contrasts, between light and dark, night and day, joy and grief, festival and funeral. But it is in the rapid transition from one to the other and their shimmering co-existence that its distinctive qualities are most fully displayed.

Romeo and Juliet owes its legendary status to the doubleness with which it represents the fast life and early death of the young lovers. Speed inspires and exhilarates. It also terrifies, as Juliet acknowledges when she first senses that things have moved too fast, 'Too like the lightning, which doth cease to be | Ere one can say "It lightens"' (II.2.119–20). Romeo and Tybalt will also go 'to't . . . like lightning' (III.1.172), and Romeo remembers the 'lightning before death' that men are often supposed to experience (V.3.90, 91). Light so swift is like fire, which can both create and destroy. 'O for a Muse of fire', the Chorus yearns at the opening of *Henry V*. 'Gallop apace, you fiery-footed steeds', begs Juliet (III.2.1). Of course the young should live fast. But *must* they die? 'What is love? 'Tis not hereafter', sings Feste in *Twelfth Night*. 'Youth's a stuff will not endure' (II.3.45, 50). But youth cut off in its prime is a 'stuff' that can endure in art, in memory, in the golden monuments the bereaved fathers agree to provide for their dead offspring (V.3.299–304). Amidst the well-populated canon of tragic lovers, Romeo and Juliet achieve their celebrity by the combination of their youth, the mutuality of their passion for each other and the absence of any shadow of infidelity between them. There simply isn't time. Their tragedy is that the first time is also the last time. They achieve the immortality of legend by dying before they have time to slow down, grow up, grow old. What a waste. Or what a way to go.

Many interpretations of the play try to decide between these conclusions. The story touches a nerve. Someone must be to blame. Stern-minded moralists try to blame the young lovers for their own early deaths. Arthur Brooke, for example, who provided Shakespeare with his immediate source for the story (see below), describes them as 'a couple of unfortunate lovers, thralling themselves to unhonest desire, neglecting the authority and advice of parents and friends'. (But to thrall yourself can be so thrilling.) The twentieth-century poet W. H. Auden thought Romeo and Juliet were damned. There have always been commentators ready to argue that Shakespeare's first audiences would have found good reason to condemn the young lovers. They are secretive, deceitful, impatient, hasty, passionate, volatile, extreme. Above all they disobey their parents. The fact that they are Italian may have made it easier for an Elizabethan audience to view them as exotic foreigners and Verona as a world elsewhere. But Italians do not have a monopoly on impatient rebellious youngsters.

Nor do Elizabethans. But in staging such a clash between parents and children, the play was dramatizing matters of urgent debate for Shakespeare's first audiences. Was marriage primarily a social, economic, political institution, to be organized by the leading members

of the families concerned, especially the fathers? In a
society so hierarchically arranged you could expect
pressure from above and beyond your immediate family,
in the form of an aristocratic patron for example, or
even, if you had the misfortune to fall within the orbit
of the court, from royalty itself. From such a perspective the idea of the young bride and groom choosing
each other for themselves was an absurdity. There are
of course many societies and cultures in the world today
in which such absence of choice is the norm. Some
members of an Elizabethan audience would certainly
have felt this way, and Shakespeare offered them some
support by making his Juliet even younger than she is in
his immediate source, lowering her age from sixteen to
thirteen. (Anxieties about 'under-age' sex have made
later adapters raise it again or omit all reference to it.)
But disapproving Elizabethans must have been dis-
appointed that Juliet's father is not endowed with more
gravity and her mother with more tenderness, and that
Romeo's parents almost entirely slip out of the picture.
The violence that the generally jovial Capulet unleashes
towards his daughter in Act III, scene 5 can be, in
performance, extremely shocking. Whatever ideas an
audience may entertain about the rights of parents to
abuse their children, it's clear there must have been plenty
of Elizabethans who identified with a different concep-
tion of marriage, newly emerging out of Protestant and
humanist beliefs in individual choice. The idea that a
young man and woman might decide for themselves has
become sufficiently familiar to readers and audiences in
the rich First World that there's a danger of forgetting
how novel and exciting it once was, what a 'prodigious
birth' it must once have been, to borrow Juliet's unforgettable phrase (I.5.140). Social historians and literary

critics used to argue about what 'an Elizabethan audience' would have believed on this, or any other matter,
conveniently ignoring the capacity of audiences for
thinking, believing and wanting different things all at
once.

In the last years of the sixteenth century Shakespeare's
play must have seemed daringly original in challenging
a lot of ancient assumptions about marriage. We should
not ignore all the taboos the young lovers defy by
marrying in such haste and secrecy, and in the theatre
we may feel anxious about our complicity with this
furtive act. Where are the witnesses to give the sacrament of marriage its blessing (II.6)? In Brooke's poem
(1562) and Baz Luhrmann's film (1996, see below) the
Nurse bears witness to the ceremony. But in
Shakespeare's play, although the Friar hopes the heavens
will smile upon 'this holy act', no one else gets to do so
because it happens in private offstage. We the audience
are the nearest thing to a witness, and this should make
us uneasy, partly responsible, a bit like the third person
on stage here apart from the lovers, Friar Laurence
himself. When it comes to judging the three characters
involved in this holy but secretive act, the verdicts 'innocent' or 'guilty' are both too simple. The theatre is not
a court of law. But it does stage questions of justice and
the difficulty of reaching judgements by enlisting the
audience as engaged witnesses who participate in the
unfolding events, the 'evidence'. This makes us attend
with particular interest not only to the lovers themselves
and the parents they disobey, but to the other characters
on stage who go between them, whose 'good counsel'
they so urgently need, most notably the Friar and the
Nurse, the surrogate father and mother, the 'old folks'.
Why are they so 'Unwieldy, slow, heavy and pale as

lead', moans Juliet (II.5.15)? But: 'Too swift arrives as
tardy as too slow', urges the Friar (II.6.15).

NARRATIVE, DRAMA AND TIME

The story of Romeo and Juliet was well known at least
to the educated members of Shakespeare's first audiences
in the 1590s. (There is no certainty about the date of its
first performance, but we have two quarto texts of the
play from 1597 and 1599; see An Account of the Text.)
Shakespeare's main immediate source was a popular poem
by Arthur Brooke, *The Tragicall Historye of Romeus and
Juliet* (first published in 1562), itself based on a French
version by Pierre Boaistuau of an Italian tale by Matteo
Bandello and others before him. These various tellings
take different positions on the rights and wrongs of the
lovers' defiance of their parents. But the plot or the
sequence of main events remained constant and in this
respect Shakespeare's play follows Brooke's poem closely:
there is the lovers' first meeting at the Capulet feast, the
brawl that leads to Romeo's banishment, the scheme to
save Juliet from an arranged marriage, Romeo's receipt
of the news of her false death, the lovers' reunion in the
tomb, the reconciliation of their two families. All Shakespeare's significant characters are also present in Brooke
and his predecessors, but some are developed out of mere
hints, most notably the figure of Mercutio, to whom
Brooke makes only a single brief reference. Shakespeare
does similar things elsewhere, as for example with the
figure of Enobarbus in *Antony and Cleopatra*, his source
for this and his other Roman plays being the Greek author
Plutarch (whose *Lives of the Noble Grecians and Romans*
were translated by Sir Thomas North in 1579).

But the single most important change wrought by Shakespeare on his sources is almost always the transformation of narrative into drama, with the consequential effects on time and timing. Performance on stage occurs in 'real time', a present tense shared by actors and audience, as written narrative does not. (It is true that this becomes complicated when a written story is read aloud to others, and hence in a sense 'performed'.) Dramatists can counteract or complement this sense of the here and now by various means that indicate the lapse of days, months or even years in the course of performance. Shakespeare does this with the help of his Choruses in *Henry V* and *The Winter's Tale*, and Anton Chekhov with the intervals that allow time to pass silently between the end of one Act and the start of another. Elsewhere, especially in the histories and tragedies, in both *Henry IV* plays, *Julius Caesar*, *King Lear* and *Macbeth*, Shakespeare can less blatantly insinuate a sense that more time is passing than is taken up by the scenes we are actually watching. This sleight of hand is mainly achieved through the shift of scene from place to place, which creates a sense that offstage space accommodates larger passages of time than onstage. Simply speaking, time passes more swiftly behind the scenes.

But this is not so in *Romeo and Juliet*. One must qualify this slightly. The Nurse says she teases Juliet 'sometimes' by comparing Romeo unfavourably with Paris, and Juliet recalls that she has also praised him to the skies 'So many thousand times' (see notes to II.4.199 and III.5.240). Together they imply a much longer, more habitual passage of time than can possibly be the literal case. Like Mercutio's 'wit of cheverel, that stretches from an inch narrow to an ell broad' (II.4.82–3), this gives time a slightly elastic quality. There is also a certain elasticizing of the time Romeo spends banished in Mantua, while Friar John is delayed in the plague-house and prevented from delivering the crucial letter. In real Elizabethan London he could not have left such a house until several weeks after the last death from plague, or recovery from it.

Apart from these slight exceptions Shakespeare has taken positive pains to compress the time and space provided by his narrative source(s), and allow little respite from it. In his usual fashion he radically condenses the time-span of the story-line he gets from his source. This means that events which in Brooke are spread out over at least nine months are concentrated into four days and nights. The action begins on Sunday morning; Romeo and Juliet meet for the first time that evening at the Capulet feast; Monday afternoon sees them married, Tybalt and Mercutio killed and Romeo banished; the lovers spend their one and only night together and separate on Tuesday morning; Juliet gets the drug from the Friar later that day, and takes it that night; Romeo gets the news of her death next day in Mantua and arrives at her tomb on Wednesday night just before she comes round, and they die, almost together; the play seems to conclude in the glooming dawn of Thursday morning. Though it does not sport a neo-Aristotelian unity of time as *The Tempest* does (in which the real time of performance matches the fictional time of the events represented), it is plotted with unusual attention to the clock. We are regularly reminded of the time of day or night, that the clock has just struck nine (I.1.161), that 'the bawdy hand of the dial is now upon the prick of noon' (II.4.109–10), or that the second cock has crowed, the curfew bell rung and it's three o'clock in the morning (IV.4.3–4). Less prosaically the young lovers mark the time of their unions and partings by the natural phenomena of light and darkness, sun and moon, and birdsong. The time of year is also specific. This is mid July, just over two weeks before Lammastide (1 August) (I.3.17), 'these hot days' when 'the mad blood [is] stirring' (III.1.4). Shakespeare is always alert to temperature, a word related to 'temper' and 'tempest', to being 'mistempered' (I.1.87) and 'distempered' (II.3.29, 36), and thus to ideas of time and timing. The bodies in this play are exposed to the elements – as the audience and performers were, for real, in the open-air public playhouses of Elizabethan London.

The result of all this condensation is that there is no time to spare, and hardly any space to breathe. After their marriage Brooke allows the lovers to meet every night for a month or two before the disastrous fight with Tybalt. Shakespeare gives them no such leisure. With characteristic cruelty he dooms Romeo to the fight with Tybalt *before* the marriage is consummated, so that the single night he shares with Juliet is correspondingly shadowed – and precious. 'Gallop apace . . .', says Juliet, hymning the night of love that lies ahead, oblivious as yet to the blood-guilt Romeo will bring to their bed (III.2.1). Queen Mab 'gallops night by night | Through lovers' brains' (I.4.70–71). And the play itself gallops apace to a lodging less ethereal than that of the classical sun god, the darkness of the Capulets' tomb. The play is full of images of high velocity, of birds and winds and wings and tennis balls. When Juliet hurtles onstage for her marriage to Romeo, Friar Laurence greets her with one of the play's most telling reflections: 'Here comes the lady. O, so light a foot | Will ne'er wear out the everlasting flint' (II.6.16–17). So far from wearing it out, the story of a life may make no impression whatever on the unyielding world over which it passes, so light, so swift, so ephemeral. The Friar's 'ever-lasting flint' here points to a grimmer truth than that which the fathers vow at the end they'll enshrine in the 'pure gold' of their children's statues.

TRAGEDY, ROPERY AND DRUDGERY

No one before Shakespeare had put so much comedy into a tragic drama. No one had put such a young couple at its centre. The play has much in common with the world of Shakespeare's comedies, with an earlier play associated with Verona (*The Two Gentlemen of Verona*), with *A Midsummer Night's Dream* (from which Mercutio's brilliant Queen Mab speech (I.4.53–95) seems like a mischievous migrant), and with the later and darker *Measure for Measure* (where two young lovers, one of whom is called Juliet, find themselves more shamefully oppressed by the tortured and debased sexuality surrounding them, in a Vienna that could be another Verona). On the face of it the efforts of young lovers to outwit their seniors sound more like matter for comedy than tragedy, and for the first half of *Romeo and Juliet* an audience who didn't know the play at all (and arrived too late to hear the prologue) could be forgiven for expecting it to end happily, with the young vindicated and the parents quashed. This is what happens in *A Midsummer Night's Dream*, a play evidently written close in time to *Romeo and Juliet*, just before or just after. The two plays reflect on each other, not least in their treatment of accident, the relations between 'hap' and 'happiness'. This is especially true of the final scenes at the tombs, the Capulets' and, in *A Midsummer Night's Dream*, Ninus'. When Bottom and his mates present to

Theseus and his court 'a tedious brief scene of young Pyramus | And his love Thisbe' (V.1.56–7), we see a travesty, a grotesque miniature version of what in the other play seems for real. Yet throughout *Romeo and Juliet*, not excluding the final scene itself, there are elements of the grotesque that verge on the comical – 'very tragical mirth' (to borrow from Bottom and his friends (V.1.57)). It would not take much to avert the catastrophe in the Capulet vault and turn the scene into a 'happy ending'. It's instructive to see the parodies and burlesques beloved by the nineteenth century doing exactly this, gleefully resurrecting all the corpses for a jolly final knees-up. In one of the best of these travesties, *The Cup of Cold Poison* by Andrew Halliday (1859), the final scene has Queen Mab rising from beneath the earth to resuscitate all the dead characters. She is followed by the insulted Ghost of Shakespeare but he's swiftly appeased by Romeo and the Nurse. (Nicely conflated with the Mrs Gamp of Dickens's *Martin Chuzzlewit*, the latter makes much of the fact that her friend 'Mrs Harris' rhymes with 'Paris'.) The Nurse triumphantly points out to the assembled company that the best defence of burlesque has been provided by Shakespeare himself: look at the last Act of *A Midsummer Night's Dream*. The abashed Bard redescends in silence. 'I had him there', she chuckles.

But in Shakespeare's play the corpses are for real, as we say, and they stay where they are until the performance is concluded, when the players get to their feet to rejoin the world of the audience. It is certainly a tragedy, officially at least. But again we must take the force of Shakespeare's originality, for in *Romeo and Juliet* he is doing extraordinary things with genre, and in this respect he is paving the way for his own later experiments in such wonderfully unpredictable plays as *Hamlet*, *Measure for Measure*, *Troilus and Cressida*, *King Lear* and *The Winter's Tale*. In his *Apology for Poetry* (written 1579–80 and published 1595) Sir Philip Sidney had objected to the way contemporary dramatists, unlike their classical forebears in Greece and Rome, mixed up the kings and the clowns, the high life and low life. He would have been particularly perplexed by a tragedy that has no kings at all and a good deal of low life, of what the Nurse calls 'ropery' (II.4.143). Like the Capulet servant entrusted with the guest-list for the old accustomed feast, the Nurse has to do a lot of 'trudging' or 'trudging about' (I.3.35, I.2.34). It's all very well for the wanton young to race and idle around, but someone has to do the dirty work: 'I am the drudge, and toil in your delight', she reminds the eager Juliet (II.5.75).

Verona does have a prince and more than one count (Anselm as well as Paris), but it is mainly composed of 'streets' and a 'household', both of them seething with low life, with ropery and drudgery. The Montagues and Capulets seem less like nobles than well-to-do citizens, the latter in particular. There is plenty of food and drink. The servant sent out with invitations to the feast boasts of his master 'the great rich Capulet' (I.2.78) and the Nurse tells Romeo that the man who 'lays hold of Juliet' will have 'the chinks' (I.5.116–17). The daughter of the house, the one surviving child, is an heiress. We get a flavour of the comfortable, unpatrician world her family move in from the guest list, with its signors, counts, their sisters and nieces and someone intriguingly called 'the lively Helena' (I.2.69). Though the play does not require a large cast – in Shakespeare's time it could have been performed, with doubling, by a company of twelve or so, with a few extras – the minor roles contribute a vital

sense of the ordinary world out of which the exceptional
events erupt. There are the quarrelsome servants,
Sampson, Gregory and Abram, and three or four citizens who try to break up their fight (I.1); there is the
Capulet servant who can't read the names on the guest
list (I.2) and the others who bustle to and fro preparing
the festivities, amongst them Anthony and Potpan, Susan
Grindstone and Nell; there is the Nurse's man Peter,
played in the 1590s by the company's resident clown,
Will Kemp (we know this from a stage direction that
names him: see note to IV.5.100); the musicians he teases
are called Simon Catling, Hugh Rebeck and James
Soundpost; the County Paris's Page and Romeo's man
Balthasar get caught up in the bloody finale. The under-
world of these minor figures is not separated from the
sphere in which the rich citizens and their families move
but densely interwined with it. These 'low' figures may
not be able to read but they can still play with words.
Notice the pleasure a Capulet servant takes in the fact
that 'Nurse' rhymes with 'curse' (I.3.102–3); another
quips that a wooden head helps when you have to fetch
logs, and his master banters back: 'A merry whoreson,
ha! | Thou shalt be loggerhead' (IV.4.18–21). The great
representative of all these figures in the play is the Nurse,
who is in some sense at the heart of the Capulet household.

   The passages involving these minor 'low' figures are
always liable to abridgement in performance, not least
because some of the jokes may be incomprehensible to
modern audiences: the opening exchange between
Sampson and Gregory, and the scene with the musicians
for instance (IV.5.96–144). Nevertheless they are essen-
tial to a full reading of Shakespeare's text. They root it
in the everyday world where people have to work, trudge

and drudge, get bossed about, tired and bored – the world where bones ache. They see the world from 'below'. They represent the mundane, creaturely and at times brutal demands of the body, for physical gratification and relief. Together they compose a perspective that complements the lovers' view of themselves and each other, against which to measure it. As their spokespersons they have two major characters (who can often steal the show in performance). The Nurse and Mercutio blatantly belong to the world of comedy in the base sense that they spend a lot of time more or less deliberately cracking jokes and witticisms. But whereas the Nurse is in social terms 'low', Mercutio is as well born as the world of the play allows, in so far as he is kin to the Prince. Nothing gives such a strong flavour of the miscellaneous everyday world of Verona as the passage in Act II, scene 4 where the Nurse and her man Peter meet Mercutio, Benvolio and Romeo in the street, and they all banter together. Both Mercutio and the Nurse are full of mirth, and this spills on to the protagonist that each of them shadows. We can mark the decisive turns that the play takes towards tragedy by noting the moments when they are violently separated, first Mercutio from Romeo (III.1), and then the Nurse from Juliet (III.5). Romeo may be banished from Verona, but Mercutio and the Nurse are banished from the play.

LOVE AND DEATH

In many ways the story of Romeo and Juliet would have seemed to Shakespeare's first audience distinctly modern, as it does to us now. But for its roots we can delve further back beyond the fifteenth- and sixteenth-century sources.

At the end of the play the scene at the Capulet monument carries the aura of ancient myths about continuing life in the tomb or revival from death, myths associated with the cycle of the seasons, and in classical antiquity with the death and rebirth of Persephone or Proserpine, daughter of the earth goddess Demeter. This last is a myth on which Shakespeare himself draws in *The Winter's Tale*. Yet if such mythic resonances are audible, the scene in the Capulet tomb trembles on the verge of parody, for by the end of the play there is not one corpse nor even two, but if Tybalt's is included as well as Paris's, no fewer than four. Performances on stage and screen sometimes omit the intruders, Tybalt and Paris, but Shakespeare seems to have wanted this tomb-womb to be crowded and charged with sex and violence. It seems less the site of new birth than a place where passion is consummated, where lovers – in the Elizabethan pun that equates death and orgasm – 'die' together, or try to.

Sexual passion had of course featured as a subject for tragedy before Shakespeare. If we look back to the Greeks, we find Helen of Troy in Homer and the tragedians, Heracles in Sophocles' *Women of Trachis* and Phaedra in Euripides' *Hippolytus*. But Aphrodite and Eros are savage, predatory, daemonic, divine. To translate such passions as 'love' may be misleading, until we reflect on how many things the word can mean in our own language. The nearest analogue in Greek tragedy to the end of *Romeo and Juliet* is the scene in the rock-tomb (offstage) at the climax of Sophocles' *Antigone*, where young Haemon arrives too late to save the eponymous heroine, and joins her in death by suicide. The ancient world provides models much closer to Shakespeare in the unfortunate lovers remembered by Ovid, especially Hero and Leander and Pyramus and Thisbe.

And in the second century AD we can find a narrative romance known as the *Ephesiaca*, by Xenophon of Ephesus, in which two young lovers are married, separated and reunited in a tomb, after the girl tries to avoid a second marriage by taking poison. Fortunately the drug just puts her to sleep so her 'death' turns out to be faked. (The ambivalence of the drug is a notably recurring feature in this story of Love and Death, Eros and Thanatos.) When Sigmund Freud was developing the concepts on which psychoanalysis would be founded, including his theory of the Oedipal complex, it was to Sophocles that he looked back for inspiration rather than to Xenophon of Ephesus. But where the conjunction of love and death was concerned, Freud was also drawing on the more recent animation of these deeply charged images, as for example by two great musical dramas, Richard Wagner's *Tristan und Isolde* (1859) and Giuseppe Verdi's *Aida* (1871). In both these operas the lovers die together united in ecstasy – in the latter, interred together in a rock-tomb. In the recent movie of *William Shakespeare's Romeo + Juliet* (1996) Baz Luhrmann has his lovers die to Wagner's 'Liebestod' (love-death), and it's significant that both his film and Franco Zeffirelli's (1968) have attracted from critics the word 'operatic'.

But the lovers in Wagner and Verdi are not youngsters, nor are they surrounded by ropery and drudgery. On the contrary, they soar up and away on the wings of music, assisted by the full force of the modern orchestra. Shakespeare's great love story has often inspired other artists to set them to music and song. The nineteenth century produced operas by Vincenzo Bellini (1830) and Charles Gounod (1867), Hector Berlioz's Dramatic Symphony (1839) and Peter Ilich Tchaikovsky's Fantasy Overture (1870), and the twentieth century Sergei

Prokofiev's great ballet (1938), Leonard Bernstein's *West Side Story* (1957), and the highly effective film scores by Nino Rota and Nellee Hooper to the movies by Zeffirelli and Luhrmann. As with most successful translations that exploit the resources of art forms and media unavailable to Shakespeare, all these draw on an element inherent in their source. In this case it is the lyrical impulse in the lovers' own most impassioned utterance, the urge to break into song for joy, for excitement, for grief. In Shakespeare their voices lift up out of the body, finding natural expression in images of soaring, flying, floating on 'love's light wings' (II.2.66) with 'wind-swift Cupid' (II.5.8). Nor are the lovers entirely alone. Mercutio's astonishing Queen Mab speech is a passage of verbal ecstasy, of spontaneous 'flight'.

But this is only one element in Shakespeare's play. The centrifugal impulses given such vivid expression by the lovers are matched by forces pulling down to earth, to the domain of decaying bodies and the worms that will feed on them, to the everlasting flint. These contradictory pressures are reflected in the play's range of verbal reference. On the one hand, there are allusions to the world of classical myth and antiquity that seem to elevate and aggrandize. Juliet speaks, more inauspiciously than she knows, of the horses of the sun god that Phaëton failed to control (III.2.1–4). There are other references to myths of disaster and transformation from Ovid: Danaë, Echo, Philomel and Proserpine. Yet Shakespeare and his contemporaries did not treat classical myth and history with uniform reverence. They often found it absurd, pretentious, grotesque. It was a way of measuring their own modernity, of distancing themselves from the oppressive solemnity of the past. And Romeo and Juliet would like to be 'modern'.

Mercutio is certainly not afflicted by reverence for the models of love represented by classical myth. He taunts Romeo with a series of heroines associated with tragedies of love: Dido, Cleopatra, Helen, Hero and Thisbe (II.4.41–2). It's only the last two who are remotely relevant. Hero and Leander were the subject of a narrative poem by Shakespeare's contemporary, the dramatist and poet Christopher Marlowe (finished after he died in 1593 by George Chapman), and Pyramus and Thisbe feature unforgettably in *A Midsummer Night's Dream*. Shakespeare had been drawn to the tragic legend of Venus and Adonis for his narrative poem of 1593, and he went on to write two more plays centred on tragic love-couples that bear some comparison with *Romeo and Juliet*, *Troilus and Cressida* and *Antony and Cleopatra*. In all three cases the lovers are separated by politics and violence. It is true that by comparison with the Trojan War and the fate of the Roman Empire, the feud of the Montagues and Capulets might seem a petty affair, however dignified by being a matter of 'ancient grudge'. But the legendary heroes who stalk the Shakespearian stage are also made to look petty: Achilles and Helen (in *Troilus and Cressida*) and Antony and Cleopatra (in the play named after them). On the other hand, petty is not how the feud appears, nor Mercutio's death, to Romeo and Juliet themselves.

How can we tell how large or small are the things we contemplate? The great models of the past are not reliable. The problem of scale is wrought into the language that Shakespeare gives his characters: aggrandizing and inflating to excess, but also deflating, debasing and shrinking. Mercutio's extraordinary Queen Mab speech epitomizes these vertiginous shifts of perspective that menace the difference between 'large' and 'small'. Other differences too, such as waking and dreaming, or day and night, or love and death.

FORMS OF SPEECH

Verona is a world without sure standards, firm foundations, agreed boundaries. It is volatile, fluid, unstable, mercurial. This applies to the language the characters speak as it does to the actions they commit. Again we have to recognize that Shakespeare was doing something unprecedented with the many forms of language he puts on show. Some of these can seem trivial, when Romeo puns on 'sole' and 'soul' (I.4.14–16), or Mercutio on 'dun' and 'done' (I.4.40–43), or Juliet (triply) on 'Ay', 'I' and 'eye' (III.2.45–50). These can be hard to get across in modern performance; indeed they are often just cut. Juliet's wordplay is particularly embarrassing because the context – she thinks the Nurse is telling her that Romeo has killed himself – is serious. But this is not necessarily a good reason for avoiding or omitting such moments. There is a long and instructive history of embarrassment with Shakespeare's wordplay that hits a high point in the eighteenth century with Dr Johnson and his friend the great actor David Garrick. The title page of the first Quarto announces 'An Excellent Conceited Tragedy of Romeo and Juliet' (where 'conceited' means something like 'verbally ingenious'). This is exactly what the taste of the Augustan age objected to, with its strong preference for rational explanation and linguistic exactitude. In the Advertisement to his 1748 adaptation Garrick said it was his aim 'to clear the original as much as possible from the jingle and quibble which were always thought the great objections to reviving it'. But just as the play stages the problem of managing the erotic energies surging through the young lovers, so editors, critics and performers repeat this drama when they try to control the linguistic energies of the text.

These energies are manifest in the exuberant variety of speech forms, and the often dizzying transitions between them. 'Blubbering and weeping, weeping and blubbering': thus the Nurse, on Juliet's grief at Romeo's banishment, yoking by violence together the dignity of 'weeping' and the shamefulness of 'blubbering' (III.3.88). At the most dignified extreme there are the sonnets spoken by the Chorus at the beginning of Acts I and II (though the latter is frequently cut in performance), and the one composed, apparently on the spur of the moment, by Romeo and Juliet on their first meeting (I.5.93–106.) Not content with this amazing feat, they complete four lines of a second one (107–10) before they are interrupted by the Nurse. Needless to say the servants never speak like this. A sonnet is a distinctly written form of verse that outside the Elizabethan theatre you'd expect to be the prerogative of nobility, or poets trying to ingratiate themselves with aristocratic patrons. How well educated the lovers must be to make this sonnet up between them on the spot. But from the start of the play Romeo has given every sign of being *over*-educated. When we first see him he speaks almost entirely in the clichés of fashionable contemporary love-poetry inspired by Petrarch (see note to II.4.38–9): 'O heavy lightness, serious vanity, | Misshapen chaos of well-seeming forms' (I.1.178–9). What is he trying to say – or not to say? At one level Romeo is giving gnomic expression to the extremes that the play will go on to embrace. But at this early stage his own understanding of them seems superficial, and his language at once a form of display and of secrecy, of guardedness. This would be a way of describing much of the ostentatious speech in the play: Mercutio's for instance.

There are all sorts of clichés, conventions and customs on display in Verona. At the other extreme there is the dirty everyday talk of the servants with which the play's action starts – a typically abrupt transition from the formality of the opening chorus to the informal prose of the streets. There are other kinds of conventional thought and expression, Tybalt's for instance, mocked by Mercutio (II.4.19–35). Friar Laurence seems at times a walking compendium of Good Advice, almost as much of a slave to the language he speaks, and through which he thinks, as the early, Petrarchan Romeo. 'O, what learning is!' exclaims the Nurse after the Friar has calmed down the suicidally inclined Romeo with a lecture on all the good reasons he has to be 'happy' (III.3.160). 'Well, we were born to die', mutters Juliet's father to Paris, helplessly (III.4.4).

But of course not all the speech is conventional. On the contrary, the world of this play seems to sponsor a kind of shameless, instinctive pleasure in the possibilities of language, in rhyme for instance, and in double meanings, especially words and expressions with a sexual underside. This ear for 'low' meaning is earthy, unromantic, tough-minded to the point of cynicism, especially where 'love' is concerned. Seen from below, the language of love may just be a way of mystifying the urges of sexual desire or of justifying the distribution of power in the family and state: children and servants are required to 'love' their elders and betters. This helps to explain the importance of all the low talk, especially the sexual innuendo, that over the years has caused such difficulty for editors (especially in editions for schools) and also for players in performance. The play is radically simplified when this is cut. Most important for their adjacency to the two young lovers are the voices of the Nurse and Mercutio, the voices of scepticism that insist on the physical, creaturely aspects of sex.

Audiences feel comfortable with the Nurse and Mercutio because they invariably know where they are – except for the latter's Queen Mab speech. But there are other characters and moments of whom and of which this is far from true, when speech is awkward, angular, precarious. Consider the lines in which Lady Capulet commends the County Paris to her daughter by comparing him to a book (I.3.82–95). In modern performances this is an obvious candidate for cutting. Yet perhaps we should attend to such passages all the more carefully because they do *not* blend easily into the dominant naturalistic idiom of our theatre (and film and television). They are the points at which the Shakespearian text is 'difficult', resistant to translation or appropriation into modern terms. With Lady Capulet here, the difficulty is the very elaborateness and protractedness of the simile. Its artifice contrasts forcibly with the easy informal diction of the other adult woman in the scene, the Nurse. This is part of its point. We only begin to understand what Juliet and her mother are up against when we hear the formality of the speech required of a well-educated lady in such a situation. There is no need for Lady Capulet to *believe* in what she is saying, but hearing it can help us understand the constraints on her conduct, and her daughter's. Or again, consider the difficulty for modern actor and audience of Juliet's triple puns on 'Ay', 'I' and 'eye', already mentioned (III.2.45–50), and her recourse to the same sort of facile oxymorons

Romeo was spinning at the start, before he met her: 'Beautiful tyrant! fiend angelical!', and so on (III.2.75). Fortunately she quickly snaps out of this extravagant idiom, but modern performance often cuts this difficult passage (III.2.73–85) or reduces it to a minimum.

One way of making sense of Juliet's 'artificial' speech here is to think of her as riddling and quibbling to mask or displace her real feelings – like Mercutio jesting on the point of death. But what of moments when characters start speaking a less self-conscious, more generous kind of poetry, as this, for example, from Benvolio, in answer to Romeo's mother: 'Madam, an hour before the worshipped sun | Peered forth the golden window of the East, . . .' (I.1.118–19). This sounds as though he might have written it beforehand. This too, a few lines later, when Romeo's father responds in similar language: 'But all so soon as the all-cheering sun | Should in the farthest East begin to draw | The shady curtains from Aurora's bed, . . .' (134–6). Could he be *copying* Benvolio, deliberately, inadvertently? At moments like this such diction may have a dramatic function surpassing the speaker's own motives or intentions, to introduce a new rhythm, perspective or tone. Yet it raises questions about the hold that characters have on their speech, and it has on them, that permeate the play as a whole. How do we know, how can we tell whether they mean what they say? Are they saying one thing and meaning another? Where do these words come from? Who or what are we listening to? The fictional character? The author?

Such questions become particularly challenging in some of the central passages between the two lovers, from the moment when Romeo first catches sight of Juliet, 'O, she doth teach the torches to burn bright! | It seems she hangs upon the cheek of night | As a rich

jewel in an Ethiop's ear –' (I.5.44–6), through the magnif-
icent lyrics of the so-called 'balcony' scene, 'But soft!
What light through yonder window breaks? | It is the
East, and Juliet is the sun!' (II.2.2–3), to the bittersweet
exchanges of the *aubade* or dawn-song, when they part
after their one night together, 'It was the nightingale, and
not the lark, | That pierced the fearful hollow of thine
ear' (III.5.2–3). We may need to recognize a radical uncertainty on the listener's part and perhaps on the speaker's
own, about what such poetry means to say, as an act of
expression and communication. This is precisely what
gives such scope to the player in performance, that the
words can be uttered and heard in so many different
ways, intended and unintended. To take a wonderful,
perplexing example: what does Juliet mean by praying
that, when she dies (or perhaps when *Romeo* does – there
is some uncertainty about the text), night should 'Take
him and cut him out in little stars' (III.2.21ff.)?

Or consider a different case, the formal lamentation
round Juliet's 'dead' body in Act IV, scene 5, a scene
that is often curtailed in performance. The passage beginning with Lady Capulet's 'Accursed, unhappy, wretched,
hateful day' to Capulet's 'And with my child my joys
are burièd!' (43–64) is certainly awkward, even
grotesque. The audience knows with Friar Laurence that
the corpse is not for real, while Capulet, his wife, the
Nurse and Paris all believe that it is. Modern performances often dodge the difficulty of a vocal formality that
is alien to naturalistic theatre, though perfectly at home
in opera or musical theatre. And in recent years several
effective productions have adopted just this way of
playing it, by according it the dignity of formal lament
familiar to musical drama, and presenting the collective
grief in such a way that we are forced to 'take it seri-

ously'. The difficulty of the scene is intrinsic to the text.
It is not a false note but a precarious balance entirely
characteristic of the play as a whole, such that we often
don't know whether to laugh or cry.

The characters are doing things here, just as Lady
Capulet was talking to her daughter, 'by the book'. That
is to say, they are obeying convention, good etiquette,
following the rules. But as with so much else in this play,
there is no way of being certain whether this is a good
thing or a bad thing. A purposeful uncertainty runs
through the play about the value of formality, ceremony,
conventional learning. When Romeo was in love with
Rosaline, or thought he was, he spoke entirely 'by the
book'. Friar Laurence tells him that it was not love but
doting, that 'Thy love did learn by rote, that could not
spell' (II.3.84). Doing things by the book can be super-
ficial, simply learned by rote, without real substance or
meaning. But Juliet has told Romeo that he kisses by the
book and this is presumably a compliment (I.5.110). The
Elizabethan sense of 'compliment', meaning 'form,
custom, ceremony', is much to the point. When Mercutio
mocks Tybalt's enslavement to the latest style of duelling,
doing everything just so, he calls him, derisively, 'the
courageous captain of compliments' (II.4.20). Mercutio
abhors such 'fashion-mongers' (32–3).

Juliet also speaks of 'compliment' when Romeo overhears her at her window: 'Fain would I dwell on form,
fain, fain deny | What I have spoke, but farewell compli-
ment' (II.2.88–9). In other words, goodbye to the conventions, the common forms. She shows what she means a
moment or two later when Romeo starts to swear he loves
her: 'Lady, by yonder blessèd moon I vow, | That tips
with silver all these fruit-tree tops –' (107–8). She stops
him and says, don't swear by the moon. He's a bit

flummoxed. A man has to swear by something. Juliet's a quick learner and a quick teacher. 'Do not swear at all. | Or if thou wilt, swear by thy gracious self, | Which is the god of my idolatry, | And I'll believe thee' (II.2.112–15). Romeo does as he's told. But Juliet's had enough of this game: 'Well, do not swear' (116). And her thoughts have taken a darker turn. In its small way this tentative banter gives a taste of the way the lovers, especially Juliet, try to escape the 'compliments', to elude the rules of the game by playing with them, improvising, dancing to new tunes of their own. Everyone and everything else in Verona is so *predictable* – the ancient grudge, the ancient feast, the ancient jokes. Everyone except Romeo and Juliet, and Mercutio.

'FAIR VERONA'

The Verona that Shakespeare creates for his lovers ensures that they are pressed for time and pressed for space. There are the city streets, dangerous, volatile public spaces where men strut, push women to the wall or accost them tauntingly, where feuds flare up, challenges are hurled down, swords are 'bandied' (III.1.87). Set against these exposed places are several refuges, most prominently the Capulet household. In one of its aspects it faces out towards the world, taking pride in its hospitality, its food and drinking and feasting. It welcomes in the outside world, even – and this is important for qualifying our sense of the family feud – the odd Montague. There is the Great Chamber where the dancing takes place and the kitchen offstage where they curse the Nurse, call for dates and quinces and look to the baked meats. But there is also the inner, 'private' space of Juliet's bedroom. How private is this? Nurses and mothers and fathers can barge their way in (though lovers too can be let in and out). Apart from the bed itself, where she will spend the night with Romeo and seem to die, the most important feature of Juliet's room is the window through which she speaks to Romeo in the orchard beneath, and through which he will come and go. This orchard is a happy successor to the sycamore grove mentioned by Benvolio at the start, where Romeo tries to hide his narcissistic, masturbatory self, 'to himself so secret and so close', as his father says (I.1.149). The Capulet garden is dangerous but more promising, in that it harbours a real woman to whom he can speak and listen. 'She speaks', he exclaims twice, in astonishment (II.2.12, 25).

The orchard is a precious, pressurized space because in fair Verona, as in Elizabethan England, privacy is hard to come by. You can't get away from loitering louts in the streets; you can't get away from parents in your bedroom; even when you go for an early morning wander someone will be watching you. All this creates in the young lovers a correspondingly intense desire to escape, to soar up and away, or to sink into darkness, or at the very least to head towards the borders and margins and edges of things. This is where *Romeo and Juliet* looks ahead to another play about sex in the city, *Measure for Measure*. In both these ultra-urban plays those locations are especially desirable which seem to offer relief from the glare of exposure, from the sense of everyone watching you. In *Measure* these include Isabella's convent, Mariana's moated grange, even the darkness of prison and prospect of death that Claudio faces; in *Romeo and Juliet*, the grove of sycamore, Friar Laurence's cell, Juliet's bedroom or at least its window ledge, the apothecary's shop in Mantua, the Capulet tomb, the sisterhood of holy nuns where the

Friar desperately promises he'll dispose of Juliet (V.3.156–7).

The ghostly Friar's 'close cell', as Romeo calls it (II.2.192), occupies a special position in the play's topography. He is the youngsters' 'holy father', the one to whom they can, indeed must, confide their secrets in the discipline of confession or 'shrift' to which reference is frequently made. There is a tenderness in his relations with the lovers, in the way he calls Romeo 'young waverer' (II.3.85) and Juliet 'pensive daughter' (IV.1.39). They trust him. His cell is the locus of a higher authority – personal, moral, medical, theological – than anything else that Verona has to offer. As we first see him at the break of day, so his cell seems to lie at the city's margin, where civil space gives on to the 'nature' he studies, the 'plants, herbs, stones' that he gathers and analyses. His cell is an altogether more inward place than the shadowy 'old Free-town, our common judgement-place', to which at the end of the first street-brawl the Prince summons Montague (though not Capulet). This latter is not a particularly impressive address, and we never see for ourselves the seat of the Prince's power, his residence. The Friar's cell harbours more authority, but this drains away from him when he leaves it, for the Capulet household (IV.5), and the tomb (V.3). By the end of his long last speech (V.3.229–69), he's a broken man.

The tomb is the play's final, triumphant refuge, but like Juliet's bedroom it is all too easily invaded. There's a certain imaginative connection between the two thresholds, the window of her room and the mouth of the tomb. 'O here | Will I set up my everlasting rest', says Romeo, as he prepares to drink the poison (V.3.109–10). This is not an innocent expression. The Nurse has used it already (IV.5.6), as she tries to wake Juliet, muttering suggestively about the lack of rest Juliet will have when the County Paris gets her into bed and 'sets up his rest'. Of the several quibbles at play in this proverbial phrase, one is drawn from gambling and another refers to firing a musket or couching a lance. Romeo's expression, on the edge of the grave, is a masterpiece of brinkman-ship, a summation of the sex and risk and violence that have writhed together through the play. Such wordplay itself takes a violent risk with language. Not to be outdone, Juliet tops him with a breathtaking final pun that equates her self-inflicted death-blow with the act of sexual penetration – as if she were raping herself: 'O happy dagger! | This is thy sheath; there rust, and let me die' (V.3.169–70).

Is there no escape from the violence of Verona, outside and in, except in the grave? No world elsewhere? Apparently not. There is Mantua, to which Romeo is banished, or more exactly, for it is all we see of this 'other' place, there is the Apothecary and his shop (V.1). The intensity of Romeo's exchange with this figure of desti-tution is out of all proportion to its length. (It is signif-icant that the Victorian burlesques make much of the Apothecary's role.) The hunger and need he represents make him a negative image of the plenty enjoyed by the Capulet household; the deadly drugs he harbours make him a dark double of Friar Laurence; in performance he has sometimes been doubled with Mercutio to create a sense of occult fatality (see p. lvi). Later in his career Shakespeare might have made more of this moment, as he might have made more of the plague-house where Friar John is crucially detained. Together these 'other' places hint at and pick up references scattered through the text to states and conditions and forces beyond civil and human control. Aching bones, famine, plague, lightning, earthquakes, the sea: the lovers' euphoria is balanced against a sense of the body's vulnerability, the ease with which it can be invaded, withered, destroyed.

Within the play there lurks the mystery of forces beyond our comprehension. In a resonant phrase the opening Chorus speaks of 'The fearful passage of their death-marked love' (9). Juliet exclaims: 'Prodigious birth of love' (I.5.140). Romeo thinks of himself as engaged on a perilous voyage into the unknown, across the ocean or into the darkness: 'wert thou as far | As that vast shore washed with the farthest sea, | I should adventure for such merchandise' (II.2.82–4). This is, or should be, a great rite of passage from youth to maturity, from one world to another, one self to another. In a sense the tragedy for all concerned is that the young couple suffer this ordeal alone – or 'high-lone', as the Nurse has it (I.3.37). Their union should belong to everyone, to all Verona. The great rite of marriage should be a public event, a 'prodigious birth' not for the lovers alone, but for the whole world around them.

For all the famous high-summer setting of the play, the dog days and the mad blood stirring, a heroine named after the month of July and born on Lammas Eve, Verona can seem like a city of the dead, or at least of the moribund. The word 'ancient' echoes through the play from the Chorus's first reference to 'ancient grudge'. Later Juliet will mark her rejection of the Nurse, her sense of betrayal, by calling her 'Ancient damnation' (III.5.235). As well as the Nurse, there are the 'ancient' men, Montague and Capulet and good cousin Capulet, well past their dancing days (I.5.31 ff.). In terms of seasonal myth they represent the 'limping winter' to which Capulet refers when he invites Paris to the feast: 'Such comfort as do lusty young men feel | When well-apparelled April on the heel | Of limping winter treads' (I.2.26–8). But no matter what the temperature in the streets, there's a permanent winter awaiting the lusty young men and women. One of them describes her family tomb as 'an ancient receptacle | Where for this many hundred years the bones | Of all my buried ancestors are packed' (IV.3.39–41).

Not all that is ancient is moribund or sterile, or simply so. The Capulets invite their friends to 'an old accustomed feast', which represents an important kind of refuge or intermission in which the grudge can be suspended and differences sunk, or to be more exact, 'masked'. Not if Tybalt has anything to do with it, of course. But what is the Capulet feast in honour of? What are they celebrating? In the Brooke source it had been clearly associated with the Christmas season, but in Shakespeare we simply don't know. It's the same with the ancient feud, the origins of which are lost in the mists of time. There is something unrooted and ungrounded about fair Verona, a portent of the modern city as Shakespeare's age was beginning to know it. The productive rhythms of communal time traditionally depend on agreed alternations between work and holiday, labour and leisure. For Shakespeare's first audience this sense of time was based on the rhythms of sowing and reaping, and on the feasts and holidays, both sacred and secular, that structured their year. The Lammas Eve that is Juliet's birthday heralds what was once a critical date in the rural calendar. The eight weeks or so from Lammas (1 August) to Michaelmas (29 September) marked the time of harvest, and at Lammas itself the loaves made from the first ripe corn were consecrated. The early English church took over what had probably been a major Celtic and Teutonic festival associated with this date (the nearest Christian equivalent being the Feast of Corpus Christi, which falls a good deal earlier in the summer, on the Thursday after Trinity Sunday). Lammastide was certainly a date with enough associations of fruition and thanksgiving to serve as a critical moment of 'passage' for a girl named after the month of July.

But fair Verona has forgotten such associations, as Elizabethan London was beginning to. How do you mark time in the city? At least partly by the rhythms of commercial, legal and administrative activities, by a court's sessions or a legal agreement such as binds Antonio to Shylock in *The Merchant of Venice*. Like other plays in which an urban setting predominates, such as *The Comedy of Errors* and *Measure for Measure*, *Romeo and Juliet* presents a world in which time is becoming increasingly man-made, man-watched, man-measured. Verona is divorced from the rhythms of seasonal recurrence and return, from the great rites through which the life of the community was once renewed, and possession of the future passed from one generation to the next, from limping winter to leaping summer and beyond. In the metaphoric topography of Verona the tomb of the Capulets lies, it turns out, at its heart. And the girl who is all the hope of the future, whom her father calls 'the hopeful lady of my earth' (I.2.15), the young woman who should be consecrated as the bride and mother of the new generations to come, she will become the bride of Death, her festival turned to funeral.

COMFORT, CONDUCT, CONSORT

If Verona is portrayed as a place cut off from some kinds or aspects of 'nature', from the forms of labour and festivity rooted in the countryside, the Friar's scientific

learning may provide a modern compensation. There is
nothing modern about his complement in this respect,
the Nurse. Her great speech about Juliet's early childhood (I.3.17–58) puts us in touch with ancient aspects of
the natural world that we don't find anywhere else in the
play. It is through the Nurse that we learn to associate
Juliet's birth with Lammastide, and her weaning not
only with an earthquake but also a joke predicting a later
rite of passage, her initiation into sex. We also learn of
the Nurse's own child Susan, who was of an age with
Juliet, and who like the majority of children in
Shakespeare's time, and too many other times, has failed
to survive infancy. Death and sex are for the Nurse
inevitabilities she has learned to greet with resignation
and even good humour, 'Sitting in the sun under the
dove-house wall' (I.3.28). Like the other elements that
go to make up Verona, the Nurse represents repetition
and predictability, but she offers a more maternal or
nurturing reassurance than anything to be got from
anyone else. Like the Friar she provides – the word once
enjoyed a stronger meaning than it does now – 'comfort'.

But the Nurse is something more and other than a
comforting presence. She is also ominous or portentous
– not necessarily of misfortune, as the word 'ominous'
now simply means for us, but in its old double or ambiva-
lent sense, presaging good *or* ill. ('Ominous' has been
reduced to predicting a bad outcome, just as 'success'
has been reduced to marking a good outcome, but in
Shakespeare's time both possibilities were open in these
words.) The Nurse marks the critical moments in Juliet's
life: birth, weaning, and now sexual initiation and
marriage. The time of the 'fall' predicted by her dead
husband in his lightly bawdy joke has now come about:
it is time for Juliet to 'fall backward'. This is right and

proper, and the way things are supposed to be in the cycle of life. But the times and events and seasons to which the Nurse alludes seem curiously to melt together. Her speech holds together birth and weaning and sex and marriage and death, but they seem barely distinct from each other, these vital, mortal moments of 'passage'.

The Nurse is one of the three mentors to whom the youngsters look for comfort, counsel or conduct. If you are to get through a 'fearful passage', you will need a guide, a 'pilot', 'conduct' or 'convoy', to use the play's own words. The Friar and the Nurse both try to serve them and fail. The third and most astonishing figure in this respect is Mercutio, whose relationship to Romeo complements that of the Nurse to Juliet. Tybalt accuses him of 'consorting' with Romeo and Mercutio takes offence (III.i.44–8); Tybalt repeats the taunt to Romeo himself (III.i.130). But Shakespeare does make the mercurial Mercutio a consort to Romeo, a kind of secret double or alter ego. In performance Mercutio can some-times steal the show, but this has not always been the case. The role has an interesting history. From the Restoration to the mid twentieth century Mercutio was suppressed, censored and sentimentalized. This is partly because of his relentless, ingenious obscenity. This acts as a foil to Romeo's spirituality, especially the bloodless and abstract form of his first crush on Rosaline. But if this 'earthiness' were all that Mercutio represented, then he would be much simpler. The Queen Mab speech makes something much stranger, more mysterious and awesome of him. It associates him with the worlds of dream, sleep and nightmare, another form of the world elsewhere occluded or ignored by Verona. There is a world of nature out there, in the winds and the sea, in lightning and earthquake, but there is another world in here, inside the head, especially the heads of troubled, passionate, imaginative – and perhaps bored – young men.

It's been said that there is something 'daemonic' about Mercutio. It may well be that this owes something to the classical deity from whom he seems to derive his name – the god Mercury or Hermes: herald and messenger of the gods, trickster, conductor of souls of the dead to Hades, patron of thieves, merchants, travellers (the name 'Romeo' means 'wanderer'), and associated with eloquence, luck, roads, wind, sleep and dreams. Above all he is the god of boundaries and frontiers. He is a figure peculiarly appropriate to a play that has so many scenes of twilight, on the edge of night and day, and so many scenes set on the edge of houses and monuments and cities, at windows and the mouth of tombs. And a play in which there are so many references to messengers and angels (which means 'messenger'), a play in which a crucial message goes fatally astray.

Wherever Mercutio comes from, there is no question about the brilliant effect of his death at the very centre of the play. It entirely transforms the nature of Romeo's guilt. (Brooke's Romeus simply kills Tybalt in a street-fight.) Given the importance of his relations with Mercutio, it contributes a wholly new sense of something that Romeo loses. *And*, it must be said, that we the audience lose. We all miss Mercutio in the second half of the play, as we all miss Hotspur in the second play of *Henry IV*. Does Mercutio need to die so that Romeo can grow up – as first Hotspur and then Falstaff have to be sacrificed for the sake of Hal's development, at the end of the two *Henry IV* plays? Does Romeo have to escape from all that same-sex bonding, the boys' gang, to confrontation with the opposite sex and a heterosexual

union? Perhaps. After all, this is one of the big stories
our culture tells us about the need to grow up and become
a proper heterosexual. Is Mercutio in love with Romeo
and jealous of his attraction to the other sex? In recent
decades more or less openly gay Mercutios have become
commonplace on stage and screen. It's worth noting that
Mercutio and Juliet never meet, that he's oblivious to
the change we see for ourselves when Romeo drops
Rosaline and falls for Juliet. However he's played on
stage, most audiences and readers now feel a real sense
of loss in Mercutio's demise, as of some vital energy,
some mental and imaginative possibility. Some critics
have gone so far as to speak of Mercutio as the play's
truly tragic character. His death is shocking and painful
in a way that Juliet's and Romeo's are not. So too the
death of Enobarbus – another character whom Shakespeare hugely develops from a mere hint in his source –
is lonely, comfortless, acrid, by comparison with those
of Antony and Cleopatra. It is possible to understand
Mercutio's famous curse very seriously, 'A plague a'both
your houses!' (III.1.106) One could even see this male-
diction coming true in the play's second half, as if it
were, at some deep level, Mercutio's revenge. For it is
the plague that prevents the vital message from Friar
Laurence reaching Romeo in Mantua.

There is certainly the sense that Romeo has some
unfinished business with Mercutio. Perhaps something
of this surfaces near the end of the play when Romeo
comes face to face with the Apothecary. Directors have
been known to elevate the Apothecary into an emblem
of Fate (as Terry Hands's Royal Shakespeare Company
production did in 1973), and to double him with Mercutio.
There is a slight verbal association between them: Romeo
speaks of the Apothecary's 'overwhelming brows'

(V.1.39); Mercutio had said of the mask he put on for the Capulet feast: 'Here are the beetle brows shall blush for me' (I.4.32). At some subliminal level these may link up with Juliet's great invocation: 'Come gentle night. Come, loving, black-browed night' (III.2.20). The Apothecary is the messenger of death, the figure who provides Romeo's 'conduct' to the realm of eternal night. There is a notable change in Romeo's language, as he looks *into* the Apothecary, and what he stands for:

> Art thou so bare and full of wretchedness,
> And fearest to die? Famine is in thy cheeks.
> Need and oppression starveth in thy eyes.
> Contempt and beggary hangs upon thy back.
> The world is not thy friend, nor the world's law. (V.1.68–72)

This is what it means to be a real outlaw, beyond the pale, an image of deprivation, misery, total abjection. If the Apothecary looks back to the 'living dead man' Dr Pinch in *The Comedy of Errors* (V.1.242), this confrontation looks ahead to the moment when King Lear comes face to face with Poor Tom, and recognizes 'unaccommodated man', real need, the thing itself (III.4.103).

MORTALITY AND MERCY

Near the start of *Measure for Measure* the Duke appoints Angelo as his deputy and says, ringingly, 'Mortality and mercy in Vienna | Live in thy tongue and heart' (I.1.44–5). *Measure for Measure* takes the closest possible interest in the corruption of human justice. It presents an entire community, and pursues the sources of its sickness at every level, from the brothel to the judgement-seat. For all its official allegiance to the genre of comedy, this interest in justice brings it closer to the world of the tragedies and histories. It keeps its hold on comedy, just, by the weight given to mercy and forgiveness in its final scenes. Whether you think it's a con trick or a brilliant political manoeuvre or a happy accident, whether you feel Vienna has been cleaned up or whitewashed or just left as it was before, the Duke holds the play together by resuming his power to punish, pardon and reward. He enforces a 'happy ending', a dream of justice and mercy, accomplished by human hands, measured by human scales.

The ending of *Romeo and Juliet* is certainly not a happy one. But is it as unhappy as it should be? There are some difficult problems of staging. Friar Laurence begins his final explanation with the fatal words: 'I will be brief' (V.3.229). He is not. But the length of his speech does provide time for the other characters onstage, especially Juliet's mother and father, to understand how this catastrophe has come about. Though its patience may be tried, an audience can be made to wonder what the parents feel about the Friar's tale, especially his description of its fatal conclusion as 'this work of heaven' (261). Can he be serious?

There are real questions stirring in this final scene, as we look back at the play as a whole, about where the blame lies. The Prince says 'All are punished' (295). In itself this has the ring of real tragedy. It affirms that the deaths we have witnessed are a collective disaster for those who are left behind in this harsh world to draw their breath in pain, like the Horatio to whom the dying Hamlet addresses these unforgettable words (*Hamlet*, V.2.343). In *Romeo and Juliet* it is not just the prime deaths of the title characters, but the other four that occur in the course

of the play (Tybalt, Mercutio, Paris, Lady Montague).
The good news is that the lovers have not died in vain.
The Friar's plot to heal the rift between the feuding families has not utterly failed. The two fathers are going to
raise statues in pure gold to each others' children, 'Poor
sacrifices of our enmity' (V.3.304). But is this really such
good news? Isn't all this sudden reconciliation discomforting, even offensive? Isn't it a bit easy, all this mercy
and forgiveness and hand-wringing? Don't we want to
see some *real* guilt? After all, the fathers have between
them made a real mess of things, Montague and Capulet
and Friar Laurence. Between them they've helped to
destroy their city's youth and vigour and promise. All
the youngsters have killed themselves or each other. Even
Benvolio has disappeared. And let's not forget the
mothers, Lady Capulet and the Nurse. Where *is* the
Nurse, by the way? In his closing lines the Prince seems
to have changed his mind when he says: 'Some shall be
pardoned, and some punishèd' (V.3.308). Who, exactly?

It is easy to feel that there isn't quite enough real guilt
in Verona. Nor is there anything we could confidently
call evil, as there will be in the Elsinore of *Hamlet*, the
Scotland of *Macbeth* and the Venice and Cyprus of
Othello. Look at the parents, especially the Capulets.
They *might* have been monsters – looming, Oedipal
authority figures, out of whose daemonic clutches their
children struggle bravely and hopelessly to break. But
Lady Capulet is no more like Clytemnestra than Hamlet's
mother is, indeed a good deal less so, and Capulet is a
bit of a buffoon. The young lovers themselves surely
aren't 'guilty', not in the way we expect tragic characters to be, whether knowingly or reluctantly or even
unconsciously. Despite brave efforts to argue that they
are justly punished for surrendering to their passion and

cheating on their parents, it's more natural to feel they
are 'a bit to blame' than that they are guilty in the way
that Othello and Lear and Macbeth are guilty. And what
is it that destroys them? Something with the grandeur
of irresistible fatality, such as we associate with the Greek
gods, with mythic or psychological or natural inevitability? Or just a chain of unlucky accidents, a street-
fight that goes wrong and a letter that goes astray – a
matter of bad timing? Fate, or accident?

There are some deep patterns and forces lurking in
the shadows of this play. But the characters themselves
are less conscious of them, and less resourceful in the
way they try to understand them, than they are in Shakespeare's later tragedies. On the brink of his fateful first
meeting with Juliet, Romeo says: 'my mind misgives |
Some consequence, yet hanging in the stars, | Shall
bitterly begin his fearful date | With this night's revels'
(I.4.106–9). When he hears the (false) news of Juliet's
death, he exclaims: 'Is it e'en so? Then I defy you, stars!'
(V.1.24). Such superstitions about 'the stars' would have
held more force for an Elizabethan audience than they
do now, but as a serious explanation for disaster (a word
we get from the Latin for 'bad star'), they have never
been truly arresting. No, the real force of this tragedy
does not lie in 'the stars', any more than the continuing
force of Greek tragedies depends on beliefs about Apollo
and Aphrodite which no longer send a shiver down our
spines. Real tragic force depends on provoking in readers
and audiences a kind of half-assent to the presence of
forces, rhythms and patterns in our lives that lie beyond
our control and comprehension. The assent is only partial
because we also wish to protest, vigorously, against the
sense of their inevitability.

There is mystery in *Romeo and Juliet*. And there is at

the end, in the final scene, a real mess such as critical interpretation and theatrical performance should not try too hard to clarify. The Friar tries to clear things up, but he has a lot to answer for. Better surely to appreciate, as something realistic and outrageous, the unresolved anger, grief and bewilderment in the face of this collective disaster, where there is no one to tidy things up conclusively, to apportion judgement, to dispense mortality and mercy in Verona. There is only poor Prince Escalus, the well-meaning nonentity. For in Verona, as in all the other tragic black-spots in our world, mortality and mercy are not confidently to be dispensed by merely human hands.

Adrian Poole

The Play in Performance

The opening Chorus famously speaks of 'the two hours' traffic of our stage'(12). It's perfectly possible to perform *Romeo and Juliet* in two hours or less, depending on how many words you get the actors to speak and how fast. (In modern performance it takes on average about three seconds to speak one line and five minutes to speak 100.) If you want them to speak every word in the text of the second Quarto (1599) that forms the basis of most modern editions, including this one (see An Account of the Text), then even at a cracking pace it will take well over three hours. But we can't know for certain how many of these words were uttered by Shakespeare's company, the Lord Chamberlain's men, when they performed this play in the second half of the 1590s, probably at the Theatre and then at the Curtain. There is an earlier and shorter version, the first Quarto (1597), that may have been designed for other venues or occasions, especially touring. This loses a good deal of the 'poetry', so that Juliet's 'Gallop apace, you fiery-footed steeds' at the start of Act III, scene 2 lasts only four lines instead of thirty-one, for example. In keeping with some modern stage and all screen versions, it puts a premium on 'action' to keep the story moving. Franco Zeffirelli's acclaimed Old Vic production (1960) cut about one-third of the traditional Shakespearian text, while his film version (1968) only *retained* about one-third. Baz Luhrmann's carefully entitled film *William Shakespeare's Romeo + Juliet* (1996) is comparably ruthless.

The Introduction has noted some aspects of Shakespeare's text(s) that have been most liable to omission over the two and a half centuries since David Garrick 'restored' it to the stage at Drury Lane in 1748. Garrick sentimentalized the play by focusing on the lovers and giving them the lengthy reunion in the tomb that Shakespeare had unaccountably omitted. He also realized the opportunity for spectacle that has attracted actor-managers, directors and impresarios who can afford extravagant scenic effects, lavish music and a large cast of extras, such as Henry Irving and Herbert Beerbohm Tree in the late Victorian and early Edwardian theatre, and Zeffirelli and Luhrmann on film. Garrick made much of the masked ball at the Capulet feast, which is authorized by Shakespeare's text, and also of Juliet's funeral procession, which is not. The solemn dirge composed for this looks ahead to the continuing importance of music in performance of the play and its offshoots in opera, ballet, musical and film. One 'spectacular' element however has undergone significant transformation over the past fifty years, both on stage and screen. Since Peter Brook's 1947 Stratford production – critics remarked on the unprecedented venom in the family quarrel and the real hatred in the fights – the streets of Verona have become more dangerous and the violence more brutal.

Productions must decide how fair or ugly to make Verona. You can make the physical setting ravishingly beautiful, an exotic picture-book vision of Renaissance Italy. This may soften the ugliness of the violence or it may heighten the contrast. Or you can emphasize the realism of the street-life, the dirt and the stench, against which the poetry and the beauty of the young lovers can stand out more sharply – unless they are corrupted by it. In any case there is a balance to be struck between the central love story and its public context, between earthy corporeal 'reality' and idealistic spiritual 'romance'.

There is also a challenge to be met in the contrasting representation of external and internal spaces, and how you get from one to the other. On one hand you have to choreograph some large public scenes – the street-fights, the feast and the final dénouement in the tomb. At the other extreme you have to establish the space for intimate encounters between the principals, most obviously for the so-called 'balcony' scene (II.2), the several scenes in Juliet's bedroom (I.3, II.5, III.2, III.5, IV.3, IV.5), at Friar Laurence's cell (II.3, II.6, III.3, IV.1), and at the Capulet tomb (V.3). The difficulties posed by these scenes and the transitions between them vary between different spaces and media. The 'bare' Elizabethan stage and the 'full' modern screen have this in common that they can both redefine space and shift location in the blink of an eye. A couple of well-known instances illustrate the nature of the stage for which Shakespeare wrote. When Romeo, Mercutio and his friends enter the Capulet house a space that was 'outside' is transformed by a brief exchange between the serving-men into 'inside' (I.5.1–16). Later, the scene at dawn after their one night together (III.5) begins with the lovers looking out of Juliet's bedroom from the upper level or gallery. When Romeo descends at line 42 he presumably climbs down the rope ladder in full view of the audience, turning the stage into the orchard for his remaining seventeen-line exchange with Juliet. But when her mother makes her entrance on to the main stage at line 64, and Juliet comes down from the window by an internal staircase, this turns the space into her bedroom. The stage has been turned outside in. In other theatres this redefinition of space can pose difficulties.

The actors are often faced with comparably rapid transitions, as for example from levity to seriousness and vice versa. Mercutio's role is particularly rich in possibilities for bewildering his listeners onstage and in the audience: how serious is he? The uncertainty culminates in his final dying moments. How quickly or slowly does the truth dawn on his friends, that whatever he's saying, his death is for real? The possibility that speakers may not always mean exactly what they say affects many of the play's verbal effects, especially those that call attention to themselves, such as clever wordplay, rhyme or self-consciously literary effect. These have a chilling effect on audiences who can't understand them, or if they do, can't share the character's pleasure in them. Productions can choose to cut them completely. But if they retain them, they have to decide what effect they wish to produce, as for example by choosing to have the opening Chorus delivered by the actor who plays the Prince, or Friar Laurence, or Romeo, or the Apothecary. In passages of dialogue that involve ostentatiously clever turns of phrase actors have to decide whether they are trying to express something about themselves, or exert some power over their listeners onstage, or both. And how do the listeners react? Our impressions of Mercutio, for example, will be radically coloured by the way Romeo, Benvolio and the others respond to him. Do they admire him? Does he make them nervous? Does he deliver the Queen Mab speech to all of them, or specifically to Romeo, or to himself, or some combination of all these?

A major change has overtaken performance of the

play in the last fifty years in the frank re-admission of its sexuality, both coarse and refined. From Garrick onwards much of the lewd talk was simply cut, as for example Mercutio's ebullient obscenities in the exchange with Benvolio after the Capulet ball (II.1). In 1935 Laurence Olivier may well have been the first Mercutio since Shakespeare's time to utter on stage the naughty couplet about Romeo's woman and the 'poppering pear' (II.1.38), and from the 1960s onwards we have heard more 'open-arses' (Q2, the 1599 edition) than 'open et ceteras' (the coyer Q1, 1597 edition, reading). At a more elevated level Juliets have also been permitted more candid excitement at the prospect of physical union. Until the twentieth century 'Gallop apace, you fiery-footed steeds' (III.2) was always edited (especially 8–16), if indeed it was to be heard at all. Few self-respecting Juliets now would forgo this dimension of the role, nor the opportunity for a frank display of physical feeling for the sexual partner of their choice. Until quite recently the lovers would play the dawn scene after their night together very properly dressed; now we are more likely to see them naked in bed.

If modern performances have seized with alacrity on the corporeal aspects of the play, they have been no more at ease than earlier generations with its later phases. Mercutio's absence is part of the problem. So too is Romeo's, from early in Act III, scene 5 throughout Act IV (see note to V.1). This throws a lot of responsibility on to Juliet (and the Friar), and the sequence of scenes surrounding her fake death can seem protracted. So too can the long passage after the lovers have died halfway through Act V, scene 3, especially Friar Laurence's explanation of what the audience already knows (229–69). Modern performances often

sustain the pace by trimming the whole play from the
parting of the lovers at III.5.59 to the end. Particular
uneasiness surrounds the sincerity of the alleged reconciliation of the two families over the lovers' corpses,
and it's become common to expose it to scorn. In 1986
Michael Bogdanov's Royal Shakespeare Company production turned this final scene into a press conference,
reducing the resolution to a shameless media event.
Luhrmann's film takes a similar line.

When are you too old to play Romeo and Juliet? The
American Julia Marlowe went on till she was fifty-seven;
her Romeo (her real-life husband) was sixty-five. Since
the discovery of the teenager in the 1950s modern audiences have grown to expect a convincing simulation of
youthful physicality. There has always been a tension
between the technical experience ideally required for the
principal roles and the juvenility the actors must represent. One day you're too young to play Juliet and the
next you're too old. Theatre audiences participate in the
make-believe of performance and so are generally more
tolerant than their cinematic counterparts. But the nub
of the challenge in this respect has never been the literal
age of the players concerned so much as the audience's
own ideas about sex, love, gender and youth.

It's instructive that for the Victorians Juliet was a relatively easy and attractive role, the one in which any
aspiring young actress would aim to make a big mark.
It's true that the role was carefully edited, as indeed was
the text as a whole, to occlude the explicit sexuality. Was
this exactly the attraction, the idea of innocent female
passion on the brink of acknowledgment? Has the role
become more difficult because actors and audiences find
it harder to recognize the moment of sexual awakening
for a young woman? Did the Victorians think of it as

'surely not yet', while we think of it as 'surely already'?
Not that there haven't been notable successes, such as
Peggy Ashcroft in 1935 and Estelle Kohler in 1967 and
1973. But the role attracts new kinds of anxieties – that
Juliet is too sexy too soon, or conversely and damn-
ingly, never sexy enough, 'too English'. Audiences
demand a sexual chemistry between the young lovers,
and when this is absent it is often Juliet who gets the
blame.

Romeo by contrast was for most of the nineteenth
century not a role that actors queued up to play, and it's
revealing that one of those who did so most successfully
was a woman, the American Charlotte Cushman. Was
Romeo just too emotional to be played by a (real) man?
A scene that caused particular problems was the one with
the Friar when Romeo grovels on the ground and tries
to kill himself: 'Art thou a man? . . . Thy tears are
womanish', the Friar exclaims (III.3.109–10). In the
twentieth century the position seems to have changed
and there have been many highly successful Romeos. It's
been said that when Gielgud and Olivier exchanged the
roles of Romeo and Mercutio in 1935 Gielgud's poetic,
gentlemanly Romeo looked to the past, while Olivier's
earthy, athletic, sensuous Romeo pointed the way to the
future. If you cut or reduce the references to Romeo's
passion for Rosaline, as was often the case in the nineteenth century, you enhance the 'innocence' he brings
to his first encounter with Juliet; modern performance
is likely to promote the sense of his prior experience.
Does the fact that Romeos can now give a freer rein both
to their passion and their vulnerability reflect a better fit
between modern conceptions of what it means to be an
attractive young man and Shakespeare's? Is it easier for
Romeos now to attract both male and female members

of an audience, no matter what their sexual inclinations, than it is for Juliets?

In this respect it is important to consider the huge variations the role of Mercutio has undergone. Restrained, censored and sentimentalized, up until the middle of the twentieth century Mercutio was a mainly charming man-about-town whose effervescence could make him, for the audience, a distinct rival to Romeo. But in recent decades he has turned into a more darkly enigmatic presence. The restoration of all the 'dirty language' has contributed to this, giving the player scope to explore the vicious implications of his feelings towards women and the all-male sociability he aggressively promotes. It's Juliet to whom he has become a rival, and not merely for Romeo's attention. Recent Mercutios have raised questions about what it takes to be a man, what it means to be a young man, of which previous audiences have seemed unconscious. It is not unknown for his ghostly presence to linger ominously over the latter phase of the play (as for example in Michael Boyd's Royal Shakespeare Company production, 2000).

The Nurse has always been a less troubling presence than Mercutio, and the stereotype on which she draws seems to have remained relatively constant. Nevertheless, there are choices to be made about quite how ancient she is, and after the imposing performances by Edith Evans in 1935 and even more venerably in 1961, some recent productions have diminished the age-gap between her and Juliet to good effect, creating more of a chance to explore the nurture that Juliet receives, or fails to receive, from her two mothers. Lady Capulet's age is also open to question, as are the relations she has with her husband and Tybalt. (Zeffirelli was the first to allow her an intimacy with Tybalt that compensates for the blankness of her marriage.) The scenes in which the three women appear together (Act 1, scene 3 in particular) represent opportunities, precious because comparatively slender, for characterizing a domestic 'female' domain to contrast with the 'male' world of the streets outside. The great moment of choice for the actor playing the Nurse comes when Juliet asks her advice and she recommends forgetting Romeo and marrying Paris – and committing bigamy (III.5.213–28). How stupid is the Nurse? How difficult does she find it to utter this worldly wisdom, if at all? Does she at some level realize, before she has finished or as she leaves, that Juliet is going to reject it, and curse her? Does it hurt?

Of the three main figures of male authority in the play, Prince Escalus is given the least to say and do, but productions must choose how impressive to make the justice he dispenses, and the display of power with which it's backed. Modern productions tend towards scepticism about, if not outright hostility towards, the 'glooming peace' over which he finally presides. There are more complex opportunities in the role of Juliet's father. At one extreme he is a violent, impatient and hateful tyrant who can't bear to be crossed, and at the other, a soft-hearted, sentimental, resourceless old man whose world is shattered when he loses his only surviving child. Comical, genial, generous, vicious, he is one of the richest portraits of a father in Shakespeare. So too, in a different way, is the ghostly father, Friar Laurence, but he carries the burden of a more ambitious moral and spiritual authority than the shallow old Capulet. He runs the risk of boring the audience, as Capulet never does. Hence the value in the rare moments of humour he's given ('God pardon sin! Wast thou with Rosaline?' II.3.40), and the more frequent possibilities for irony which make an audience warm towards him, establishing not only his good intentions, but the intelligence with which he puts them to work. If one of the main questions about the role is the depth of his love for the son and the daughter who look up to him, then another must be how deeply he considers the risks all three of them run. How big is his heart and how large is his brain? And how candid is he in defeat? Does he put too much faith in his drugs and then try to avoid responsibility by speaking of 'this work of heaven'? If he is allowed to give his final speech in full, how exactly does he balance the elements of impeachment and purging, 'Myself condemnèd and myself excused' (V.3.227)?

The single biggest challenge about the play in performance at the start of the twenty-first century is simply its legendary status as 'the greatest love story the world has ever known'. Audiences bring to it more powerful preconceptions than to any other play of Shakespeare's with the possible exception of *Hamlet*, and certainly more powerful preconceptions about young love. They also bring images, conscious, fugitive or deeply buried, of the two lovers separated from each other in the so-called 'balcony' scene and united by death in the tomb. Everybody knows them; these are celebrities. Hence the pressure, as always with productions of Shakespeare but here more than ever, to do something different.

Of the many successful instances over the past fifty years of doing something different with *Romeo and Juliet*, one of the most influential has been *West Side Story*, the musical by Jerome Robbins and Leonard Bernstein first staged in 1957 and filmed in 1961. Jaded journalists have been known to say they prefer it to Shakespeare's play. It's true that in a sense Shakespeare's play is only another telling of the Romeo and Juliet story. So too are the films

by Zeffirelli and Luhrmann that have effectively modernized it – like *West Side Story*, but using some of
Shakespeare's words. All these versions can be compared
with the narratives on which Shakespeare himself gratefully drew (especially Brooke). But for better or worse
Shakespeare's is not just another version. It is the one
that has carried most authority, against which others are
measured, and out of which therefore new performances, on stage, screen or any other medium, can
constantly be generated.

Adrian Poole

Further Reading

Brian Gibbons's Arden edition (1980) and G. Blakemore Evans's New Cambridge edition (1984) provide readers with comprehensively edited texts. Evans has a lengthy, illustrated section on the history of the play in the theatre and a detailed examination of Shakespeare's sources. Gibbons focuses on the play's physicality – what he calls its appetitiveness – both in linguistic and theatrical terms. Evans notes how critical opinion 'has ranged from simple adulation to measured disapproval' and investigates the critical obsession with the play as a failed or experimental tragedy either of fate or character or both. These editions provide material – as do the pages on the play in *William Shakespeare: A Textual Companion* (1987) by Stanley Wells and Gary Taylor – which should be read to supplement the textual discussion in this edition's Account of the Text, especially regarding the influence of the first Quarto (1597) and the Folio (1623) on the shape of any 'final' text. None of these three, however, goes as far as Cedric Watts, in his Harvester New Critical Introduction (1991), who, after arguing that 'the play is textually more protean, variable and flexible than we may at first have supposed', suggests that the only 'honest' edition of *Romeo and Juliet* would be printings of both Q1 and Q2 (the first [1597] and second [1599] editions). Shades of *King Lear*.

For many critics the fault lines of textual instability mesh with those of generic uncertainty and linguistic experimentation. In *Shakespeare's Early Tragedies* (1968) Nicholas Brooke talks dismissively of the play's 'obtrusive poeticalness' in its dramatizing of the world of the love sonnets, comparable, he says, to the way *Titus Andronicus* dramatizes the world of Lucrece. (Gibbons thinks Sidney's sonnet-sequence, *Astrophil and Stella*, is particularly significant for *Romeo and Juliet*.) H. A. Mason's *Shakespeare's Tragedies of Love* (1970) examines and praises the power of this poeticalness and has an interesting discussion of the play's relationship to its major source, Arthur Brooke's poem *The Tragicall Historye of Romeus and Juliet* (1562). A tendency to simple adulation can be discerned in Douglas Cole's collection of essays on the play, *Twentieth-Century Interpretations* (1970). And in *The Osier Cage: Rhetorical Devices in 'Romeo and Juliet'* (1966) Robert O. Evans praises Romeo and Juliet as great rhetoricians whose use of language proclaims 'the transcendence of the intellectual portions of their souls above the others', while in *Passion Lends Them Power: A Study of Shakespeare's Love Tragedies* (1976) Derick Marsh believes that the play succeeds 'in giving new meaning to the typical lovers' cliché of "I cannot live without you"'. Works like these look back to E. E. Stoll's *Shakespeare's Young Lovers* (1935): 'It is poetically, dramatically, not psychologically, that the characters are meant to interest us.'

What interests many critics – especially those closer to measured disapproval in their response to the play than to simple adulation – is the way *Romeo and Juliet* resists or muddles classification. Such a view rejects determinate interpretations, whether they treat the play as a pure tragedy of Fate, as does Bertrand Evans in

Shakespeare's Tragic Practice (1979), as one of free
agency, as in Franklin Dickey's *Not Wisely But Too Well:
Shakespeare's Love Tragedies* (1957), as a 'Christian'
tragedy, as does James Seward in *Tragic Vision in 'Romeo
and Juliet'* (1973), or as a 'medieval' one, as in John
Lawlor's essay on the play in *Early Shakespeare*
(Stratford-upon-Avon Studies 3, ed. J. R. Brown and B.
Harris, 1961). Instead, this line of criticism seizes upon
the play's resistance to easy classification as in itself a
classifying strategy. Hence Neil Taylor and Bryan
Loughrey's assertion in their collection of essays in the
Casebook Series, *Shakespeare's Early Tragedies: 'Richard
III', 'Titus Andronicus', and 'Romeo and Juliet'* (1990),
that 'the tragedy is an enactment of painfully contradictory facts', especially the facts of providence and
unpredictability. Cedric Watts's fine study also notes the
structural paradox whereby 'inelegant' chance and co-
incidence occur in a context of constant suggestions of
divine ordaining in a style combining 'aspiring lyricism
and realistic muscularity'. In sentences of measured
adulation Watts proclaims the play to be the most thrilling
tragedy since Aeschylus, Sophocles and Euripides; it is
'so memorably enhancive of sexuality as to make the
explanations of Marxists and Freudians alike seem
descendants of Mercutio's cynical bawdry and the
Nurse's mundane practicality'.

A significant muddling agent generically speaking is
the amount of comedy in the play. In her classic study,
The Comic Matrix of Shakespeare's Tragedies (1979),
Susan Snyder thinks that *Romeo and Juliet* 'becomes,
rather than is, tragic' – because of Mercutio's death 'a
well-developed comic movement is diverted into tragedy
by mischance'. Maynard Mack in *Everybody's Shakespeare: Reflections Chiefly on the Tragedies* (1993) argues

that the play has all 'the attractions of high comedy'. A. C. Hamilton's *The Early Shakespeare* (1967) thinks the play to be a tragic counterpart to the early comedies. In Jill Levenson's book in the Shakespeare in Performance Series (1987) she quotes from George Santayana's 'Carnival' (1922): 'everything in nature is lyrical in its ideal essence, tragic in its fate, and comic in its existence'. She makes much – rightly – of the play's wit, a wit that 'prevents *Romeo and Juliet* from becoming an intense two-hour dirge for young love', from 'settling into melancholy'. At the same time she argues that in the verse that the lovers speak they grow from 'ordinary to archetypal'. Joseph Porter's work *Shakespeare's Mercutio: His History and Drama* (1988) focuses on the character who (with the Nurse) is a source for so much of the play's astringent humour. Porter perhaps spends too much of the book pursuing the figure of Mercury in history and literature on the somewhat flimsy basis of the mercuriality of Mercutio's combinations: 'an opposition to love, an amiable erotic permissiveness, and a phallocentrism that admits traces of homoeroticism' – none the less his defence of Mercutio is an admirable corrective to a reductive reading of the play.

Michael Taylor

To the Arden (1980) and New Cambridge (1984) editions can now be added Jill L. Levenson's fine Oxford Shakespeare edition (2000). In addition to her extensive introduction and substantial annotations, Levenson answers the challenge issued by Cedric Watts at the head of this entry for an 'honest' edition that would print the texts of both Q1 and Q2. Levenson's own earlier study

of the play in performance has been supplemented by
further work including James N. Loehlin's annotated
edition in the series Shakespeare in Production (2002)
and Russell Jackson's study of the play's fifteen productions by the Royal Shakespeare Company between 1947
and 2000 in the series Shakespeare at Stratford (2003).
Loehlin includes discussion of the films by Zeffirelli and
others that feature largely in the proliferating literature
on 'Shakespeare and Film', and he sees the cultural position of Shakespeare's play at the beginning of the twenty-
first century summed up in two films from the late 1990s,
Baz Luhrmann's *William Shakespeare's Romeo + Juliet*
and John Madden's *Shakespeare in Love*. Helpful accounts
of the films (and 'offshoots') based on Shakespeare's
play are provided by several of the contributors to the
Cambridge Companion to Shakespeare on Film, ed. Russell
Jackson (2000). Other recent studies have sought to
measure the differences between Shakespeare's time and
our own, especially where ideas, values and beliefs about
love, sex, marriage, families and identity are concerned.
To Cedric Watts's excellent short book on the play can
be added one by Sasha Roberts in the series Writers and
Their Work (1998). Roberts stresses the multiple possibilities in a text that too many interpretations (including
performances) have sought to simplify, arguing that it
'allows for considerable complexity in the depiction of
marital, patriarchal, matriarchal, and filial relations, and
engages with contemporary concerns about the nature
of power and its abuse within the family'. There has
been an important issue of *Shakespeare Survey*, edited by
Stanley Wells, devoted to *'Romeo and Juliet' and Its
Afterlife* (1996).

                                        Adrian Poole

THE MOST EXCELLENT AND LAMENTABLE TRAGEDY OF ROMEO AND JULIET

The Characters in the Play

Escalus, PRINCE of Verona
MERCUTIO, kinsman of the Prince and friend of Romeo
PARIS, a young count, kinsman of the Prince and Mercutio, and suitor of Juliet
PAGE to Count Paris

MONTAGUE, head of a Veronese family at feud with the Capulets
LADY MONTAGUE
ROMEO, son of Montague
BENVOLIO, nephew of Montague and friend of Romeo and Mercutio
ABRAM, servant of Montague
BALTHASAR, servant of Montague attending on Romeo

CAPULET, head of a Veronese family at feud with the Montagues
LADY CAPULET
JULIET, daughter of Capulet
TYBALT, nephew of Lady Capulet
FOLLOWER
COUSIN CAPULET, an old man of the Capulet family
NURSE of Juliet, her foster-mother
PETER, servant of Capulet attending on the Nurse

SAMPSON
GREGORY
Clown, a SERVANT   } of the Capulet household
SERVINGMEN

FRIAR LAURENCE, a Franciscan
FRIAR JOHN, a Franciscan
An APOTHECARY of Mantua
FIDDLER and MUSICIANS (Simon Catling, Hugh Rebeck, James Soundpost)
Members of the WATCH
CITIZENS of Verona
Maskers, torchbearers, pages, servants

CHORUS

The Prologue

Enter Chorus

CHORUS

Two households, both alike in dignity
  In fair Verona, where we lay our scene,
From ancient grudge break to new mutiny,
  Where civil blood makes civil hands unclean.
From forth the fatal loins of these two foes
  A pair of star-crossed lovers take their life;
Whose misadventured piteous overthrows
  Doth with their death bury their parents' strife.
The fearful passage of their death-marked love
  And the continuance of their parents' rage,   10
Which, but their children's end, naught could remove,
  Is now the two hours' traffic of our stage;
The which if you with patient ears attend,
What here shall miss, our toil shall strive to mend. *Exit*

Enter Sampson and Gregory, with swords and buck-
lers, of the house of Capulet

SAMPSON Gregory, on my word, we'll not carry coals.

GREGORY No. For then we should be colliers.

SAMPSON I mean, an we be in choler, we'll draw.

GREGORY Ay, while you live, draw your neck out of collar.

SAMPSON I strike quickly, being moved.

GREGORY But thou art not quickly moved to strike.

SAMPSON A dog of the house of Montague moves me.

GREGORY To move is to stir, and to be valiant is to stand.
Therefore, if thou art moved, thou runnest away.

SAMPSON A dog of that house shall move me to stand. I
will take the wall of any man or maid of Montague's.

GREGORY That shows thee a weak slave. For the weakest
goes to the wall.

SAMPSON 'Tis true; and therefore women, being the
weaker vessels, are ever thrust to the wall. Therefore I
will push Montague's men from the wall, and thrust his
maids to the wall.

GREGORY The quarrel is between our masters, and us
their men.

SAMPSON 'Tis all one. I will show myself a tyrant. When
I have fought with the men, I will be civil with the
maids – I will cut off their heads.

GREGORY The heads of the maids?

SAMPSON Ay, the heads of the maids, or their maiden-
heads. Take it in what sense thou wilt.

GREGORY They must take it in sense that feel it.

SAMPSON Me they shall feel while I am able to stand; and
'tis known I am a pretty piece of flesh.

GREGORY 'Tis well thou art not fish; if thou hadst, thou
30   hadst been poor-John. Draw thy tool. Here comes of
the house of Montagues.

Enter Abram and another Servingman

SAMPSON My naked weapon is out. Quarrel. I will back
thee.

GREGORY How? Turn thy back and run?

SAMPSON Fear me not.

GREGORY No, marry. I fear thee!

SAMPSON Let us take the law of our sides. Let them
begin.

GREGORY I will frown as I pass by, and let them take it as
40   they list.

SAMPSON Nay, as they dare. I will bite my thumb at them;
which is disgrace to them if they bear it.

ABRAM Do you bite your thumb at us, sir?

SAMPSON I do bite my thumb, sir.

ABRAM Do you bite your thumb at us, sir?

SAMPSON (*aside to Gregory*) Is the law of our side if I say
'Ay'?

GREGORY (*aside to Sampson*) No.

SAMPSON No, sir, I do not bite my thumb at you, sir. But
50   I bite my thumb, sir.

GREGORY Do you quarrel, sir?

ABRAM Quarrel, sir? No, sir.

SAMPSON But if you do, sir, I am for you. I serve as good
a man as you.

ABRAM No better.

SAMPSON Well, sir.

Enter Benvolio

GREGORY (*aside to Sampson*) Say 'better'. Here comes one
of my master's kinsmen.

SAMPSON Yes, better, sir.

ABRAM You lie.   60

SAMPSON Draw, if you be men. Gregory, remember thy
washing blow.

They fight

BENVOLIO Part, fools!
Put up your swords. You know not what you do.

Enter Tybalt

TYBALT

What, art thou drawn among these heartless hinds?
Turn thee, Benvolio, look upon thy death.

BENVOLIO

I do but keep the peace. Put up thy sword,
Or manage it to part these men with me.

TYBALT

What, drawn, and talk of peace? I hate the word
As I hate hell, all Montagues, and thee.   70
Have at thee, coward!

They fight

Enter three or four Citizens with clubs or partisans

CITIZENS Clubs, bills, and partisans! Strike! Beat them
down! Down with the Capulets! Down with the Montagues!

Enter old Capulet in his gown, and his wife

CAPULET

What noise is this? Give me my long sword, ho!

LADY CAPULET

A crutch, a crutch! Why call you for a sword?

Enter old Montague and his wife

CAPULET

My sword, I say! Old Montague is come
And flourishes his blade in spite of me.

MONTAGUE

Thou villain Capulet! – Hold me not. Let me go.

LADY MONTAGUE

80   Thou shalt not stir one foot to seek a foe.

Enter Prince Escalus, with his train

PRINCE

Rebellious subjects, enemies to peace,
Profaners of this neighbour-stainèd steel –
Will they not hear? What, ho – you men, you beasts,
That quench the fire of your pernicious rage
With purple fountains issuing from your veins!
On pain of torture, from those bloody hands
Throw your mistempered weapons to the ground
And hear the sentence of your movèd prince.
Three civil brawls, bred of an airy word

90   By thee, old Capulet, and Montague,
Have thrice disturbed the quiet of our streets
And made Verona's ancient citizens
Cast by their grave-beseeming ornaments
To wield old partisans, in hands as old,
Cankered with peace, to part your cankered hate.
If ever you disturb our streets again,
Your lives shall pay the forfeit of the peace.
For this time all the rest depart away.
You, Capulet, shall go along with me;

100   And, Montague, come you this afternoon,
To know our farther pleasure in this case,
To old Free-town, our common judgement-place.
Once more, on pain of death, all men depart.

Exeunt all but Montague, his wife, and Benvolio

MONTAGUE

Who set this ancient quarrel new abroach?
Speak, nephew, were you by when it began?

BENVOLIO

Here were the servants of your adversary
And yours, close fighting ere I did approach.
I drew to part them. In the instant came
The fiery Tybalt, with his sword prepared;
Which, as he breathed defiance to my ears,   110
He swung about his head and cut the winds,
Who nothing hurt withal, hissed him in scorn.
While we were interchanging thrusts and blows,
Came more and more, and fought on part and part,
Till the Prince came, who parted either part.

LADY MONTAGUE

O where is Romeo? Saw you him today?
Right glad I am he was not at this fray.

BENVOLIO

Madam, an hour before the worshipped sun
Peered forth the golden window of the East,
A troubled mind drive me to walk abroad;   120
Where, underneath the grove of sycamore
That westward rooteth from this city side,
So early walking did I see your son.
Towards him I made. But he was ware of me
And stole into the covert of the wood.
I, measuring his affections by my own,
Which then most sought where most might not be found,
Being one too many by my weary self,
Pursued my humour, not pursuing his,
And gladly shunned who gladly fled from me.   130

MONTAGUE

Many a morning hath he there been seen
With tears augmenting the fresh morning's dew,

Adding to clouds more clouds with his deep sighs.
But all so soon as the all-cheering sun
Should in the farthest East begin to draw
The shady curtains from Aurora's bed,
Away from light steals home my heavy son
And private in his chamber pens himself,
Shuts up his windows, locks fair daylight out,
140   And makes himself an artificial night.
Black and portentous must this humour prove
Unless good counsel may the cause remove.

BENVOLIO
My noble uncle, do you know the cause?

MONTAGUE
I neither know it nor can learn of him.

BENVOLIO
Have you importuned him by any means?

MONTAGUE
Both by myself and many other friends.
But he, his own affections' counsellor,
Is to himself – I will not say how true –
But to himself so secret and so close,
150   So far from sounding and discovery,
As is the bud bit with an envious worm
Ere he can spread his sweet leaves to the air
Or dedicate his beauty to the sun.
Could we but learn from whence his sorrows grow,
We would as willingly give cure as know.
    Enter Romeo

BENVOLIO
See, where he comes. So please you step aside.
I'll know his grievance, or be much denied.

MONTAGUE
I would thou wert so happy by thy stay
To hear true shrift. Come, madam, let's away.

Exeunt Montague and wife

BENVOLIO

Good morrow, cousin.

ROMEO   Is the day so young?   160

BENVOLIO

But new struck nine.

ROMEO   Ay me! sad hours seem long.

Was that my father that went hence so fast?

BENVOLIO

It was. What sadness lengthens Romeo's hours?

ROMEO

Not having that which having makes them short.

BENVOLIO

In love?

ROMEO

Out –

BENVOLIO

Of love?

ROMEO

Out of her favour where I am in love.

BENVOLIO

Alas that love, so gentle in his view,

Should be so tyrannous and rough in proof!   170

ROMEO

Alas that love, whose view is muffled, still

Should without eyes see pathways to his will!

Where shall we dine? O me, what fray was here?

Yet tell me not, for I have heard it all.

Here's much to-do with hate, but more with love.

Why then, O brawling love, O loving hate,

O anything, of nothing first create!

O heavy lightness, serious vanity,

Misshapen chaos of well-seeming forms,

Feather of lead, bright smoke, cold fire, sick health,   180

Still-waking sleep, that is not what it is!
This love feel I, that feel no love in this.
Dost thou not laugh?

BENVOLIO   No, coz, I rather weep.

ROMEO

Good heart, at what?

BENVOLIO   At thy good heart's oppression.

ROMEO

Why, such is love's transgression.
Griefs of mine own lie heavy in my breast,
Which thou wilt propagate, to have it pressed
With more of thine. This love that thou hast shown
Doth add more grief to too much of mine own.
Love is a smoke made with the fume of sighs;
Being purged, a fire sparkling in lovers' eyes;
Being vexed, a sea nourished with lovers' tears.
What is it else? A madness most discreet,
A choking gall and a preserving sweet.
Farewell, my coz.

BENVOLIO   Soft! I will go along.
An if you leave me so, you do me wrong.

ROMEO

Tut, I have left myself. I am not here.
This is not Romeo, he's some other where.

BENVOLIO

Tell me in sadness, who is that you love?

ROMEO

What, shall I groan and tell thee?

BENVOLIO   Groan? Why, no.
But sadly tell me who.

ROMEO

Bid a sick man in sadness make his will.
Ah, word ill urged to one that is so ill!
In sadness, cousin, I do love a woman.

BENVOLIO

    I aimed so near when I supposed you loved.

ROMEO

    A right good markman. And she's fair I love.

BENVOLIO

    A right fair mark, fair coz, is soonest hit.

ROMEO

    Well, in that hit you miss. She'll not be hit

    With Cupid's arrow. She hath Dian's wit,

    And, in strong proof of chastity well armed,   210

    From love's weak childish bow she lives uncharmed.

    She will not stay the siege of loving terms,

    Nor bide th'encounter of assailing eyes,

    Nor ope her lap to saint-seducing gold.

    O, she is rich in beauty; only poor

    That, when she dies, with beauty dies her store.

BENVOLIO

    Then she hath sworn that she will still live chaste?

ROMEO

    She hath; and in that sparing makes huge waste.

    For beauty, starved with her severity,

    Cuts beauty off from all posterity.   220

    She is too fair, too wise, wisely too fair,

    To merit bliss by making me despair.

    She hath forsworn to love; and in that vow

    Do I live dead that live to tell it now.

BENVOLIO

    Be ruled by me – forget to think of her.

ROMEO

    O, teach me how I should forget to think!

BENVOLIO

    By giving liberty unto thine eyes.

    Examine other beauties.

ROMEO   'Tis the way

To call hers, exquisite, in question more.
230 These happy masks that kiss fair ladies' brows,
Being black, puts us in mind they hide the fair.
He that is strucken blind cannot forget
The precious treasure of his eyesight lost.
Show me a mistress that is passing fair,
What doth her beauty serve but as a note
Where I may read who passed that passing fair?
Farewell. Thou canst not teach me to forget.

BENVOLIO
I'll pay that doctrine, or else die in debt.   *Exeunt*

I.2   *Enter Capulet, County Paris, and the Clown, a*
Servant

CAPULET
But Montague is bound as well as I,
In penalty alike; and 'tis not hard, I think,
For men so old as we to keep the peace.

PARIS
Of honourable reckoning are you both,
And pity 'tis you lived at odds so long.
But now, my lord, what say you to my suit?

CAPULET
But saying o'er what I have said before:
My child is yet a stranger in the world;
She hath not seen the change of fourteen years.
10 Let two more summers wither in their pride
Ere we may think her ripe to be a bride.

PARIS
Younger than she are happy mothers made.

CAPULET
And too soon marred are those so early made.

Earth hath swallowed all my hopes but she;
She's the hopeful lady of my earth.
But woo her, gentle Paris, get her heart.
My will to her consent is but a part,
And, she agreed, within her scope of choice
Lies my consent and fair according voice.
This night I hold an old accustomed feast,   20
Whereto I have invited many a guest,
Such as I love; and you among the store,
One more, most welcome, makes my number more.
At my poor house look to behold this night
Earth-treading stars that make dark heaven light.
Such comfort as do lusty young men feel
When well-apparelled April on the heel
Of limping winter treads, even such delight
Among fresh female buds shall you this night
Inherit at my house. Hear all; all see;   30
And like her most whose merit most shall be;
Which, on more view of many, mine, being one,
May stand in number, though in reckoning none.
Come, go with me. (*To Servant*) Go, sirrah, trudge about
Through fair Verona; find those persons out
Whose names are written there, and to them say,
My house and welcome on their pleasure stay.

Exeunt Capulet and Paris

SERVANT Find them out whose names are written here! It
is written that the shoemaker should meddle with his
yard and the tailor with his last, the fisher with his pencil   40
and the painter with his nets. But I am sent to find those
persons whose names are here writ, and can never find
what names the writing person hath here writ. I must to
the learned. In good time!

Enter Benvolio and Romeo

BENVOLIO

Tut, man, one fire burns out another's burning.

One pain is lessened by another's anguish.

Turn giddy, and be holp by backward turning.

One desperate grief cures with another's languish.

Take thou some new infection to thy eye,

50   And the rank poison of the old will die.

ROMEO

Your plantain leaf is excellent for that.

BENVOLIO

For what, I pray thee?

ROMEO   For your broken shin.

BENVOLIO

Why, Romeo, art thou mad?

ROMEO

Not mad, but bound more than a madman is;

Shut up in prison, kept without my food,

Whipped and tormented and – Good-e'en, good fellow.

SERVANT

God gi' good-e'en. I pray, sir, can you read?

ROMEO

Ay, mine own fortune in my misery.

SERVANT Perhaps you have learned it without book. But

60   I pray, can you read anything you see?

ROMEO

Ay, if I know the letters and the language.

SERVANT Ye say honestly. Rest you merry.

ROMEO

Stay, fellow. I can read.

He reads the letter

*Signor Martino and his wife and daughters. County Anselm
and his beauteous sisters. The lady widow of Utruvio.
Signor Placentio and his lovely nieces. Mercutio and his*

brother Valentine. Mine uncle Capulet, his wife, and daugh-
ters. My fair niece Rosaline and Livia. Signor Valentio and
his cousin Tybalt. Lucio and the lively Helena.

A fair assembly. Whither should they come?   70
SERVANT Up.
ROMEO Whither? To supper?
SERVANT To our house.
ROMEO Whose house?
SERVANT My master's.
ROMEO Indeed I should have asked thee that before.
SERVANT Now I'll tell you without asking. My master is
   the great rich Capulet; and if you be not of the house of
   Montagues, I pray come and crush a cup of wine. Rest
   you merry.   *Exit Servant* 80
BENVOLIO
   At this same ancient feast of Capulet's
   Sups the fair Rosaline whom thou so loves,
   With all the admirèd beauties of Verona.
   Go thither, and with unattainted eye
   Compare her face with some that I shall show,
   And I will make thee think thy swan a crow.
ROMEO
   When the devout religion of mine eye
      Maintains such falsehood, then turn tears to fires;
   And these, who, often drowned, could never die,
      Transparent heretics, be burnt for liars!   90
   One fairer than my love? The all-seeing sun
   Ne'er saw her match since first the world begun.
BENVOLIO
   Tut, you saw her fair, none else being by,
   Herself poised with herself in either eye.
   But in that crystal scales let there be weighed
   Your lady's love against some other maid

That I will show you shining at this feast,
And she shall scant show well that now seems best.

ROMEO

I'll go along, no such sight to be shown,
But to rejoice in splendour of mine own.   *Exeunt*

100

I.3   *Enter Lady Capulet and Nurse*

LADY CAPULET

Nurse, where's my daughter? Call her forth to me.

NURSE

Now, by my maidenhead at twelve year old,
I bade her come. What, lamb! What, ladybird! –
God forbid! – Where's this girl? What, Juliet!
     Enter Juliet

JULIET

How now? Who calls?

NURSE

Your mother.

JULIET

Madam, I am here. What is your will?

LADY CAPULET

This is the matter – Nurse, give leave awhile.
We must talk in secret. – Nurse, come back again.
I have remembered me, thou's hear our counsel.
Thou knowest my daughter's of a pretty age.

10

NURSE

Faith, I can tell her age unto an hour.

LADY CAPULET

She's not fourteen.

NURSE   I'll lay fourteen of my teeth –
And yet, to my teen be it spoken, I have but four –
She's not fourteen. How long is it now
To Lammastide?

LADY CAPULET   A fortnight and odd days.
NURSE
    Even or odd, of all days in the year,
    Come Lammas Eve at night shall she be fourteen.
    Susan and she – God rest all Christian souls! –
    Were of an age. Well, Susan is with God.   20
    She was too good for me. But, as I said,
    On Lammas Eve at night shall she be fourteen.
    That shall she, marry! I remember it well.
    'Tis since the earthquake now eleven years;
    And she was weaned – I never shall forget it –
    Of all the days of the year, upon that day.
    For I had then laid wormwood to my dug,
    Sitting in the sun under the dovehouse wall.
    My lord and you were then at Mantua.
    Nay, I do bear a brain. But, as I said,   30
    When it did taste the wormwood on the nipple
    Of my dug and felt it bitter, pretty fool,
    To see it tetchy and fall out wi' th'dug!
    Shake, quoth the dovehouse! 'Twas no need, I trow,
    To bid me trudge.
    And since that time it is eleven years.
    For then she could stand high-lone. Nay, by th'rood,
    She could have run and waddled all about.
    For even the day before she broke her brow.
    And then my husband – God be with his soul!   40
    'A was a merry man – took up the child.
    'Yea,' quoth he, 'dost thou fall upon thy face?
    Thou wilt fall backward when thou hast more wit.
    Wilt thou not, Jule?' And, by my holidam,
    The pretty wretch left crying and said 'Ay.'
    To see now how a jest shall come about!
    I warrant, an I should live a thousand years,
    I never should forget it. 'Wilt thou not, Jule?' quoth he,

And, pretty fool, it stinted and said 'Ay.'

LADY CAPULET

50   Enough of this. I pray thee hold thy peace.

NURSE

Yes, madam. Yet I cannot choose but laugh
To think it should leave crying and say 'Ay.'
And yet, I warrant, it had upon it brow
A bump as big as a young cockerel's stone,
A perilous knock. And it cried bitterly.
'Yea,' quoth my husband, 'fallest upon thy face?
Thou wilt fall backward when thou comest to age.
Wilt thou not, Jule?' It stinted, and said 'Ay.'

JULIET

And stint thou too, I pray thee, Nurse, say I.

NURSE

60   Peace, I have done. God mark thee to his grace!
Thou wast the prettiest babe that e'er I nursed.
An I might live to see thee married once,
I have my wish.

LADY CAPULET

Marry, that 'marry' is the very theme
I came to talk of. Tell me, daughter Juliet,
How stands your dispositions to be married?

JULIET

It is an honour that I dream not of.

NURSE

An honour! Were not I thine only nurse,
I would say thou hadst sucked wisdom from thy teat.

LADY CAPULET

70   Well, think of marriage now. Younger than you,
Here in Verona, ladies of esteem
Are made already mothers. By my count,
I was your mother much upon these years
That you are now a maid. Thus then in brief:

The valiant Paris seeks you for his love.

NURSE

A man, young lady! Lady, such a man
As all the world – why, he's a man of wax.

LADY CAPULET

Verona's summer hath not such a flower.

NURSE

Nay, he's a flower; in faith, a very flower.

LADY CAPULET

What say you? Can you love the gentleman?   80
This night you shall behold him at our feast.
Read o'er the volume of young Paris' face,
And find delight writ there with beauty's pen.
Examine every married lineament,
And see how one another lends content.
And what obscured in this fair volume lies
Find written in the margent of his eyes.
This precious book of love, this unbound lover,
To beautify him only lacks a cover.
The fish lives in the sea, and 'tis much pride   90
For fair without the fair within to hide.
That book in many's eyes doth share the glory,
That in gold clasps locks in the golden story.
So shall you share all that he doth possess,
By having him making yourself no less.

NURSE

No less? Nay, bigger! Women grow by men.

LADY CAPULET

Speak briefly, can you like of Paris' love?

JULIET

I'll look to like, if looking liking move.
But no more deep will I endart mine eye
Than your consent gives strength to make it fly.   100

Enter Servingman

SERVINGMAN Madam, the guests are come, supper served
up, you called, my young lady asked for, the Nurse
cursed in the pantry, and everything in extremity. I
must hence to wait. I beseech you follow straight.

LADY CAPULET
We follow thee.   *Exit Servingman*
          Juliet, the County stays.

NURSE
Go, girl, seek happy nights to happy days.   *Exeunt*

I.4   *Enter Romeo, Mercutio, Benvolio, with five or six other*
             maskers, and torchbearers

ROMEO
What, shall this speech be spoke for our excuse?
Or shall we on without apology?

BENVOLIO
The date is out of such prolixity.
We'll have no Cupid hoodwinked with a scarf,
Bearing a Tartar's painted bow of lath,
Scaring the ladies like a crowkeeper,
Nor no without-book prologue, faintly spoke
After the prompter, for our entrance.
But, let them measure us by what they will,
We'll measure them a measure and be gone.

ROMEO
Give me a torch. I am not for this ambling.
Being but heavy, I will bear the light.

MERCUTIO
Nay, gentle Romeo, we must have you dance.

ROMEO
Not I, believe me. You have dancing shoes
With nimble soles. I have a soul of lead
So stakes me to the ground I cannot move.

MERCUTIO

    You are a lover. Borrow Cupid's wings
    And soar with them above a common bound.

ROMEO

    I am too sore empiercèd with his shaft
    To soar with his light feathers; and so bound   20
    I cannot bound a pitch above dull woe.
    Under love's heavy burden do I sink.

MERCUTIO

    And, to sink in it, should you burden love –
    Too great oppression for a tender thing.

ROMEO

    Is love a tender thing? It is too rough,
    Too rude, too boisterous, and it pricks like thorn.

MERCUTIO

    If love be rough with you, be rough with love.
    Prick love for pricking, and you beat love down.
    Give me a case to put my visage in.
    A visor for a visor! What care I   30
    What curious eye doth quote deformities?
    Here are the beetle brows shall blush for me.

BENVOLIO

    Come, knock and enter; and no sooner in
    But every man betake him to his legs.

ROMEO

    A torch for me! Let wantons light of heart
    Tickle the senseless rushes with their heels.
    For I am proverbed with a grandsire phrase –
    I'll be a candle-holder and look on;
    The game was ne'er so fair, and I am done.

MERCUTIO

    Tut, dun's the mouse, the constable's own word!   40
    If thou art Dun, we'll draw thee from the mire
    Of – save your reverence – love, wherein thou stickest

Up to the ears. Come, we burn daylight, ho!
ROMEO
    Nay, that's not so.
MERCUTIO   I mean, sir, in delay
    We waste our lights in vain, like lamps by day.
    Take our good meaning, for our judgement sits
    Five times in that ere once in our five wits.
ROMEO
    And we mean well in going to this masque,
    But 'tis no wit to go.
MERCUTIO   Why, may one ask?
ROMEO
50 I dreamt a dream tonight.
MERCUTIO   And so did I.
ROMEO
    Well, what was yours?
MERCUTIO   That dreamers often lie.
ROMEO
    In bed asleep, while they do dream things true.
MERCUTIO
    O, then I see Queen Mab hath been with you.
    She is the fairies' midwife, and she comes
    In shape no bigger than an agate stone
    On the forefinger of an alderman,
    Drawn with a team of little atomies
    Over men's noses as they lie asleep.
    Her chariot is an empty hazelnut,
60 Made by the joiner squirrel or old grub,
    Time out o'mind the fairies' coachmakers.
    Her wagon spokes made of long spinners' legs;
    The cover, of the wings of grasshoppers;
    Her traces, of the smallest spider web;
    Her collars, of the moonshine's watery beams;
    Her whip, of cricket's bone; the lash, of film;

Her wagoner, a small grey-coated gnat,
Not half so big as a round little worm
Pricked from the lazy finger of a maid.
And in this state she gallops night by night   70
Through lovers' brains, and then they dream of love;
O'er courtiers' knees, that dream on curtsies straight;
O'er lawyers' fingers, who straight dream on fees;
O'er ladies' lips, who straight on kisses dream,
Which oft the angry Mab with blisters plagues,
Because their breaths with sweetmeats tainted are.
Sometime she gallops o'er a courtier's nose,
And then dreams he of smelling out a suit.
And sometime comes she with a tithe-pig's tail
Tickling a parson's nose as 'a lies asleep;   80
Then he dreams of another benefice.
Sometime she driveth o'er a soldier's neck;
And then dreams he of cutting foreign throats,
Of breaches, ambuscados, Spanish blades,
Of healths five fathom deep; and then anon
Drums in his ear, at which he starts and wakes,
And being thus frighted, swears a prayer or two
And sleeps again. This is that very Mab
That plaits the manes of horses in the night
And bakes the elf-locks in foul sluttish hairs,   90
Which once untangled much misfortune bodes.
This is the hag, when maids lie on their backs,
That presses them and learns them first to bear,
Making them women of good carriage.
This is she —

ROMEO   Peace, peace, Mercutio, peace!
Thou talkest of nothing.

MERCUTIO   True. I talk of dreams;
Which are the children of an idle brain,
Begot of nothing but vain fantasy;

Which is as thin of substance as the air,
100   And more inconstant than the wind, who woos
Even now the frozen bosom of the North
And, being angered, puffs away from thence,
Turning his side to the dew-dropping South.

BENVOLIO
This wind you talk of blows us from ourselves.
Supper is done, and we shall come too late.

ROMEO
I fear, too early. For my mind misgives
Some consequence, yet hanging in the stars,
Shall bitterly begin his fearful date
With this night's revels and expire the term
110   Of a despisèd life, closed in my breast,
By some vile forfeit of untimely death.
But He that hath the steerage of my course
Direct my sail! On, lusty gentlemen!

BENVOLIO
Strike, drum.

I.5   *They march about the stage; and Servingmen come*
          forth with napkins

FIRST SERVINGMAN Where's Potpan, that he helps not
   to take away? He shift a trencher! He scrape a trencher!

SECOND SERVINGMAN When good manners shall lie all
   in one or two men's hands, and they unwashed too, 'tis
   a foul thing.

FIRST SERVINGMAN Away with the joint-stools; remove
   the court-cupboard; look to the plate. Good thou, save
   me a piece of marchpane; and, as thou loves me, let the
   porter let in Susan Grindstone and Nell.
                              Exit Second Servingman

Anthony, and Potpan!   10
   Enter two more Servingmen

THIRD SERVINGMAN Ay, boy, ready.

FIRST SERVINGMAN You are looked for and called for, asked for and sought for, in the Great Chamber.

FOURTH SERVINGMAN We cannot be here and there too. Cheerly, boys! Be brisk a while, and the longer liver take all.

                Exeunt Third and Fourth Servingmen
     Enter Capulet, his wife, Juliet, Tybalt, Nurse, and all the guests and gentlewomen to the maskers

CAPULET

Welcome, gentlemen! Ladies that have their toes
Unplagued with corns will walk a bout with you.
Ah, my mistresses, which of you all
Will now deny to dance? She that makes dainty,   20
She, I'll swear, hath corns. Am I come near ye now?
Welcome, gentlemen! I have seen the day
That I have worn a visor and could tell
A whispering tale in a fair lady's ear,
Such as would please. 'Tis gone, 'tis gone, 'tis gone!
You are welcome, gentlemen! Come, musicians, play.
   Music plays, and they dance
A hall, a hall! Give room! and foot it, girls.
More light, you knaves! and turn the tables up;
And quench the fire, the room is grown too hot.
Ah, sirrah, this unlooked-for sport comes well.   30
Nay, sit, nay, sit, good cousin Capulet,
For you and I are past our dancing days.
How long is't now since last yourself and I
Were in a mask?

COUSIN CAPULET By'r Lady, thirty years.

CAPULET

What, man? 'Tis not so much, 'tis not so much.

'Tis since the nuptial of Lucentio,
Come Pentecost as quickly as it will,
Some five-and-twenty years; and then we masked.

COUSIN CAPULET
'Tis more, 'tis more. His son is elder, sir.
His son is thirty.

CAPULET   Will you tell me that?
His son was but a ward two years ago.

ROMEO (*to Servingman*)
What lady's that, which doth enrich the hand
Of yonder knight?

SERVINGMAN   I know not, sir.

ROMEO
O, she doth teach the torches to burn bright!
It seems she hangs upon the cheek of night
As a rich jewel in an Ethiop's ear –
Beauty too rich for use, for earth too dear!
So shows a snowy dove trooping with crows
As yonder lady o'er her fellows shows.
The measure done, I'll watch her place of stand
And, touching hers, make blessèd my rude hand.
Did my heart love till now? Forswear it, sight!
For I ne'er saw true beauty till this night.

TYBALT
This, by his voice, should be a Montague.
Fetch me my rapier, boy. What, dares the slave
Come hither, covered with an antic face,
To fleer and scorn at our solemnity?
Now, by the stock and honour of my kin,
To strike him dead I hold it not a sin.

CAPULET
Why, how now, kinsman? Wherefore storm you so?

TYBALT
Uncle, this is a Montague, our foe.

A villain, that is hither come in spite
To scorn at our solemnity this night.

CAPULET

Young Romeo is it?

TYBALT   'Tis he, that villain Romeo.

CAPULET

Content thee, gentle coz, let him alone.
'A bears him like a portly gentleman.
And, to say truth, Verona brags of him
To be a virtuous and well-governed youth.
I would not for the wealth of all this town
Here in my house do him disparagement.   70
Therefore be patient; take no note of him.
It is my will, the which if thou respect,
Show a fair presence and put off these frowns,
An ill-beseeming semblance for a feast.

TYBALT

It fits when such a villain is a guest.
I'll not endure him.

CAPULET   He shall be endured.
What, goodman boy! I say he shall. Go to!
Am I the master here, or you? Go to!
You'll not endure him! God shall mend my soul!
You'll make a mutiny among my guests!   80
You will set cock-a-hoop! You'll be the man!

TYBALT

Why, uncle, 'tis a shame.

CAPULET   Go to, go to!
You are a saucy boy. Is't so, indeed?
This trick may chance to scathe you. I know what.
You must contrary me! Marry, 'tis time —
Well said, my hearts! — You are a princox, go!
Be quiet, or — More light, more light! — For shame!
I'll make you quiet, what! — Cheerly, my hearts!

TYBALT

    Patience perforce with wilful choler meeting

90   Makes my flesh tremble in their different greeting.

    I will withdraw. But this intrusion shall,

    Now seeming sweet, convert to bitterest gall. *Exit Tybalt*

ROMEO

    If I profane with my unworthiest hand

        This holy shrine, the gentle sin is this.

    My lips, two blushing pilgrims, ready stand

        To smooth that rough touch with a tender kiss.

JULIET

    Good pilgrim, you do wrong your hand too much,

        Which mannerly devotion shows in this.

    For saints have hands that pilgrims' hands do touch,

100   And palm to palm is holy palmers' kiss.

ROMEO

    Have not saints lips, and holy palmers too?

JULIET

    Ay, pilgrim, lips that they must use in prayer.

ROMEO

    O, then, dear saint, let lips do what hands do!

        They pray: grant thou, lest faith turn to despair.

JULIET

    Saints do not move, though grant for prayers' sake.

ROMEO

    Then move not while my prayer's effect I take.

    He kisses her

    Thus from my lips, by thine my sin is purged.

JULIET

    Then have my lips the sin that they have took.

ROMEO

    Sin from my lips? O trespass sweetly urged!

        Give me my sin again.

He kisses her

JULIET   You kiss by th'book.   110

NURSE

  Madam, your mother craves a word with you.

ROMEO

  What is her mother?

NURSE   Marry, bachelor,

  Her mother is the lady of the house,

  And a good lady, and a wise and virtuous.

  I nursed her daughter that you talked withal.

  I tell you, he that can lay hold of her

  Shall have the chinks.

ROMEO   Is she a Capulet?

  O dear account! My life is my foe's debt.

BENVOLIO

  Away, be gone. The sport is at the best.

ROMEO

  Ay, so I fear. The more is my unrest.   120

CAPULET

  Nay, gentlemen, prepare not to be gone.

  We have a trifling foolish banquet towards.

    They whisper in his ear

  Is it e'en so? Why then, I thank you all.

  I thank you, honest gentlemen. Good night.

  More torches here! Come on then, let's to bed.

  Ah, sirrah, by my fay, it waxes late.

  I'll to my rest.   *Exeunt all but Juliet and Nurse*

JULIET

  Come hither, Nurse. What is yond gentleman?

NURSE

  The son and heir of old Tiberio.

JULIET

  What's he that now is going out of door?   130

NURSE
    Marry, that, I think, be young Petruchio.

JULIET
    What's he that follows here, that would not dance?

NURSE
    I know not.

JULIET
    Go ask his name. – If he be marrièd,
    My grave is like to be my wedding bed.

NURSE
    His name is Romeo, and a Montague,
    The only son of your great enemy.

JULIET
    My only love, sprung from my only hate!
    Too early seen unknown, and known too late!
140   Prodigious birth of love it is to me
    That I must love a loathèd enemy.

NURSE
    What's this, what's this?

JULIET   A rhyme I learnt even now
    Of one I danced withal.
        One calls within: 'Juliet'
NURSE   Anon, anon!
    Come, let's away. The strangers all are gone.   *Exeunt*

*

II   *Enter Chorus*
CHORUS
    Now old desire doth in his deathbed lie,
        And young affection gapes to be his heir.
    That fair for which love groaned for and would die,
        With tender Juliet matched, is now not fair.

Now Romeo is beloved and loves again,
    Alike bewitchèd by the charm of looks.
But to his foe supposed he must complain,
    And she steal love's sweet bait from fearful hooks.
Being held a foe, he may not have access
    To breathe such vows as lovers use to swear,   10
And she as much in love, her means much less
    To meet her new belovèd anywhere.
But passion lends them power, time means, to meet,
Tempering extremities with extreme sweet.   *Exit*

Enter Romeo alone   II.I

ROMEO
    Can I go forward when my heart is here?
    Turn back, dull earth, and find thy centre out.
    Enter Benvolio with Mercutio. Romeo withdraws

BENVOLIO
    Romeo! My cousin Romeo! Romeo!

MERCUTIO   He is wise,
    And, on my life, hath stolen him home to bed.

BENVOLIO
    He ran this way and leapt this orchard wall.
    Call, good Mercutio.

MERCUTIO   Nay, I'll conjure too.
    Romeo! Humours! Madman! Passion! Lover!
    Appear thou in the likeness of a sigh.
    Speak but one rhyme, and I am satisfied.
    Cry but 'Ay me!' Pronounce but 'love' and 'dove'.   10
    Speak to my gossip Venus one fair word,
    One nickname for her purblind son and heir,
    Young Abraham Cupid, he that shot so trim
    When King Cophetua loved the beggar maid.
    He heareth not, he stirreth not, he moveth not.

The ape is dead, and I must conjure him.
I conjure thee by Rosaline's bright eyes,
By her high forehead and her scarlet lip,
By her fine foot, straight leg, and quivering thigh,
And the demesnes that there adjacent lie,
That in thy likeness thou appear to us!

BENVOLIO

An if he hear thee, thou wilt anger him.

MERCUTIO

This cannot anger him. 'Twould anger him
To raise a spirit in his mistress' circle
Of some strange nature, letting it there stand
Till she had laid it and conjured it down.
That were some spite. My invocation
Is fair and honest. In his mistress' name,
I conjure only but to raise up him.

BENVOLIO

Come, he hath hid himself among these trees
To be consorted with the humorous night.
Blind is his love and best befits the dark.

MERCUTIO

If love be blind, love cannot hit the mark.
Now will he sit under a medlar tree
And wish his mistress were that kind of fruit
As maids call medlars when they laugh alone.
O, Romeo, that she were, O that she were
An open-arse and thou a poppering pear!
Romeo, good night. I'll to my truckle-bed.
This field-bed is too cold for me to sleep.
Come, shall we go?

BENVOLIO   Go then, for 'tis in vain
To seek him here that means not to be found.

Exeunt Benvolio and Mercutio

ROMEO (*coming forward*)   II.2

    He jests at scars that never felt a wound.

      Enter Juliet above

    But soft! What light through yonder window breaks?

    It is the East, and Juliet is the sun!

    Arise, fair sun, and kill the envious moon,

    Who is already sick and pale with grief

    That thou her maid art far more fair than she.

    Be not her maid, since she is envious.

    Her vestal livery is but sick and green,

    And none but fools do wear it. Cast it off.

    It is my lady. O, it is my love!   10

    O that she knew she were!

    She speaks. Yet she says nothing. What of that?

    Her eye discourses. I will answer it.

    I am too bold. 'Tis not to me she speaks.

    Two of the fairest stars in all the heaven,

    Having some business, do entreat her eyes

    To twinkle in their spheres till they return.

    What if her eyes were there, they in her head?

    The brightness of her cheek would shame those stars

    As daylight doth a lamp. Her eyes in heaven   20

    Would through the airy region stream so bright

    That birds would sing and think it were not night.

    See how she leans her cheek upon her hand!

    O that I were a glove upon that hand,

    That I might touch that cheek!

JULIET   Ay me!

ROMEO   She speaks.

    O, speak again, bright angel! – for thou art

    As glorious to this night, being o'er my head,

    As is a wingèd messenger of heaven

    Unto the white-upturnèd wondering eyes

    Of mortals that fall back to gaze on him   30

When he bestrides the lazy, puffing clouds
And sails upon the bosom of the air.

JULIET

O Romeo, Romeo! – wherefore art thou Romeo?
Deny thy father and refuse thy name.
Or, if thou wilt not, be but sworn my love,
And I'll no longer be a Capulet.

ROMEO (*aside*)

Shall I hear more, or shall I speak at this?

JULIET

'Tis but thy name that is my enemy.
Thou art thyself, though not a Montague.
40   What's Montague? It is nor hand nor foot
Nor arm nor face nor any other part
Belonging to a man. O, be some other name!
What's in a name? That which we call a rose
By any other word would smell as sweet.
So Romeo would, were he not Romeo called,
Retain that dear perfection which he owes
Without that title. Romeo, doff thy name;
And for thy name, which is no part of thee,
Take all myself.

ROMEO   I take thee at thy word.
50   Call me but love, and I'll be new baptized.
Henceforth I never will be Romeo.

JULIET

What man art thou that, thus bescreened in night,
So stumblest on my counsel?

ROMEO   By a name
I know not how to tell thee who I am.
My name, dear saint, is hateful to myself,
Because it is an enemy to thee.
Had I it written, I would tear the word.

JULIET

   My ears have yet not drunk a hundred words
   Of thy tongue's uttering, yet I know the sound.
   Art thou not Romeo, and a Montague?   60

ROMEO

   Neither, fair maid, if either thee dislike.

JULIET

   How camest thou hither, tell me, and wherefore?
   The orchard walls are high and hard to climb,
   And the place death, considering who thou art,
   If any of my kinsmen find thee here.

ROMEO

   With love's light wings did I o'erperch these walls.
   For stony limits cannot hold love out,
   And what love can do, that dares love attempt.
   Therefore thy kinsmen are no stop to me.

JULIET

   If they do see thee, they will murder thee.   70

ROMEO

   Alack, there lies more peril in thine eye
   Than twenty of their swords! Look thou but sweet,
   And I am proof against their enmity.

JULIET

   I would not for the world they saw thee here.

ROMEO

   I have night's cloak to hide me from their eyes.
   And but thou love me, let them find me here.
   My life were better ended by their hate
   Than death proroguèd, wanting of thy love.

JULIET

   By whose direction foundest thou out this place?

ROMEO

   By love, that first did prompt me to inquire.   80
   He lent me counsel, and I lent him eyes.

I am no pilot; yet, wert thou as far
As that vast shore washed with the farthest sea,
I should adventure for such merchandise.

JULIET

Thou knowest the mask of night is on my face,
Else would a maiden blush bepaint my cheek
For that which thou hast heard me speak tonight.
Fain would I dwell on form – fain, fain deny
What I have spoke. But farewell compliment!
Dost thou love me? I know thou wilt say 'Ay.'
And I will take thy word. Yet, if thou swearest,
Thou mayst prove false. At lovers' perjuries,
They say, Jove laughs. O gentle Romeo,
If thou dost love, pronounce it faithfully.
Or if thou thinkest I am too quickly won,
I'll frown, and be perverse, and say thee nay,
So thou wilt woo. But else, not for the world.
In truth, fair Montague, I am too fond,
And therefore thou mayst think my 'haviour light.
But trust me, gentleman, I'll prove more true
Than those that have more cunning to be strange.
I should have been more strange, I must confess,
But that thou overheardest, ere I was ware,
My true-love passion. Therefore pardon me,
And not impute this yielding to light love,
Which the dark night hath so discoverèd.

ROMEO

Lady, by yonder blessèd moon I vow,
That tips with silver all these fruit-tree tops –

JULIET

O, swear not by the moon, th'inconstant moon,
That monthly changes in her circled orb,
Lest that thy love prove likewise variable.

ROMEO
    What shall I swear by?
JULIET   Do not swear at all.
    Or if thou wilt, swear by thy gracious self,
    Which is the god of my idolatry,
    And I'll believe thee.
ROMEO   If my heart's dear love –
JULIET
    Well, do not swear. Although I joy in thee,
    I have no joy of this contract tonight.
    It is too rash, too unadvised, too sudden;
    Too like the lightning, which doth cease to be
    Ere one can say 'It lightens.' Sweet, good night!   120
    This bud of love, by summer's ripening breath,
    May prove a beauteous flower when next we meet.
    Good night, good night! As sweet repose and rest
    Come to thy heart as that within my breast!
ROMEO
    O, wilt thou leave me so unsatisfied?
JULIET
    What satisfaction canst thou have tonight?
ROMEO
    Th'exchange of thy love's faithful vow for mine.
JULIET
    I gave thee mine before thou didst request it.
    And yet I would it were to give again.
ROMEO
    Wouldst thou withdraw it? For what purpose, love?   130
JULIET
    But to be frank and give it thee again.
    And yet I wish but for the thing I have.
    My bounty is as boundless as the sea,
    My love as deep. The more I give to thee,
    The more I have, for both are infinite.

I hear some noise within. Dear love, adieu!
   Nurse calls within
Anon, good Nurse! – Sweet Montague, be true.
Stay but a little, I will come again.   *Exit Juliet*

ROMEO
O blessèd, blessèd night! I am afeard,
Being in night, all this is but a dream,
Too flattering-sweet to be substantial.
   Enter Juliet above

JULIET
Three words, dear Romeo, and good night indeed.
If that thy bent of love be honourable,
Thy purpose marriage, send me word tomorrow,
By one that I'll procure to come to thee,
Where and what time thou wilt perform the rite,
And all my fortunes at thy foot I'll lay
And follow thee my lord throughout the world.

NURSE (*within*)
Madam!

JULIET
I come, anon – But if thou meanest not well,
I do beseech thee –

NURSE (*within*)   Madam!

JULIET   By and by I come –
To cease thy strife and leave me to my grief.
Tomorrow will I send.

ROMEO   So thrive my soul –

JULIET
A thousand times good night!   *Exit Juliet*

ROMEO
A thousand times the worse, to want thy light!
Love goes toward love as schoolboys from their books;
But love from love, toward school with heavy looks.
   Enter Juliet above again

JULIET

Hist! Romeo, hist! O for a falconer's voice,
To lure this tassel-gentle back again!
Bondage is hoarse and may not speak aloud,   160
Else would I tear the cave where Echo lies
And make her airy tongue more hoarse than mine
With repetition of 'My Romeo!'

ROMEO

It is my soul that calls upon my name.
How silver-sweet sound lovers' tongues by night,
Like softest music to attending ears!

JULIET

Romeo!

ROMEO   My nyas?

JULIET   What o'clock tomorrow
Shall I send to thee?

ROMEO   By the hour of nine.

JULIET

I will not fail. 'Tis twenty year till then.
I have forgot why I did call thee back.   170

ROMEO

Let me stand here till thou remember it.

JULIET

I shall forget, to have thee still stand there,
Remembering how I love thy company.

ROMEO

And I'll still stay, to have thee still forget,
Forgetting any other home but this.

JULIET

'Tis almost morning. I would have thee gone.
And yet no farther than a wanton's bird,
That lets it hop a little from his hand,
Like a poor prisoner in his twisted gyves,

180 And with a silken thread plucks it back again,
    So loving-jealous of his liberty.

ROMEO
    I would I were thy bird.

JULIET   Sweet, so would I.
    Yet I should kill thee with much cherishing.
    Good night, good night! Parting is such sweet sorrow
    That I shall say goodnight till it be morrow.

                                        Exit Juliet

ROMEO
    Sleep dwell upon thine eyes, peace in thy breast!
    Would I were sleep and peace, so sweet to rest!
    The grey-eyed morn smiles on the frowning night,
    Chequering the eastern clouds with streaks of light,
190 And darkness fleckled like a drunkard reels
    From forth day's pathway made by Titan's wheels.
    Hence will I to my ghostly Friar's close cell,
    His help to crave and my dear hap to tell.   *Exit*

II.3   *Enter Friar Laurence alone, with a basket*

FRIAR
    Now, ere the sun advance his burning eye
    The day to cheer and night's dank dew to dry,
    I must up-fill this osier cage of ours
    With baleful weeds and precious-juicèd flowers.
    The earth that's nature's mother is her tomb.
    What is her burying grave, that is her womb;
    And from her womb children of divers kind
    We sucking on her natural bosom find,
    Many for many virtues excellent,
10 None but for some, and yet all different.
    O mickle is the powerful grace that lies
    In plants, herbs, stones, and their true qualities.

For naught so vile that on the earth doth live
But to the earth some special good doth give;
Nor aught so good but, strained from that fair use,
Revolts from true birth, stumbling on abuse.
Virtue itself turns vice, being misapplied,
And vice sometime's by action dignified.
Within the infant rind of this weak flower
Poison hath residence, and medicine power.   20
For this, being smelt, with that part cheers each part;
Being tasted, stays all senses with the heart.
Two such opposèd kings encamp them still
In man as well as herbs – grace and rude will.
And where the worser is predominant,
Full soon the canker death eats up that plant.
    Enter Romeo

ROMEO
    Good morrow, father.

FRIAR   Benedicite!
    What early tongue so sweet saluteth me?
    Young son, it argues a distempered head
    So soon to bid good morrow to thy bed.   30
    Care keeps his watch in every old man's eye,
    And where care lodges, sleep will never lie.
    But where unbruisèd youth with unstuffed brain
    Doth couch his limbs, there golden sleep doth reign.
    Therefore thy earliness doth me assure
    Thou art uproused with some distemperature.
    Or if not so, then here I hit it right –
    Our Romeo hath not been in bed tonight.

ROMEO
    The last is true. The sweeter rest was mine.

FRIAR
    God pardon sin! Wast thou with Rosaline?   40

ROMEO

    With Rosaline, my ghostly father? No.
    I have forgot that name and that name's woe.

FRIAR

    That's my good son! But where hast thou been then?

ROMEO

    I'll tell thee ere thou ask it me again.
    I have been feasting with mine enemy,
    Where on a sudden one hath wounded me
    That's by me wounded. Both our remedies
    Within thy help and holy physic lies.
    I bear no hatred, blessèd man, for, lo,
50   My intercession likewise steads my foe.

FRIAR

    Be plain, good son, and homely in thy drift.
    Riddling confession finds but riddling shrift.

ROMEO

    Then plainly know my heart's dear love is set
    On the fair daughter of rich Capulet.
    As mine on hers, so hers is set on mine,
    And all combined, save what thou must combine
    By holy marriage. When, and where, and how
    We met, we wooed, and made exchange of vow,
    I'll tell thee as we pass. But this I pray,
60   That thou consent to marry us today.

FRIAR

    Holy Saint Francis! What a change is here!
    Is Rosaline, that thou didst love so dear,
    So soon forsaken? Young men's love then lies
    Not truly in their hearts, but in their eyes.
    Jesu Maria! What a deal of brine
    Hath washed thy sallow cheeks for Rosaline!
    How much salt water thrown away in waste
    To season love, that of it doth not taste!

The sun not yet thy sighs from heaven clears.
Thy old groans yet ring in mine ancient ears.   70
Lo, here upon thy cheek the stain doth sit
Of an old tear that is not washed off yet.
If e'er thou wast thyself, and these woes thine,
Thou and these woes were all for Rosaline.
And art thou changed? Pronounce this sentence then:
Women may fall when there's no strength in men.

ROMEO
Thou chidst me oft for loving Rosaline.

FRIAR
For doting, not for loving, pupil mine.

ROMEO
And badest me bury love.

FRIAR   Not in a grave
To lay one in, another out to have.   80

ROMEO
I pray thee chide me not. Her I love now
Doth grace for grace and love for love allow.
The other did not so.

FRIAR   O, she knew well
Thy love did read by rote, that could not spell.
But come, young waverer, come, go with me.
In one respect I'll thy assistant be.
For this alliance may so happy prove
To turn your households' rancour to pure love.

ROMEO
O, let us hence! I stand on sudden haste.

FRIAR
Wisely and slow. They stumble that run fast.   *Exeunt*   90

II.4   *Enter Benvolio and Mercutio*

MERCUTIO Where the devil should this Romeo be? Came
he not home tonight?

BENVOLIO
Not to his father's. I spoke with his man.

MERCUTIO
Why, that same pale hard-hearted wench, that Rosaline,
Torments him so that he will sure run mad.

BENVOLIO
Tybalt, the kinsman to old Capulet,
Hath sent a letter to his father's house.

MERCUTIO A challenge, on my life.

BENVOLIO Romeo will answer it.

10   MERCUTIO Any man that can write may answer a letter.

BENVOLIO Nay, he will answer the letter's master, how he
dares, being dared.

MERCUTIO Alas, poor Romeo, he is already dead! –
stabbed with a white wench's black eye; run through the
ear with a love song; the very pin of his heart cleft with
the blind bow-boy's butt-shaft. And is he a man to encounter Tybalt?

BENVOLIO Why, what is Tybalt!

MERCUTIO More than Prince of Cats, I can tell you. O,
20   he's the courageous captain of compliments. He fights as
you sing pricksong: keeps time, distance, and proportion. He rests his minim rests, one, two, and the third in
your bosom. The very butcher of a silk button. A duellist, a duellist. A gentleman of the very first house, of the
first and second cause. Ah, the immortal *passado*! the
punto reverso! the *hay*!

BENVOLIO The what?

MERCUTIO The pox of such antic, lisping, affecting fantasticoes, these new tuners of accent! 'By Jesu, a very
30   good blade! a very tall man! a very good whore!' Why, is

not this a lamentable thing, grandsire, that we should be thus afflicted with these strange flies, these fashion-mongers, these 'pardon-me's', who stand so much on the new form that they cannot sit at ease on the old bench? O their bones, their bones!

Enter Romeo

BENVOLIO Here comes Romeo, here comes Romeo!

MERCUTIO Without his roe, like a dried herring. O flesh, flesh, how art thou fishified! Now is he for the numbers that Petrarch flowed in. Laura, to his lady, was a kitchen wench – marry, she had a better love to berhyme her – Dido a dowdy, Cleopatra a gypsy, Helen and Hero hildings and harlots, Thisbe a grey eye or so, but not to the purpose. Signor Romeo, *bon jour*. There's a French salutation to your French slop. You gave us the counterfeit fairly last night. 40

ROMEO Good morrow to you both. What counterfeit did I give you?

MERCUTIO The slip, sir, the slip. Can you not conceive?

ROMEO Pardon, good Mercutio. My business was great, and in such a case as mine a man may strain courtesy. 50

MERCUTIO That's as much as to say, such a case as yours constrains a man to bow in the hams.

ROMEO Meaning, to curtsy.

MERCUTIO Thou hast most kindly hit it.

ROMEO A most courteous exposition.

MERCUTIO Nay, I am the very pink of courtesy.

ROMEO Pink for flower.

MERCUTIO Right.

ROMEO Why, then is my pump well-flowered.

MERCUTIO Sure wit, follow me this jest now till thou hast worn out thy pump, that, when the single sole of it is worn, the jest may remain, after the wearing, solely singular. 60

ROMEO O single-soled jest, solely singular for the singleness!

MERCUTIO Come between us, good Benvolio! My wits
faint.

ROMEO Swits and spurs, swits and spurs! or I'll cry a
match.

70 MERCUTIO Nay, if our wits run the wild-goose chase, I
am done. For thou hast more of the wild goose in one of
thy wits than, I am sure, I have in my whole five. Was I
with you there for the goose?

ROMEO Thou wast never with me for anything when
thou wast not there for the goose.

MERCUTIO I will bite thee by the ear for that jest.

ROMEO Nay, good goose, bite not.

MERCUTIO Thy wit is a very bitter sweeting. It is a most
sharp sauce.

80 ROMEO And is it not, then, well served in to a sweet
goose?

MERCUTIO O, here's a wit of cheverel, that stretches from
an inch narrow to an ell broad!

ROMEO I stretch it out for that word 'broad', which, added
to the goose, proves thee far and wide a broad goose.

MERCUTIO Why, is not this better now than groaning for
love? Now art thou sociable. Now art thou Romeo. Now
art thou what thou art, by art as well as by nature. For
this drivelling love is like a great natural that runs lolling

90 up and down to hide his bauble in a hole.

BENVOLIO Stop there, stop there!

MERCUTIO Thou desirest me to stop in my tale against
the hair.

BENVOLIO Thou wouldst else have made thy tale large.

MERCUTIO O, thou art deceived! I would have made it
short; for I was come to the whole depth of my tale, and
meant indeed to occupy the argument no longer.

ROMEO Here's goodly gear!

    Enter Nurse and her man, Peter

  A sail, a sail!

MERCUTIO Two, two. A shirt and a smock.   100

NURSE Peter!

PETER Anon.

NURSE My fan, Peter.

MERCUTIO Good Peter, to hide her face. For her fan's the
    fairer face.

NURSE God ye good-morrow, gentlemen.

MERCUTIO God ye good-e'en, fair gentlewoman.

NURSE Is it good-e'en?

MERCUTIO 'Tis no less, I tell ye. For the bawdy hand of
    the dial is now upon the prick of noon.   110

NURSE Out upon you! What a man are you!

ROMEO One, gentlewoman, that God hath made for him-
    self to mar.

NURSE By my troth, it is well said. 'For himself to mar,'
    quoth 'a? Gentlemen, can any of you tell me where I
    may find the young Romeo?

ROMEO I can tell you. But young Romeo will be older
    when you have found him than he was when you sought
    him. I am the youngest of that name, for fault of a
    worse.   120

NURSE You say well.

MERCUTIO Yea, is the worst well? Very well took, i'faith,
    wisely, wisely!

NURSE If you be he, sir, I desire some confidence with
    you.

BENVOLIO She will endite him to some supper.

MERCUTIO A bawd, a bawd, a bawd! So ho!

ROMEO What hast thou found?

MERCUTIO No hare, sir; unless a hare, sir, in a lenten pie,
    that is something stale and hoar ere it be spent.   130

He walks by them and sings
>   An old hare hoar,
>   And an old hare hoar,
>   Is very good meat in Lent.
>   But a hare that is hoar
>   Is too much for a score
>   When it hoars ere it be spent.

Romeo, will you come to your father's? We'll to dinner
thither.

ROMEO I will follow you.

MERCUTIO Farewell, ancient lady. Farewell. (*He sings*)
Lady, lady, lady.   *Exeunt Mercutio and Benvolio*

NURSE I pray you, sir, what saucy merchant was this that
was so full of his ropery?

ROMEO A gentleman, Nurse, that loves to hear himself
talk and will speak more in a minute than he will stand
to in a month.

NURSE An 'a speak anything against me, I'll take him
down, an 'a were lustier than he is, and twenty such
Jacks; and if I cannot, I'll find those that shall. Scurvy
knave! I am none of his flirt-gills. I am none of his
skains-mates. (*She turns to Peter her man*) And thou
must stand by too, and suffer every knave to use me at
his pleasure!

PETER I saw no man use you at his pleasure. If I had, my
weapon should quickly have been out. I warrant you,
I dare draw as soon as another man, if I see occasion in
a good quarrel, and the law on my side.

NURSE Now, afore God, I am so vexed that every part
about me quivers. Scurvy knave! Pray you, sir, a word;
and, as I told you, my young lady bid me inquire you
out. What she bid me say, I will keep to myself. But
first let me tell ye, if ye should lead her in a fool's paradise, as they say, it were a very gross kind of behaviour,

as they say. For the gentlewoman is young; and therefore, if you should deal double with her, truly it were an
ill thing to be offered to any gentlewoman, and very
weak dealing.

ROMEO Nurse, commend me to thy lady and mistress. I
protest unto thee –

NURSE Good heart, and i'faith I will tell her as much.   170
Lord, Lord! She will be a joyful woman.

ROMEO What wilt thou tell her, Nurse? Thou dost not
mark me.

NURSE I will tell her, sir, that you do protest, which, as I
take it, is a gentlemanlike offer.

ROMEO
Bid her devise
Some means to come to shrift this afternoon,
And there she shall at Friar Laurence' cell
Be shrived and married. Here is for thy pains.

NURSE
No, truly, sir. Not a penny.   180

ROMEO
Go to! I say you shall.

NURSE
This afternoon, sir? Well, she shall be there.

ROMEO
And stay, good Nurse, behind the abbey wall.
Within this hour my man shall be with thee
And bring thee cords made like a tackled stair,
Which to the high topgallant of my joy
Must be my convoy in the secret night.
Farewell. Be trusty, and I'll quit thy pains.
Farewell. Commend me to thy mistress.

NURSE
Now God in heaven bless thee! Hark you, sir.   190

ROMEO
    What sayest thou, my dear Nurse?

NURSE
    Is your man secret? Did you ne'er hear say,
    Two may keep counsel, putting one away?

ROMEO
    Warrant thee my man's as true as steel.

NURSE Well, sir, my mistress is the sweetest lady. Lord,
    Lord! when 'twas a little prating thing – O there is a
    nobleman in town, one Paris, that would fain lay knife
    aboard. But she, good soul, had as lief see a toad, a very
    toad, as see him. I anger her sometimes, and tell her that
200   Paris is the properer man. But I'll warrant you, when I
    say so, she looks as pale as any clout in the versal world.
    Doth not rosemary and Romeo begin both with a letter?

ROMEO Ay, Nurse. What of that? Both with an 'R'.

NURSE Ah, mocker! That's the dog's name. 'R' is for the –
    No, I know it begins with some other letter; and she hath
    the prettiest sententious of it, of you and rosemary, that
    it would do you good to hear it.

ROMEO Commend me to thy lady.   *Exit Romeo*

NURSE Ay, a thousand times. Peter!

210 PETER Anon.

NURSE Before, and apace.   *Exeunt*

II.5   *Enter Juliet*

JULIET
    The clock struck nine when I did send the Nurse.
    In half an hour she promised to return.
    Perchance she cannot meet him. That's not so.
    O, she is lame! Love's heralds should be thoughts,
    Which ten times faster glides than the sun's beams
    Driving back shadows over louring hills.

Therefore do nimble-pinioned doves draw love,
And therefore hath the wind-swift Cupid wings.
Now is the sun upon the highmost hill
Of this day's journey, and from nine till twelve   10
Is three long hours, yet she is not come.
Had she affections and warm youthful blood,
She would be as swift in motion as a ball.
My words would bandy her to my sweet love,
And his to me.
But old folks, many feign as they were dead –
Unwieldy, slow, heavy and pale as lead.
    Enter Nurse and Peter
O God, she comes! O honey Nurse, what news?
Hast thou met with him? Send thy man away.

NURSE

Peter, stay at the gate.   *Exit Peter*   20

JULIET

Now, good sweet Nurse – O Lord, why lookest thou sad?
Though news be sad, yet tell them merrily.
If good, thou shamest the music of sweet news
By playing it to me with so sour a face.

NURSE

I am aweary. Give me leave a while.
Fie, how my bones ache! What a jaunce have I!

JULIET

I would thou hadst my bones, and I thy news.
Nay, come, I pray thee speak. Good, good Nurse, speak.

NURSE

Jesu, what haste! Can you not stay a while?
Do you not see that I am out of breath?   30

JULIET

How art thou out of breath when thou hast breath
To say to me that thou art out of breath?
The excuse that thou dost make in this delay

Is longer than the tale thou dost excuse.
Is thy news good or bad? Answer to that.
Say either, and I'll stay the circumstance.
Let me be satisfied, is't good or bad?

NURSE Well, you have made a simple choice. You know
not how to choose a man. Romeo? No, not he. Though
his face be better than any man's, yet his leg excels all
men's; and for a hand and a foot, and a body, though
they be not to be talked on, yet they are past compare.
He is not the flower of courtesy, but, I'll warrant him, as
gentle as a lamb. Go thy ways, wench. Serve God. What,
have you dined at home?

JULIET
No, no. But all this did I know before.
What says he of our marriage? What of that?

NURSE
Lord, how my head aches! What a head have I!
It beats as it would fall in twenty pieces.
My back a't'other side – ah, my back, my back!
Beshrew your heart for sending me about
To catch my death with jauncing up and down!

JULIET
I'faith, I am sorry that thou art not well.
Sweet, sweet, sweet Nurse, tell me, what says my love?

NURSE Your love says, like an honest gentleman, and a
courteous, and a kind, and a handsome, and, I warrant,
a virtuous – Where is your mother?

JULIET
Where is my mother? Why, she is within.
Where should she be? How oddly thou repliest!
'Your love says, like an honest gentleman,
"Where is your mother?"'

NURSE   O God's Lady dear!
Are you so hot? Marry come up, I trow.

Is this the poultice for my aching bones?
Henceforward do your messages yourself.

JULIET

Here's such a coil! Come, what says Romeo?

NURSE

Have you got leave to go to shrift today?

JULIET

I have.

NURSE

Then hie you hence to Friar Laurence' cell.
There stays a husband to make you a wife.
Now comes the wanton blood up in your cheeks.   70
They'll be in scarlet straight at any news.
Hie you to church. I must another way,
To fetch a ladder, by the which your love
Must climb a bird's nest soon when it is dark.
I am the drudge, and toil in your delight.
But you shall bear the burden soon at night.
Go. I'll to dinner. Hie you to the cell.

JULIET

Hie to high fortune! Honest Nurse, farewell.   *Exeunt*

Enter Friar Laurence and Romeo   II.6

FRIAR

So smile the heavens upon this holy act
That after-hours with sorrow chide us not!

ROMEO

Amen, amen! But come what sorrow can,
It cannot countervail the exchange of joy
That one short minute gives me in her sight.
Do thou but close our hands with holy words,
Then love-devouring death do what he dare –
It is enough I may but call her mine.

FRIAR

    These violent delights have violent ends

10   And in their triumph die, like fire and powder,

    Which as they kiss consume. The sweetest honey

    Is loathsome in his own deliciousness

    And in the taste confounds the appetite.

    Therefore love moderately. Long love doth so.

    Too swift arrives as tardy as too slow.

       Enter Juliet somewhat fast. She embraces Romeo

    Here comes the lady. O, so light a foot

    Will ne'er wear out the everlasting flint.

    A lover may bestride the gossamers

    That idles in the wanton summer air,

20   And yet not fall. So light is vanity.

JULIET

    Good even to my ghostly confessor.

FRIAR

    Romeo shall thank thee, daughter, for us both.

JULIET

    As much to him, else is his thanks too much.

ROMEO

    Ah, Juliet, if the measure of thy joy

    Be heaped like mine, and that thy skill be more

    To blazon it, then sweeten with thy breath

    This neighbour air, and let rich music's tongue

    Unfold the imagined happiness that both

    Receive in either by this dear encounter.

JULIET

30   Conceit, more rich in matter than in words,

    Brags of his substance, not of ornament.

    They are but beggars that can count their worth.

    But my true love is grown to such excess

    I cannot sum up sum of half my wealth.

FRIAR

Come, come with me, and we will make short work.
For, by your leaves, you shall not stay alone
Till Holy Church incorporate two in one.   *Exeunt*

*

Enter Mercutio, Benvolio, and their men   III.I

BENVOLIO

I pray thee, good Mercutio, let's retire.
The day is hot, the Capels are abroad.
And if we meet we shall not 'scape a brawl,
For now, these hot days, is the mad blood stirring.

MERCUTIO Thou art like one of these fellows that, when
he enters the confines of a tavern, claps me his sword
upon the table and says 'God send me no need of thee!',
and by the operation of the second cup draws him on the
drawer, when indeed there is no need.

BENVOLIO Am I like such a fellow?   10

MERCUTIO Come, come, thou art as hot a Jack in thy
mood as any in Italy; and as soon moved to be moody,
and as soon moody to be moved.

BENVOLIO And what to?

MERCUTIO Nay, an there were two such, we should have
none shortly, for one would kill the other. Thou! Why,
thou wilt quarrel with a man that hath a hair more or a
hair less in his beard than thou hast. Thou wilt quarrel
with a man for cracking nuts, having no other reason but
because thou hast hazel eyes. What eye but such an eye   20
would spy out such a quarrel? Thy head is as full of
quarrels as an egg is full of meat; and yet thy head hath
been beaten as addle as an egg for quarrelling. Thou
hast quarrelled with a man for coughing in the street,

because he hath wakened thy dog that hath lain asleep in
the sun. Didst thou not fall out with a tailor for wearing
his new doublet before Easter; with another for tying
his new shoes with old riband? And yet thou wilt tutor
me from quarrelling!

30 BENVOLIO An I were so apt to quarrel as thou art, any
man should buy the fee simple of my life for an hour
and a quarter.

MERCUTIO The fee simple? O simple!

Enter Tybalt and others

BENVOLIO By my head, here comes the Capulets.

MERCUTIO By my heel, I care not.

TYBALT
Follow me close, for I will speak to them.
Gentlemen, good-e'en. A word with one of you.

MERCUTIO And but one word with one of us? Couple it
with something. Make it a word and a blow.

40 TYBALT You shall find me apt enough to that, sir, an you
will give me occasion.

MERCUTIO Could you not take some occasion without
giving?

TYBALT
Mercutio, thou consortest with Romeo.

MERCUTIO Consort? What, dost thou make us minstrels?
An thou make minstrels of us, look to hear nothing but
discords. Here's my fiddlestick. Here's that shall make
you dance. Zounds, consort!

BENVOLIO
We talk here in the public haunt of men.
50 Either withdraw unto some private place,
Or reason coldly of your grievances,
Or else depart. Here all eyes gaze on us.

MERCUTIO
Men's eyes were made to look, and let them gaze.

I will not budge for no man's pleasure, I.
Enter Romeo

TYBALT
Well, peace be with you, sir. Here comes my man.

MERCUTIO
But I'll be hanged, sir, if he wear your livery.
Marry, go before to field, he'll be your follower!
Your worship in that sense may call him 'man'.

TYBALT
Romeo, the love I bear thee can afford
No better term than this: thou art a villain.   60

ROMEO
Tybalt, the reason that I have to love thee
Doth much excuse the appertaining rage
To such a greeting. Villain am I none.
Therefore farewell, I see thou knowest me not.

TYBALT
Boy, this shall not excuse the injuries
That thou hast done me. Therefore turn and draw.

ROMEO
I do protest I never injured thee,
But love thee better than thou canst devise
Till thou shalt know the reason of my love.
And so, good Capulet, which name I tender   70
As dearly as mine own, be satisfied.

MERCUTIO
O calm, dishonourable, vile submission!
Alla stoccata carries it away.
  He draws
Tybalt, you ratcatcher, will you walk?

TYBALT
What wouldst thou have with me?

MERCUTIO Good King of Cats, nothing but one of your
nine lives. That I mean to make bold withal, and, as you

shall use me hereafter, dry-beat the rest of the eight.
Will you pluck your sword out of his pilcher by the ears?
Make haste, lest mine be about your ears ere it be out.

TYBALT

I am for you.

He draws

ROMEO

Gentle Mercutio, put thy rapier up.

MERCUTIO

Come, sir, your *passado*!

They fight

ROMEO

Draw, Benvolio. Beat down their weapons.
Gentlemen, for shame! Forbear this outrage!
Tybalt, Mercutio, the Prince expressly hath
Forbid this bandying in Verona streets.
Hold, Tybalt! Good Mercutio!

Tybalt under Romeo's arm thrusts Mercutio

A FOLLOWER

Away, Tybalt!   *Exit Tybalt with his followers*

MERCUTIO

I am hurt.
A plague a'both houses! I am sped.
Is he gone and hath nothing?

BENVOLIO   What, art thou hurt?

MERCUTIO

Ay, ay, a scratch, a scratch. Marry, 'tis enough.
Where is my page? Go, villain, fetch a surgeon.

Exit Page

ROMEO

Courage, man. The hurt cannot be much.

MERCUTIO No, 'tis not so deep as a well, nor so wide as
a church door. But 'tis enough. 'Twill serve. Ask for me
tomorrow, and you shall find me a grave man. I am pep-

pered, I warrant, for this world. A plague a'both your
houses! Zounds, a dog, a rat, a mouse, a cat, to scratch   100
a man to death! A braggart, a rogue, a villain, that fights
by the book of arithmetic! Why the devil came you between us? I was hurt under your arm.

ROMEO

I thought all for the best.

MERCUTIO

Help me into some house, Benvolio,
Or I shall faint. A plague a'both your houses!
They have made worms' meat of me.
I have it, and soundly too. Your houses!

>   *Exit Mercutio with Benvolio*

ROMEO

This gentleman, the Prince's near ally,
My very friend, hath got this mortal hurt   110
In my behalf – my reputation stained
With Tybalt's slander – Tybalt, that an hour
Hath been my cousin. O sweet Juliet,
Thy beauty hath made me effeminate
And in my temper softened valour's steel!
>   *Enter Benvolio*

BENVOLIO

O Romeo, Romeo, brave Mercutio is dead!
That gallant spirit hath aspired the clouds,
Which too untimely here did scorn the earth.

ROMEO

This day's black fate on more days doth depend.
This but begins the woe others must end.   120
>   *Enter Tybalt*

BENVOLIO

Here comes the furious Tybalt back again.

ROMEO

Alive in triumph, and Mercutio slain!

Away to heaven respective lenity,
And fire-eyed fury be my conduct now!
Now, Tybalt, take the 'villain' back again
That late thou gavest me. For Mercutio's soul
Is but a little way above our heads,
Staying for thine to keep him company.
Either thou or I, or both, must go with him.

TYBALT

130   Thou, wretched boy, that didst consort him here,
Shalt with him hence.

ROMEO   This shall determine that.

They fight. Tybalt falls

BENVOLIO

Romeo, away, be gone!
The citizens are up, and Tybalt slain.
Stand not amazed. The Prince will doom thee death
If thou art taken. Hence, be gone, away!

ROMEO

O, I am fortune's fool!

BENVOLIO   Why dost thou stay?

Exit Romeo

Enter Citizens

CITIZENS

Which way ran he that killed Mercutio?
Tybalt, that murderer, which way ran he?

BENVOLIO

There lies that Tybalt.

CITIZEN   Up, sir, go with me.

140   I charge thee in the Prince's name obey.

Enter Prince, Montague, Capulet, their wives, and all

PRINCE

Where are the vile beginners of this fray?

BENVOLIO

O noble Prince, I can discover all

The unlucky manage of this fatal brawl.
There lies the man, slain by young Romeo,
That slew thy kinsman, brave Mercutio.

LADY CAPULET

Tybalt, my cousin! O my brother's child!
O Prince! O cousin! Husband! O, the blood is spilled
Of my dear kinsman! Prince, as thou art true,
For blood of ours shed blood of Montague.
O cousin, cousin!   150

PRINCE

Benvolio, who began this bloody fray?

BENVOLIO

Tybalt, here slain, whom Romeo's hand did slay.
Romeo, that spoke him fair, bid him bethink
How nice the quarrel was, and urged withal
Your high displeasure. All this — utterèd
With gentle breath, calm look, knees humbly bowed —
Could not take truce with the unruly spleen
Of Tybalt deaf to peace, but that he tilts
With piercing steel at bold Mercutio's breast;
Who, all as hot, turns deadly point to point,   160
And, with a martial scorn, with one hand beats
Cold death aside and with the other sends
It back to Tybalt, whose dexterity
Retorts it. Romeo he cries aloud,
'Hold, friends! Friends, part!' and swifter than his tongue
His agile arm beats down their fatal points,
And 'twixt them rushes; underneath whose arm
An envious thrust from Tybalt hit the life
Of stout Mercutio, and then Tybalt fled.
But by and by comes back to Romeo,   170
Who had but newly entertained revenge,
And to't they go like lightning. For, ere I
Could draw to part them, was stout Tybalt slain.

And as he fell, did Romeo turn and fly.
This is the truth, or let Benvolio die.

LADY CAPULET
He is a kinsman to the Montague.
Affection makes him false. He speaks not true.
Some twenty of them fought in this black strife,
And all those twenty could but kill one life.
180   I beg for justice, which thou, Prince, must give.
Romeo slew Tybalt. Romeo must not live.

PRINCE
Romeo slew him. He slew Mercutio.
Who now the price of his dear blood doth owe?

MONTAGUE
Not Romeo, Prince. He was Mercutio's friend;
His fault concludes but what the law should end,
The life of Tybalt.

PRINCE   And for that offence
Immediately we do exile him hence.
I have an interest in your hate's proceeding,
My blood for your rude brawls doth lie a-bleeding.
190   But I'll amerce you with so strong a fine
That you shall all repent the loss of mine.
I will be deaf to pleading and excuses.
Nor tears nor prayers shall purchase out abuses.
Therefore use none. Let Romeo hence in haste,
Else, when he is found, that hour is his last.
Bear hence this body, and attend our will.
Mercy but murders, pardoning those that kill.   *Exeunt*

III.2   *Enter Juliet alone*

JULIET
Gallop apace, you fiery-footed steeds,
Towards Phoebus' lodging! Such a waggoner

As Phaëton would whip you to the West
And bring in cloudy night immediately.
Spread thy close curtain, love-performing night,
That runaway's eyes may wink, and Romeo
Leap to these arms untalked of and unseen.
Lovers can see to do their amorous rites
By their own beauties; or, if love be blind,
It best agrees with night. Come, civil night,   10
Thou sober-suited matron, all in black,
And learn me how to lose a winning match,
Played for a pair of stainless maidenhoods.
Hood my unmanned blood, bating in my cheeks,
With thy black mantle till strange love grow bold,
Think true love acted simple modesty.
Come, night. Come, Romeo. Come, thou day in night;
For thou wilt lie upon the wings of night
Whiter than new snow upon a raven's back.
Come, gentle night. Come, loving, black-browed night.   20
Give me my Romeo. And when I shall die,
Take him and cut him out in little stars,
And he will make the face of heaven so fine
That all the world will be in love with night
And pay no worship to the garish sun.
O I have bought the mansion of a love,
But not possessed it; and though I am sold,
Not yet enjoyed. So tedious is this day
As is the night before some festival
To an impatient child that hath new robes   30
And may not wear them.

Enter Nurse, wringing her hands, with the ladder of cords
                              O here comes my Nurse,
And she brings news; and every tongue that speaks
But Romeo's name speaks heavenly eloquence.

Now, Nurse, what news? What, hast thou there the cords
That Romeo bid thee fetch?

NURSE   Ay, ay, the cords.

She throws them down

JULIET

Ay me! what news? Why dost thou wring thy hands?

NURSE

Ah, weraday! He's dead, he's dead, he's dead!
We are undone, lady, we are undone!
Alack the day! he's gone, he's killed, he's dead!

JULIET

40   Can heaven be so envious?

NURSE   Romeo can,
Though heaven cannot. O Romeo, Romeo!
Who ever would have thought it? Romeo!

JULIET

What devil art thou that dost torment me thus?
This torture should be roared in dismal hell.
Hath Romeo slain himself? Say thou but 'Ay,'
And that bare vowel 'I' shall poison more
Than the death-darting eye of cockatrice.
I am not I, if there be such an 'I'
Or those eyes shut that makes thee answer 'Ay.'

50   If he be slain, say 'Ay'; or if not, 'No.'
Brief sounds determine of my weal or woe.

NURSE

I saw the wound. I saw it with mine eyes –
God save the mark! – here on his manly breast.
A piteous corse, a bloody piteous corse;
Pale, pale as ashes, all bedaubed in blood,
All in gore-blood. I swounded at the sight.

JULIET

O, break, my heart! Poor bankrupt, break at once!
To prison, eyes; ne'er look on liberty!

Vile earth, to earth resign; end motion here,
And thou and Romeo press one heavy bier!   60

NURSE

O Tybalt, Tybalt, the best friend I had!
O courteous Tybalt, honest gentleman!
That ever I should live to see thee dead!

JULIET

What storm is this that blows so contrary?
Is Romeo slaughtered, and is Tybalt dead,
My dearest cousin and my dearer lord?
Then, dreadful trumpet, sound the General Doom!
For who is living, if those two are gone?

NURSE

Tybalt is gone, and Romeo banishèd;
Romeo that killed him, he is banishèd.   70

JULIET

O God! Did Romeo's hand shed Tybalt's blood?

NURSE

It did, it did! Alas the day, it did!

JULIET

O serpent heart, hid with a flowering face!
Did ever dragon keep so fair a cave?
Beautiful tyrant! fiend angelical!
Dove-feathered raven! Wolvish-ravening lamb!
Despisèd substance of divinest show!
Just opposite to what thou justly seemest –
A damnèd saint, an honourable villain!
O nature, what hadst thou to do in hell   80
When thou didst bower the spirit of a fiend
In mortal paradise of such sweet flesh?
Was ever book containing such vile matter
So fairly bound? O, that deceit should dwell
In such a gorgeous palace!

NURSE   There's no trust,

No faith, no honesty in men; all perjured,
All forsworn, all naught, all dissemblers.
Ah, where's my man? Give me some aqua vitae.
These griefs, these woes, these sorrows make me old.
90   Shame come to Romeo!

JULIET   Blistered be thy tongue
For such a wish! He was not born to shame.
Upon his brow shame is ashamed to sit.
For 'tis a throne where honour may be crowned
Sole monarch of the universal earth.
O, what a beast was I to chide at him!

NURSE
Will you speak well of him that killed your cousin?

JULIET
Shall I speak ill of him that is my husband?
Ah, poor my lord, what tongue shall smooth thy name
When I, thy three-hours wife, have mangled it?
100 But wherefore, villain, didst thou kill my cousin?
That villain cousin would have killed my husband.
Back, foolish tears, back to your native spring!
Your tributary drops belong to woe,
Which you, mistaking, offer up to joy.
My husband lives, that Tybalt would have slain;
And Tybalt's dead, that would have slain my husband.
All this is comfort. Wherefore weep I then?
Some word there was, worser than Tybalt's death,
That murdered me. I would forget it fain.
110 But O, it presses to my memory
Like damnèd guilty deeds to sinners' minds!
'Tybalt is dead, and Romeo – banishèd.'
That 'banishèd', that one word 'banishèd',
Hath slain ten thousand Tybalts. Tybalt's death
Was woe enough, if it had ended there;
Or, if sour woe delights in fellowship

And needly will be ranked with other griefs,
Why followed not, when she said 'Tybalt's dead,'
Thy father, or thy mother, nay, or both,
Which modern lamentation might have moved?   120
But with a rearward following Tybalt's death,
'Romeo is banishèd' – to speak that word
Is father, mother, Tybalt, Romeo, Juliet,
All slain, all dead. 'Romeo is banishèd' –
There is no end, no limit, measure, bound,
In that word's death. No words can that woe sound.
Where is my father and my mother, Nurse?

NURSE

Weeping and wailing over Tybalt's corse.
Will you go to them? I will bring you thither.

JULIET

Wash they his wounds with tears. Mine shall be spent,   130
When theirs are dry, for Romeo's banishment.
Take up those cords. Poor ropes, you are beguiled,
Both you and I, for Romeo is exiled.
He made you for a highway to my bed,
But I, a maid, die maiden-widowèd.
Come, cords. Come, nurse. I'll to my wedding bed,
And death, not Romeo, take my maidenhead!

NURSE

Hie to your chamber. I'll find Romeo
To comfort you. I wot well where he is.
Hark ye, your Romeo will be here at night.   140
I'll to him. He is hid at Laurence' cell.

JULIET

O, find him! Give this ring to my true knight
And bid him come to take his last farewell.

                              Exit Juliet with Nurse

III.3   *Enter Friar Laurence*

FRIAR
      Romeo, come forth. Come forth, thou fearful man.
      Affliction is enamoured of thy parts,
      And thou art wedded to calamity.

          Enter Romeo

ROMEO
      Father, what news? What is the Prince's doom?
      What sorrow craves acquaintance at my hand
      That I yet know not?

FRIAR   Too familiar
      Is my dear son with such sour company.
      I bring thee tidings of the Prince's doom.

ROMEO
      What less than doomsday is the Prince's doom?

FRIAR
10   A gentler judgement vanished from his lips:
      Not body's death, but body's banishment.

ROMEO
      Ha, banishment? Be merciful, say 'death'.
      For exile hath more terror in his look,
      Much more than death. Do not say 'banishment'.

FRIAR
      Hence from Verona art thou banishèd.
      Be patient, for the world is broad and wide.

ROMEO
      There is no world without Verona walls,
      But purgatory, torture, hell itself.
      Hence banishèd is banished from the world,
20   And world's exile is death. Then 'banishèd'
      Is death mistermed. Calling death 'banishèd',
      Thou cuttest my head off with a golden axe
      And smilest upon the stroke that murders me.

FRIAR

    O deadly sin! O rude unthankfulness!
    Thy fault our law calls death. But the kind Prince,
    Taking thy part, hath rushed aside the law,
    And turned that black word 'death' to banishment.
    This is dear mercy, and thou seest it not.

ROMEO

    'Tis torture, and not mercy. Heaven is here,
    Where Juliet lives. And every cat and dog   30
    And little mouse, every unworthy thing,
    Live here in heaven and may look on her.
    But Romeo may not. More validity,
    More honourable state, more courtship lives
    In carrion flies than Romeo. They may seize
    On the white wonder of dear Juliet's hand
    And steal immortal blessing from her lips,
    Who, even in pure and vestal modesty,
    Still blush, as thinking their own kisses sin.
    This may flies do, when I from this must fly.   40
    And sayest thou yet that exile is not death?
    But Romeo may not, he is banishèd.
    Flies may do this but I from this must fly.
    They are free men. But I am banishèd.
    Hadst thou no poison mixed, no sharp-ground knife,
    No sudden mean of death, though ne'er so mean,
    But 'banishèd' to kill me – 'banishèd'?
    O Friar, the damnèd use that word in hell.
    Howling attends it! How hast thou the heart,
    Being a divine, a ghostly confessor,   50
    A sin-absolver, and my friend professed,
    To mangle me with that word 'banishèd'?

FRIAR

    Thou fond mad man, hear me a little speak.

ROMEO

O, thou wilt speak again of banishment.

FRIAR

I'll give thee armour to keep off that word —
Adversity's sweet milk, philosophy,
To comfort thee, though thou art banishèd.

ROMEO

Yet 'banishèd'? Hang up philosophy!
Unless philosophy can make a Juliet,
60   Displant a town, reverse a prince's doom,
It helps not, it prevails not. Talk no more.

FRIAR

O, then I see that madmen have no ears.

ROMEO

How should they, when that wise men have no eyes?

FRIAR

Let me dispute with thee of thy estate.

ROMEO

Thou canst not speak of that thou dost not feel.
Wert thou as young as I, Juliet thy love,
An hour but married, Tybalt murderèd,
Doting like me, and like me banishèd,
Then mightst thou speak; then mightst thou tear thy hair,
70   And fall upon the ground, as I do now,
Taking the measure of an unmade grave.

Knock

FRIAR

Arise. One knocks. Good Romeo, hide thyself.

ROMEO

Not I; unless the breath of heartsick groans
Mist-like infold me from the search of eyes.

Knock

FRIAR

Hark, how they knock! — Who's there? — Romeo, arise.

Thou wilt be taken. – Stay a while! – Stand up.
> *Knock*

Run to my study. – By and by! – God's will,
What simpleness is this! – I come, I come!
> *Knock*

Who knocks so hard? Whence come you? What's your
    will?

NURSE

Let me come in, and you shall know my errand.   80
I come from Lady Juliet.

FRIAR   Welcome then.
> *Enter Nurse*

NURSE

O holy Friar, O, tell me, holy Friar,
Where's my lady's lord, where's Romeo?

FRIAR

There on the ground, with his own tears made drunk.

NURSE

O, he is even in my mistress' case,
Just in her case! O woeful sympathy!
Piteous predicament! Even so lies she,
Blubbering and weeping, weeping and blubbering.
Stand up, stand up! Stand, an you be a man.
For Juliet's sake, for her sake, rise and stand!   90
Why should you fall into so deep an O?
> *He rises*

ROMEO

Nurse –

NURSE   Ah sir! ah sir! Death's the end of all.

ROMEO

Spakest thou of Juliet? How is it with her?
Doth not she think me an old murderer,
Now I have stained the childhood of our joy
With blood removed but little from her own?

Where is she? and how doth she? and what says
My concealed lady to our cancelled love?

NURSE

O, she says nothing, sir, but weeps and weeps,
100   And now falls on her bed, and then starts up,
And Tybalt calls, and then on Romeo cries,
And then down falls again.

ROMEO   As if that name,
Shot from the deadly level of a gun,
Did murder her; as that name's cursèd hand
Murdered her kinsman. O, tell me, Friar, tell me,
In what vile part of this anatomy
Doth my name lodge? Tell me, that I may sack
The hateful mansion.

*He offers to stab himself, and the Nurse snatches the
dagger away*

FRIAR   Hold thy desperate hand.
Art thou a man? Thy form cries out thou art.
110   Thy tears are womanish. Thy wild acts denote
The unreasonable fury of a beast.
Unseemly woman in a seeming man!
And ill-beseeming beast in seeming both!
Thou hast amazed me. By my holy order,
I thought thy disposition better tempered.
Hast thou slain Tybalt? Wilt thou slay thyself?
And slay thy lady that in thy life lives,
By doing damnèd hate upon thyself?
Why railest thou on thy birth, the heaven, and earth?
120   Since birth and heaven and earth, all three, do meet
In thee at once; which thou at once wouldst lose.
Fie, fie, thou shamest thy shape, thy love, thy wit,
Which, like a usurer, aboundest in all,
And usest none in that true use indeed
Which should bedeck thy shape, thy love, thy wit.

Thy noble shape is but a form of wax,
Digressing from the valour of a man;
Thy dear love sworn but hollow perjury,
Killing that love which thou hast vowed to cherish;
Thy wit, that ornament to shape and love,   130
Misshapen in the conduct of them both,
Like powder in a skilless soldier's flask
Is set afire by thine own ignorance,
And thou dismembered with thine own defence.
What, rouse thee, man! Thy Juliet is alive,
For whose dear sake thou wast but lately dead.
There art thou happy. Tybalt would kill thee,
But thou slewest Tybalt. There art thou happy.
The law, that threatened death, becomes thy friend
And turns it to exile. There art thou happy.   140
A pack of blessings light upon thy back.
Happiness courts thee in her best array.
But, like a mishavèd and sullen wench,
Thou pouts upon thy fortune and thy love.
Take heed, take heed, for such die miserable.
Go, get thee to thy love, as was decreed.
Ascend her chamber. Hence and comfort her.
But look thou stay not till the Watch be set,
For then thou canst not pass to Mantua,
Where thou shalt live till we can find a time   150
To blaze your marriage, reconcile your friends,
Beg pardon of the Prince, and call thee back
With twenty hundred thousand times more joy
Than thou wentest forth in lamentation.
Go before, Nurse. Commend me to thy lady,
And bid her hasten all the house to bed,
Which heavy sorrow makes them apt unto.
Romeo is coming.

NURSE

 O Lord, I could have stayed here all the night

160 To hear good counsel. O, what learning is! –

 My lord, I'll tell my lady you will come.

ROMEO

 Do so, and bid my sweet prepare to chide.

   The Nurse begins to go in and turns back again

NURSE

 Here, sir, a ring she bid me give you, sir.

 Hie you, make haste, for it grows very late. *Exit Nurse*

ROMEO

 How well my comfort is revived by this!

FRIAR

 Go hence. Good night. And here stands all your state:

 Either be gone before the Watch be set,

 Or by the break of day disguised from hence.

 Sojourn in Mantua. I'll find out your man,

170 And he shall signify from time to time

 Every good hap to you that chances here.

 Give me thy hand. 'Tis late. Farewell. Good night.

ROMEO

 But that a joy past joy calls out on me,

 It were a grief so brief to part with thee.

 Farewell.   *Exeunt*

III.4   *Enter old Capulet, his wife, and Paris*

CAPULET

 Things have fallen out, sir, so unluckily

 That we have had no time to move our daughter.

 Look you, she loved her kinsman Tybalt dearly,

 And so did I. Well, we were born to die.

 'Tis very late. She'll not come down tonight.

I promise you, but for your company,
I would have been abed an hour ago.

PARIS

These times of woe afford no times to woo.
Madam, good night. Commend me to your daughter.

LADY CAPULET

I will, and know her mind early tomorrow.   10
Tonight she's mewed up to her heaviness.

Paris offers to go in and Capulet calls him again

CAPULET

Sir Paris, I will make a desperate tender
Of my child's love. I think she will be ruled
In all respects by me. Nay more, I doubt it not.
Wife, go you to her ere you go to bed.
Acquaint her here of my son Paris' love,
And bid her — mark you me? — on Wednesday next —
But soft! what day is this?

PARIS   Monday, my lord.

CAPULET

Monday! Ha, ha! Well, Wednesday is too soon.
A'Thursday let it be. A'Thursday, tell her,   20
She shall be married to this noble earl.
Will you be ready? Do you like this haste?
We'll keep no great ado — a friend or two.
For hark you, Tybalt being slain so late,
It may be thought we held him carelessly,
Being our kinsman, if we revel much.
Therefore we'll have some half a dozen friends,
And there an end. But what say you to Thursday?

PARIS

My lord, I would that Thursday were tomorrow.

CAPULET

Well, get you gone. A'Thursday be it, then.   30
Go you to Juliet ere you go to bed.

Prepare her, wife, against this wedding day.
Farewell, my lord. – Light to my chamber, ho!
Afore me, it is so very late that we
May call it early by and by. Good night.   *Exeunt*

III.5   *Enter Romeo and Juliet aloft, at the window*

JULIET
Wilt thou be gone? It is not yet near day.
It was the nightingale, and not the lark,
That pierced the fearful hollow of thine ear.
Nightly she sings on yond pomegranate tree.
Believe me, love, it was the nightingale.

ROMEO
It was the lark, the herald of the morn;
No nightingale. Look, love, what envious streaks
Do lace the severing clouds in yonder East.
Night's candles are burnt out, and jocund day
10   Stands tiptoe on the misty mountain tops.
I must be gone and live, or stay and die.

JULIET
Yond light is not daylight; I know it, I.
It is some meteor that the sun exhales
To be to thee this night a torchbearer
And light thee on thy way to Mantua.
Therefore stay yet. Thou needest not to be gone.

ROMEO
Let me be ta'en, let me be put to death.
I am content, so thou wilt have it so.
I'll say yon grey is not the morning's eye;
20   'Tis but the pale reflex of Cynthia's brow.
Nor that is not the lark whose notes do beat
The vaulty heaven so high above our heads.
I have more care to stay than will to go.

Come, death, and welcome! Juliet wills it so.
How is't, my soul? Let's talk. It is not day.

JULIET

It is, it is! Hie hence, be gone, away!
It is the lark that sings so out of tune,
Straining harsh discords and unpleasing sharps.
Some say the lark makes sweet division.
This doth not so, for she divideth us.   30
Some say the lark and loathèd toad change eyes.
O, now I would they had changed voices too,
Since arm from arm that voice doth us affray,
Hunting thee hence with hunt's-up to the day.
O, now be gone! More light and light it grows.

ROMEO

More light and light: more dark and dark our woes.
    Enter Nurse hastily

NURSE

Madam!

JULIET

Nurse?

NURSE

Your lady mother is coming to your chamber.
The day is broke. Be wary. Look about.   *Exit Nurse*   40

JULIET

Then, window, let day in, and let life out.

ROMEO

Farewell, farewell! One kiss, and I'll descend.
    He goes down

JULIET

Art thou gone so, love-lord, aye husband-friend?
I must hear from thee every day in the hour,
For in a minute there are many days.
O by this count I shall be much in years
Ere I again behold my Romeo.

ROMEO

    Farewell!

    I will omit no opportunity

50   That may convey my greetings, love, to thee.

JULIET

    O, thinkest thou we shall ever meet again?

ROMEO

    I doubt it not; and all these woes shall serve

    For sweet discourses in our times to come.

JULIET

    O God, I have an ill-divining soul!

    Methinks I see thee, now thou art so low,

    As one dead in the bottom of a tomb.

    Either my eyesight fails, or thou lookest pale.

ROMEO

    And trust me, love, in my eye so do you.

    Dry sorrow drinks our blood. Adieu, adieu! *Exit Romeo*

JULIET

60   O Fortune, Fortune! All men call thee fickle.

    If thou art fickle, what dost thou with him

    That is renowned for faith? Be fickle, Fortune,

    For then I hope thou wilt not keep him long

    But send him back.

      She goes down from the window

      Enter Juliet's mother

LADY CAPULET   Ho, daughter! Are you up?

JULIET

    Who is't that calls? It is my lady mother.

    Is she not down so late, or up so early?

    What unaccustomed cause procures her hither?

LADY CAPULET

    Why, how now, Juliet?

JULIET   Madam, I am not well.

LADY CAPULET

Evermore weeping for your cousin's death?
What, wilt thou wash him from his grave with tears?   70
An if thou couldst, thou couldst not make him live.
Therefore have done. Some grief shows much of love;
But much of grief shows still some want of wit.

JULIET

Yet let me weep for such a feeling loss.

LADY CAPULET

So shall you feel the loss, but not the friend
Which you weep for.

JULIET   Feeling so the loss,
I cannot choose but ever weep the friend.

LADY CAPULET

Well, girl, thou weepest not so much for his death
As that the villain lives which slaughtered him.

JULIET

What villain, madam?

LADY CAPULET   That same villain Romeo.   80

JULIET (*aside*)

Villain and he be many miles asunder. –
God pardon! I do, with all my heart.
And yet no man like he doth grieve my heart.

LADY CAPULET

That is because the traitor murderer lives.

JULIET

Ay, madam, from the reach of these my hands.
Would none but I might venge my cousin's death!

LADY CAPULET

We will have vengeance for it, fear thou not.
Then weep no more. I'll send to one in Mantua,
Where that same banished runagate doth live,
Shall give him such an unaccustomed dram   90

That he shall soon keep Tybalt company.
And then I hope thou wilt be satisfied.

JULIET

Indeed I never shall be satisfied
With Romeo till I behold him – dead –
Is my poor heart so for a kinsman vexed.
Madam, if you could find out but a man
To bear a poison, I would temper it –
That Romeo should, upon receipt thereof,
Soon sleep in quiet. O, how my heart abhors
100   To hear him named and cannot come to him,
To wreak the love I bore my cousin
Upon his body that hath slaughtered him!

LADY CAPULET

Find thou the means, and I'll find such a man.
But now I'll tell thee joyful tidings, girl.

JULIET

And joy comes well in such a needy time.
What are they, beseech your ladyship?

LADY CAPULET

Well, well, thou hast a careful father, child:
One who, to put thee from thy heaviness,
Hath sorted out a sudden day of joy
110   That thou expects not nor I looked not for.

JULIET

Madam, in happy time! What day is that?

LADY CAPULET

Marry, my child, early next Thursday morn
The gallant, young, and noble gentleman,
The County Paris, at Saint Peter's Church,
Shall happily make thee there a joyful bride.

JULIET

Now by Saint Peter's Church, and Peter too,
He shall not make me there a joyful bride!

I wonder at this haste, that I must wed
Ere he that should be husband comes to woo.
I pray you tell my lord and father, madam,   120
I will not marry yet; and when I do, I swear
It shall be Romeo, whom you know I hate,
Rather than Paris. These are news indeed!

LADY CAPULET

Here comes your father. Tell him so yourself,
And see how he will take it at your hands.

Enter Capulet and Nurse

CAPULET

When the sun sets the earth doth drizzle dew,
But for the sunset of my brother's son
It rains downright.
How now? A conduit, girl? What, still in tears?
Evermore showering? In one little body   130
Thou counterfeitest a bark, a sea, a wind.
For still thy eyes, which I may call the sea,
Do ebb and flow with tears. The bark thy body is,
Sailing in this salt flood. The winds, thy sighs,
Who, raging with thy tears and they with them,
Without a sudden calm will overset
Thy tempest-tossèd body. How now, wife?
Have you delivered to her our decree?

LADY CAPULET

Ay, sir. But she will none, she gives you thanks.
I would the fool were married to her grave!   140

CAPULET

Soft! Take me with you, take me with you, wife.
How? Will she none? Doth she not give us thanks?
Is she not proud? Doth she not count her blest,
Unworthy as she is, that we have wrought
So worthy a gentleman to be her bride?

JULIET

Not proud you have, but thankful that you have.
Proud can I never be of what I hate,
But thankful even for hate that is meant love.

CAPULET

How, how, how, how, chopped logic? What is this?
150 'Proud' – and 'I thank you' – and 'I thank you not' –
And yet 'not proud'? Mistress minion you,
Thank me no thankings, nor proud me no prouds,
But fettle your fine joints 'gainst Thursday next
To go with Paris to Saint Peter's Church,
Or I will drag thee on a hurdle thither.
Out, you green-sickness carrion! Out, you baggage!
You tallow-face!

LADY CAPULET   Fie, fie! What, are you mad?

JULIET

Good father, I beseech you on my knees,
Hear me with patience but to speak a word.

CAPULET

160 Hang thee, young baggage! Disobedient wretch!
I tell thee what – get thee to church a'Thursday
Or never after look me in the face.
Speak not, reply not, do not answer me!
My fingers itch. Wife, we scarce thought us blest
That God had lent us but this only child.
But now I see this one is one too much,
And that we have a curse in having her.
Out on her, hilding!

NURSE   God in heaven bless her!
You are to blame, my lord, to rate her so.

CAPULET

170 And why, my Lady Wisdom? Hold your tongue,
Good Prudence. Smatter with your gossips, go!

NURSE

I speak no treason.

CAPULET   O, God-i-good-e'en!

NURSE

May not one speak?

CAPULET   Peace, you mumbling fool!

Utter your gravity o'er a gossip's bowl,

For here we need it not.

LADY CAPULET   You are too hot.

CAPULET

God's bread! It makes me mad.

Day, night; hour, tide, time; work, play;

Alone, in company; still my care hath been

To have her matched. And having now provided

A gentleman of noble parentage,   180

Of fair demesnes, youthful, and nobly trained,

Stuffed, as they say, with honourable parts,

Proportioned as one's thought would wish a man —

And then to have a wretched puling fool,

A whining mammet, in her fortune's tender,

To answer 'I'll not wed, I cannot love;

I am too young, I pray you pardon me'!

But, an you will not wed, I'll pardon you!

Graze where you will, you shall not house with me.

Look to't, think on't. I do not use to jest.   190

Thursday is near. Lay hand on heart. Advise.

An you be mine, I'll give you to my friend.

An you be not, hang, beg, starve, die in the streets,

For, by my soul, I'll ne'er acknowledge thee,

Nor what is mine shall never do thee good.

Trust to't. Bethink you. I'll not be forsworn.   *Exit Capulet*

JULIET

Is there no pity sitting in the clouds

That sees into the bottom of my grief?

O sweet my mother, cast me not away!
200   Delay this marriage for a month, a week.
Or if you do not, make the bridal bed
In that dim monument where Tybalt lies.

LADY CAPULET
Talk not to me, for I'll not speak a word.
Do as thou wilt, for I have done with thee.

Exit Lady Capulet

JULIET
O God! – O Nurse, how shall this be prevented?
My husband is on earth, my faith in heaven.
How shall that faith return again to earth
Unless that husband send it me from heaven
By leaving earth? Comfort me, counsel me.
210   Alack, alack, that heaven should practise stratagems
Upon so soft a subject as myself!
What sayest thou? Hast thou not a word of joy?
Some comfort, Nurse.

NURSE   Faith, here it is.
Romeo is banished; and all the world to nothing
That he dares ne'er come back to challenge you.
Or if he do, it needs must be by stealth.
Then, since the case so stands as now it doth,
I think it best you married with the County.
O, he's a lovely gentleman!
220   Romeo's a dishclout to him. An eagle, madam,
Hath not so green, so quick, so fair an eye
As Paris hath. Beshrew my very heart,
I think you are happy in this second match,
For it excels your first; or if it did not,
Your first is dead – or 'twere as good he were
As living here and you no use of him.

JULIET
Speakest thou from thy heart?

NURSE
    And from my soul too. Else beshrew them both.
JULIET
    Amen!
NURSE
    What?   230
JULIET
    Well, thou hast comforted me marvellous much.
    Go in; and tell my lady I am gone,
    Having displeased my father, to Laurence' cell,
    To make confession and to be absolved.
NURSE
    Marry, I will; and this is wisely done.   *Exit Nurse*
JULIET
    Ancient damnation! O most wicked fiend!
    Is it more sin to wish me thus forsworn,
    Or to dispraise my lord with that same tongue
    Which she hath praised him with above compare
    So many thousand times? Go, counsellor!   240
    Thou and my bosom henceforth shall be twain.
    I'll to the Friar to know his remedy.
    If all else fail, myself have power to die.   *Exit*

*

Enter Friar Laurence and County Paris   IV.I
FRIAR
    On Thursday, sir? The time is very short.
PARIS
    My father Capulet will have it so,
    And I am nothing slow to slack his haste.
FRIAR
    You say you do not know the lady's mind.

Uneven is the course. I like it not.

PARIS

Immoderately she weeps for Tybalt's death,
And therefore have I little talked of love;
For Venus smiles not in a house of tears.
Now, sir, her father counts it dangerous
That she do give her sorrow so much sway,
And in his wisdom hastes our marriage
To stop the inundation of her tears,
Which, too much minded by herself alone,
May be put from her by society.
Now do you know the reason of this haste.

FRIAR (*aside*)

I would I knew not why it should be slowed. –
Look, sir, here comes the lady toward my cell.

    Enter Juliet

PARIS

Happily met, my lady and my wife!

JULIET

That may be, sir, when I may be a wife.

PARIS

That 'may be' must be, love, on Thursday next.

JULIET

What must be shall be.

FRIAR   That's a certain text.

PARIS

Come you to make confession to this father?

JULIET

To answer that, I should confess to you.

PARIS

Do not deny to him that you love me.

JULIET

I will confess to you that I love him.

PARIS

So will ye, I am sure, that you love me.

JULIET

If I do so, it will be of more price,

Being spoke behind your back, than to your face.

PARIS

Poor soul, thy face is much abused with tears.

JULIET

The tears have got small victory by that,   30

For it was bad enough before their spite.

PARIS

Thou wrongest it more than tears with that report.

JULIET

That is no slander, sir, which is a truth.

And what I spake, I spake it to my face.

PARIS

Thy face is mine, and thou hast slandered it.

JULIET

It may be so, for it is not mine own. –

Are you at leisure, holy father, now,

Or shall I come to you at evening mass?

FRIAR

My leisure serves me, pensive daughter, now. –

My lord, we must entreat the time alone.   40

PARIS

God shield I should disturb devotion! –

Juliet, on Thursday early will I rouse ye.

Till then, adieu, and keep this holy kiss.   *Exit Paris*

JULIET

O shut the door! and when thou hast done so,

Come weep with me. Past hope, past cure, past help!

FRIAR

O, Juliet, I already know thy grief.

It strains me past the compass of my wits.

I hear thou must, and nothing may prorogue it,
On Thursday next be married to this County.

JULIET

50   Tell me not, Friar, that thou hearest of this,
Unless thou tell me how I may prevent it.
If in thy wisdom thou canst give no help,
Do thou but call my resolution wise
And with this knife I'll help it presently.
God joined my heart and Romeo's, thou our hands;
And ere this hand, by thee to Romeo's sealed,
Shall be the label to another deed,
Or my true heart with treacherous revolt
Turn to another, this shall slay them both.
60   Therefore, out of thy long-experienced time,
Give me some present counsel; or, behold,
'Twixt my extremes and me this bloody knife
Shall play the umpire, arbitrating that
Which the commission of thy years and art
Could to no issue of true honour bring.
Be not so long to speak. I long to die
If what thou speakest speak not of remedy.

FRIAR

Hold, daughter. I do spy a kind of hope,
Which craves as desperate an execution
70   As that is desperate which we would prevent.
If, rather than to marry County Paris,
Thou hast the strength of will to slay thyself,
Then is it likely thou wilt undertake
A thing like death to chide away this shame,
That copest with death himself to 'scape from it.
And, if thou darest, I'll give thee remedy.

JULIET

O bid me leap, rather than marry Paris,
From off the battlements of any tower,

Or walk in thievish ways, or bid me lurk
Where serpents are. Chain me with roaring bears,   80
Or hide me nightly in a charnel house,
O'ercovered quite with dead men's rattling bones,
With reeky shanks and yellow chapless skulls.
Or bid me go into a new-made grave
And hide me with a dead man in his tomb –
Things that, to hear them told, have made me tremble –
And I will do it without fear or doubt,
To live an unstained wife to my sweet love.

FRIAR

Hold, then. Go home, be merry, give consent
To marry Paris. Wednesday is tomorrow.   90
Tomorrow night look that thou lie alone.
Let not the Nurse lie with thee in thy chamber.
Take thou this vial, being then in bed,
And this distilling liquor drink thou off;
When presently through all thy veins shall run
A cold and drowsy humour. For no pulse
Shall keep his native progress, but surcease.
No warmth, no breath, shall testify thou livest.
The roses in thy lips and cheeks shall fade
To wanny ashes, thy eyes' windows fall   100
Like death when he shuts up the day of life.
Each part, deprived of supple government,
Shall, stiff and stark and cold, appear like death.
And in this borrowed likeness of shrunk death
Thou shalt continue two-and-forty hours,
And then awake as from a pleasant sleep.
Now, when the bridegroom in the morning comes
To rouse thee from thy bed, there art thou dead.
Then, as the manner of our country is,
In thy best robes uncovered on the bier   110
Thou shalt be borne to that same ancient vault

Where all the kindred of the Capulets lie.
In the meantime, against thou shalt awake,
Shall Romeo by my letters know our drift.
And hither shall he come. And he and I
Will watch thy waking, and that very night
Shall Romeo bear thee hence to Mantua.
And this shall free thee from this present shame,
If no inconstant toy nor womanish fear
120 Abate thy valour in the acting it.

JULIET
Give me, give me! O tell not me of fear!

FRIAR
Hold. Get you gone. Be strong and prosperous
In this resolve. I'll send a friar with speed
To Mantua, with my letters to thy lord.

JULIET
Love give me strength, and strength shall help afford.
Farewell, dear father.   *Exeunt*

IV.2   *Enter Capulet, Lady Capulet, Nurse, and two or three
          Servingmen*

CAPULET
So many guests invite as here are writ.   *Exit a Servingman*
Sirrah, go hire me twenty cunning cooks.

SERVINGMAN You shall have none ill, sir. For I'll try if
they can lick their fingers.

CAPULET How! Canst thou try them so?

SERVINGMAN Marry, sir, 'tis an ill cook that cannot lick
his own fingers. Therefore he that cannot lick his fingers
goes not with me.

CAPULET
Go, begone.   *Exit Servingman*
10   We shall be much unfurnished for this time.

What, is my daughter gone to Friar Laurence?

NURSE

Ay, forsooth.

CAPULET

Well, he may chance to do some good on her.
A peevish self-willed harlotry it is.

Enter Juliet

NURSE

See where she comes from shrift with merry look.

CAPULET

How now, my headstrong! Where have you been
gadding?

JULIET

Where I have learnt me to repent the sin
Of disobedient opposition
To you and your behests, and am enjoined
By holy Laurence to fall prostrate here   20
To beg your pardon. Pardon, I beseech you!
Henceforward I am ever ruled by you.

CAPULET

Send for the County. Go tell him of this.
I'll have this knot knit up tomorrow morning.

JULIET

I met the youthful lord at Laurence' cell
And gave him what becomèd love I might,
Not stepping o'er the bounds of modesty.

CAPULET

Why, I am glad on't. This is well. Stand up.
This is as't should be. Let me see, the County.
Ay, marry, go, I say, and fetch him hither.   30
Now, afore God, this reverend holy Friar,
All our whole city is much bound to him.

JULIET

Nurse, will you go with me into my closet

To help me sort such needful ornaments
As you think fit to furnish me tomorrow?

LADY CAPULET
No, not till Thursday. There is time enough.

CAPULET
Go, Nurse, go with her. We'll to church tomorrow.

Exeunt Juliet and Nurse

LADY CAPULET
We shall be short in our provision.
'Tis now near night.

CAPULET   Tush, I will stir about,
40 And all things shall be well, I warrant thee, wife.
Go thou to Juliet, help to deck up her.
I'll not to bed tonight. Let me alone.
I'll play the housewife for this once. What, ho!
They are all forth. Well, I will walk myself
To County Paris, to prepare up him
Against tomorrow. My heart is wondrous light,
Since this same wayward girl is so reclaimed.   *Exeunt*

IV.3   *Enter Juliet and Nurse*

JULIET
Ay, those attires are best. But, gentle Nurse,
I pray thee leave me to myself tonight.
For I have need of many orisons
To move the heavens to smile upon my state,
Which, well thou knowest, is cross and full of sin.

Enter Lady Capulet

LADY CAPULET
What, are you busy, ho? Need you my help?

JULIET
No, madam. We have culled such necessaries
As are behoveful for our state tomorrow.

So please you, let me now be left alone,
And let the Nurse this night sit up with you.   10
For I am sure you have your hands full all
In this so sudden business.

LADY CAPULET   Good night.
  Go thee to bed, and rest. For thou hast need.

Exeunt Lady Capulet and Nurse

JULIET

Farewell! God knows when we shall meet again.
I have a faint cold fear thrills through my veins
That almost freezes up the heat of life.
I'll call them back again to comfort me.
Nurse! – What should she do here?
My dismal scene I needs must act alone.
Come, vial.   20
What if this mixture do not work at all?
Shall I be married then tomorrow morning?
No, no! This shall forbid it. Lie thou there.

She lays down a knife

What if it be a poison which the Friar
Subtly hath ministered to have me dead,
Lest in this marriage he should be dishonoured
Because he married me before to Romeo?
I fear it is. And yet methinks it should not,
For he hath still been tried a holy man.
How if, when I am laid into the tomb,   30
I wake before the time that Romeo
Come to redeem me? There's a fearful point!
Shall I not then be stifled in the vault,
To whose foul mouth no healthsome air breathes in,
And there die strangled ere my Romeo comes?
Or, if I live, is it not very like
The horrible conceit of death and night,
Together with the terror of the place –

As in a vault, an ancient receptacle
40   Where for this many hundred years the bones
Of all my buried ancestors are packed;
Where bloody Tybalt, yet but green in earth,
Lies festering in his shroud; where, as they say,
At some hours in the night spirits resort –
Alack, alack, is it not like that I,
So early waking – what with loathsome smells,
And shrieks like mandrakes torn out of the earth,
That living mortals, hearing them, run mad –
O, if I wake, shall I not be distraught,
50   Environèd with all these hideous fears,
And madly play with my forefathers' joints,
And pluck the mangled Tybalt from his shroud,
And, in this rage, with some great kinsman's bone
As with a club dash out my desperate brains?
O, look! Methinks I see my cousin's ghost
Seeking out Romeo, that did spit his body
Upon a rapier's point. Stay, Tybalt, stay!
Romeo, Romeo, Romeo.
Here's drink. I drink to thee.
    She falls upon her bed within the curtains

IV.4   *Enter Lady Capulet and Nurse, with herbs*
LADY CAPULET
    Hold, take these keys and fetch more spices, Nurse.
NURSE
    They call for dates and quinces in the pastry.
        Enter Capulet
CAPULET
    Come, stir, stir, stir! The second cock hath crowed.
    The curfew bell hath rung. 'Tis three o'clock.

Look to the baked meats, good Angelica.
Spare not for cost.

NURSE   Go, you cot-quean, go.
Get you to bed! Faith, you'll be sick tomorrow
For this night's watching.

CAPULET

No, not a whit. What, I have watched ere now
All night for lesser cause, and ne'er been sick.   10

LADY CAPULET

Ay, you have been a mouse-hunt in your time.
But I will watch you from such watching now.

Exeunt Lady Capulet and Nurse

CAPULET

A jealous hood, a jealous hood!

Enter three or four Servingmen with spits and logs and baskets

Now, fellow,
What is there?

FIRST SERVINGMAN

Things for the cook, sir; but I know not what.

CAPULET

Make haste, make haste.   *Exit First Servingman*
Sirrah, fetch drier logs.
Call Peter. He will show thee where they are.

SECOND SERVINGMAN

I have a head, sir, that will find out logs
And never trouble Peter for the matter.

CAPULET

Mass! and well said. A merry whoreson, ha!   20
Thou shalt be loggerhead.   *Exit Second Servingman*
Good Father! 'tis day.
The County will be here with music straight,
For so he said he would.

Music plays

                    I hear him near.
Nurse! Wife! What, ho! What, Nurse, I say!
    Enter Nurse
Go waken Juliet. Go and trim her up.
I'll go and chat with Paris. Hie, make haste,
Make haste! The bridegroom he is come already.
Make haste, I say.   *Exit Capulet*

IV. 5   *Nurse goes to curtains*

NURSE
        Mistress! What, mistress! Juliet! Fast, I warrant her, she.
        Why, lamb! Why, lady! Fie, you slug-abed!
        Why, love, I say! Madam! Sweetheart! Why, bride!
        What, not a word? You take your pennyworths now.
        Sleep for a week. For the next night, I warrant,
        The County Paris hath set up his rest
        That you shall rest but little. God forgive me!
        Marry, and amen! How sound is she asleep!
        I needs must wake her. Madam, madam, madam!
10   Ay, let the County take you in your bed.
        He'll fright you up, i'faith. Will it not be?
        What, dressed, and in your clothes, and down again?
        I must needs wake you. Lady! lady! lady!
        Alas, alas! Help, help! My lady's dead!
        O weraday that ever I was born!
        Some aqua vitae, ho! My lord! My lady!
            Enter Lady Capulet

LADY CAPULET
    What noise is here?
NURSE   O lamentable day!
LADY CAPULET
    What is the matter?
NURSE   Look, look! O heavy day!

LADY CAPULET

O me, O me! My child, my only life!
Revive, look up, or I will die with thee!   20
Help, help! Call help.

Enter Capulet

CAPULET

For shame, bring Juliet forth. Her lord is come.

NURSE

She's dead, deceased. She's dead, alack the day!

LADY CAPULET

Alack the day, she's dead, she's dead, she's dead!

CAPULET

Ha! let me see her. Out alas! she's cold,
Her blood is settled, and her joints are stiff.
Life and these lips have long been separated.
Death lies on her like an untimely frost
Upon the sweetest flower of all the field.

NURSE

O lamentable day!

LADY CAPULET   O woeful time!   30

CAPULET

Death, that hath ta'en her hence to make me wail,
Ties up my tongue and will not let me speak.

Enter Friar Laurence and the County Paris

FRIAR

Come, is the bride ready to go to church?

CAPULET

Ready to go, but never to return.
O son, the night before thy wedding day
Hath death lain with thy wife. There she lies,
Flower as she was, deflowerèd by him.
Death is my son-in-law. Death is my heir.
My daughter he hath wedded. I will die
And leave him all. Life, living, all is death's.   40

PARIS

    Have I thought long to see this morning's face,
    And doth it give me such a sight as this?

LADY CAPULET

    Accursed, unhappy, wretched, hateful day!
    Most miserable hour that e'er time saw
    In lasting labour of his pilgrimage!
    But one, poor one, one poor and loving child,
    But one thing to rejoice and solace in,
    And cruel death hath catched it from my sight.

NURSE

    O woe! O woeful, woeful, woeful day!
50   Most lamentable day, most woeful day
    That ever, ever I did yet behold!
    O day, O day, O day! O hateful day!
    Never was seen so black a day as this.
    O woeful day! O woeful day!

PARIS

    Beguiled, divorcèd, wrongèd, spited, slain!
    Most detestable Death, by thee beguiled,
    By cruel, cruel thee quite overthrown.
    O love! O life! – not life, but love in death!

CAPULET

    Despised, distressèd, hated, martyred, killed!
60   Uncomfortable time, why camest thou now
    To murder, murder our solemnity?
    O child! O child! my soul, and not my child!
    Dead art thou – alack, my child is dead,
    And with my child my joys are burièd!

FRIAR

    Peace, ho, for shame! Confusion's cure lives not
    In these confusions. Heaven and yourself
    Had part in this fair maid. Now heaven hath all,
    And all the better is it for the maid.

Your part in her you could not keep from death,
But heaven keeps his part in eternal life.   70
The most you sought was her promotion,
For 'twas your heaven she should be advanced.
And weep ye now, seeing she is advanced
Above the clouds, as high as heaven itself?
O, in this love, you love your child so ill
That you run mad, seeing that she is well.
She's not well married that lives married long,
But she's best married that dies married young.
Dry up your tears and stick your rosemary
On this fair corse, and, as the custom is,   80
In all her best array bear her to church.
For though fond nature bids us all lament,
Yet nature's tears are reason's merriment.

CAPULET

All things that we ordainèd festival
Turn from their office to black funeral.
Our instruments to melancholy bells;
Our wedding cheer to a sad burial feast;
Our solemn hymns to sullen dirges change;
Our bridal flowers serve for a buried corse;
And all things change them to the contrary.   90

FRIAR

Sir, go you in; and, madam, go with him;
And go, Sir Paris. Every one prepare
To follow this fair corse unto her grave.
The heavens do lour upon you for some ill.
Move them no more by crossing their high will.

                 Exeunt all except the Nurse, casting
             rosemary on her and shutting the curtains
    Enter Musicians

FIRST MUSICIAN

Faith, we may put up our pipes and be gone.

NURSE

    Honest good fellows, ah, put up, put up!
    For well you know this is a pitiful case.

FIDDLER

    Ay, by my troth, the case may be amended.   *Exit Nurse*
    Enter Peter

100 PETER Musicians, O musicians, 'Heart's ease', 'Heart's
    ease'! O, an you will have me live, play 'Heart's ease'.

FIDDLER Why 'Heart's ease'?

PETER O musicians, because my heart itself plays 'My
    heart is full'. O play me some merry dump to comfort
    me.

FIRST MUSICIAN Not a dump we! 'Tis no time to play
    now.

PETER You will not then?

FIRST MUSICIAN No.

110 PETER I will then give it you soundly.

FIRST MUSICIAN What will you give us?

PETER No money, on my faith, but the gleek. I will give
    you the minstrel.

FIRST MUSICIAN Then will I give you the serving-
    creature.

PETER Then will I lay the serving-creature's dagger on
    your pate. I will carry no crotchets. I'll re you, I'll fa you.
    Do you note me?

FIRST MUSICIAN An you re us and fa us, you note us.

120 SECOND MUSICIAN Pray you put up your dagger, and
    put out your wit.

PETER Then have at you with my wit! I will dry-beat you
    with an iron wit, and put up my iron dagger. Answer me
    like men.

      'When griping griefs the heart doth wound,
        And doleful dumps the mind oppress,
      Then music with her silver sound' –

Why 'silver sound'? Why 'music with her silver sound'?
What say you, Simon Catling?
FIRST MUSICIAN Marry, sir, because silver hath a sweet   130
sound.
PETER Pretty! What say you, Hugh Rebeck?
SECOND MUSICIAN I say 'silver sound' because musi-
cians sound for silver.
PETER Pretty too! What say you, James Soundpost?
THIRD MUSICIAN Faith, I know not what to say.
PETER O, I cry you mercy! You are the singer. I will say
for you. It is 'music with her silver sound' because musi-
cians have no gold for sounding.
        'Then music with her silver sound   140
           With speedy help doth lend redress.'   *Exit Peter*
FIRST MUSICIAN What a pestilent knave is this same!
SECOND MUSICIAN Hang him, Jack! Come, we'll in here,
tarry for the mourners, and stay dinner.   *Exeunt*

                            *

Enter Romeo   V.1
ROMEO
If I may trust the flattering truth of sleep,
My dreams presage some joyful news at hand.
My bosom's lord sits lightly in his throne,
And all this day an unaccustomed spirit
Lifts me above the ground with cheerful thoughts.
I dreamt my lady came and found me dead –
Strange dream that gives a dead man leave to think! –
And breathed such life with kisses in my lips
That I revived and was an emperor.
Ah me! how sweet is love itself possessed,   10
When but love's shadows are so rich in joy!

Enter Balthasar, Romeo's man, booted

News from Verona! How now, Balthasar?
Dost thou not bring me letters from the Friar?
How doth my lady? Is my father well?
How doth my lady Juliet? That I ask again,
For nothing can be ill if she be well.

BALTHASAR
Then she is well, and nothing can be ill.
Her body sleeps in Capel's monument,
And her immortal part with angels lives.
I saw her laid low in her kindred's vault
And presently took post to tell it you.
O, pardon me for bringing these ill news,
Since you did leave it for my office, sir.

ROMEO
Is it e'en so? Then I defy you, stars!
Thou knowest my lodging. Get me ink and paper,
And hire posthorses. I will hence tonight.

BALTHASAR
I do beseech you, sir, have patience.
Your looks are pale and wild and do import
Some misadventure.

ROMEO   Tush, thou art deceived.
Leave me and do the thing I bid thee do.
Hast thou no letters to me from the Friar?

BALTHASAR
No, my good lord.

ROMEO   No matter. Get thee gone
And hire those horses. I'll be with thee straight.

                              Exit Balthasar

Well, Juliet, I will lie with thee tonight.
Let's see for means. O mischief, thou art swift
To enter in the thoughts of desperate men.
I do remember an apothecary,

And hereabouts 'a dwells, which late I noted
In tattered weeds, with overwhelming brows,
Culling of simples. Meagre were his looks.   40
Sharp misery had worn him to the bones.
And in his needy shop a tortoise hung,
An alligator stuffed, and other skins
Of ill-shaped fishes; and about his shelves
A beggarly account of empty boxes,
Green earthen pots, bladders, and musty seeds,
Remnants of packthread, and old cakes of roses
Were thinly scattered, to make up a show.
Noting this penury, to myself I said,
'An if a man did need a poison now   50
Whose sale is present death in Mantua,
Here lives a caitiff wretch would sell it him.'
O, this same thought did but forerun my need,
And this same needy man must sell it me.
As I remember, this should be the house.
Being holiday, the beggar's shop is shut.
What, ho! Apothecary!
          Enter Apothecary
APOTHECARY   Who calls so loud?
ROMEO
Come hither, man. I see that thou art poor.
Hold, there is forty ducats. Let me have
A dram of poison, such soon-speeding gear   60
As will disperse itself through all the veins,
That the life-weary taker may fall dead
And that the trunk may be discharged of breath
As violently as hasty powder fired
Doth hurry from the fatal cannon's womb.
APOTHECARY
Such mortal drugs I have. But Mantua's law
Is death to any he that utters them.

ROMEO

Art thou so bare and full of wretchedness
And fearest to die? Famine is in thy cheeks.
70 Need and oppression starveth in thy eyes.
Contempt and beggary hangs upon thy back.
The world is not thy friend, nor the world's law.
The world affords no law to make thee rich.
Then be not poor, but break it and take this.

APOTHECARY

My poverty but not my will consents.

ROMEO

I pay thy poverty and not thy will.

APOTHECARY

Put this is any liquid thing you will
And drink it off, and if you had the strength
Of twenty men it would dispatch you straight.

ROMEO

80 There is thy gold – worse poison to men's souls,
Doing more murder in this loathsome world,
Than these poor compounds that thou mayst not sell.
I sell thee poison. Thou hast sold me none.
Farewell. Buy food and get thyself in flesh.
Come, cordial and not poison, go with me
To Juliet's grave. For there must I use thee.   *Exeunt*

V.2   *Enter Friar John*

FRIAR JOHN Holy Franciscan Friar, brother, ho!
      Enter Friar Laurence

FRIAR LAURENCE

This same should be the voice of Friar John.
Welcome from Mantua. What says Romeo?
Or, if his mind be writ, give me his letter.

JOHN

    Going to find a bare-foot brother out,
    One of our order, to associate me
    Here in this city visiting the sick,
    And finding him, the searchers of the town,
    Suspecting that we both were in a house
    Where the infectious pestilence did reign,   10
    Sealed up the doors, and would not let us forth,
    So that my speed to Mantua there was stayed.

LAURENCE

    Who bare my letter, then, to Romeo?

JOHN

    I could not send it – here it is again –
    Nor get a messenger to bring it thee,
    So fearful were they of infection.

LAURENCE

    Unhappy fortune! By my brotherhood,
    The letter was not nice, but full of charge,
    Of dear import; and the neglecting it
    May do much danger. Friar John, go hence.   20
    Get me an iron crow and bring it straight
    Unto my cell.

JOHN   Brother, I'll go and bring it thee.

                              Exit Friar John

LAURENCE

    Now must I to the monument alone.
    Within this three hours will fair Juliet wake.
    She will beshrew me much that Romeo
    Hath had no notice of these accidents.
    But I will write again to Mantua,
    And keep her at my cell till Romeo come.
    Poor living corse, closed in a dead man's tomb!   *Exit*

V.3   *Enter Paris and his Page, with flowers and sweet water*

PARIS
Give me thy torch, boy. Hence, and stand aloof.
Yet put it out, for I would not be seen.
Under yond yew trees lay thee all along,
Holding thy ear close to the hollow ground.
So shall no foot upon the churchyard tread,
Being loose, unfirm, with digging up of graves,
But thou shalt hear it. Whistle then to me,
As signal that thou hearest something approach.
Give me those flowers. Do as I bid thee, go.

PAGE *(aside)*
10   I am almost afraid to stand alone
Here in the churchyard. Yet I will adventure.   *Page retires*

PARIS
Sweet flower, with flowers thy bridal bed I strew –
    O woe! thy canopy is dust and stones –
Which with sweet water nightly I will dew;
    Or, wanting that, with tears distilled by moans.
The obsequies that I for thee will keep
Nightly shall be to strew thy grave and weep.
    Page whistles
The boy gives warning something doth approach.
What cursèd foot wanders this way tonight
20   To cross my obsequies and true love's rite?
What, with a torch? Muffle me, night, awhile. *Paris retires*
    Enter Romeo and Balthasar, with a torch, a
    mattock, and a crow of iron

ROMEO
Give me that mattock and the wrenching iron.
Hold, take this letter. Early in the morning
See thou deliver it to my lord and father.
Give me the light. Upon thy life I charge thee,
Whate'er thou hearest or seest, stand all aloof

And do not interrupt me in my course.
Why I descend into this bed of death
Is partly to behold my lady's face,
But chiefly to take thence from her dead finger   30
A precious ring, a ring that I must use
In dear employment. Therefore hence, be gone.
But if thou, jealous, dost return to pry
In what I farther shall intend to do,
By heaven, I will tear thee joint by joint
And strew this hungry churchyard with thy limbs.
The time and my intents are savage-wild,
More fierce and more inexorable far
Than empty tigers or the roaring sea.

BALTHASAR
I will be gone, sir, and not trouble ye.   40

ROMEO
So shalt thou show me friendship. Take thou that.
Live, and be prosperous; and farewell, good fellow.

BALTHASAR (*aside*)
For all this same, I'll hide me hereabout.
His looks I fear, and his intents I doubt. *Balthasar retires*

ROMEO
Thou detestable maw, thou womb of death,
Gorged with the dearest morsel of the earth,
Thus I enforce thy rotten jaws to open,
And in despite I'll cram thee with more food.
   Romeo begins to open the tomb

PARIS
This is that banished haughty Montague
That murdered my love's cousin – with which grief   50
It is supposèd the fair creature died –
And here is come to do some villainous shame
To the dead bodies. I will apprehend him.
Stop thy unhallowed toil, vile Montague!

Can vengeance be pursued further than death?
Condemnèd villain, I do apprehend thee.
Obey, and go with me. For thou must die.

ROMEO

I must indeed; and therefore came I hither.
Good gentle youth, tempt not a desperate man.
60   Fly hence and leave me. Think upon these gone.
Let them affright thee. I beseech thee, youth,
Put not another sin upon my head
By urging me to fury. O, be gone!
By heaven, I love thee better than myself,
For I come hither armed against myself.
Stay not, be gone. Live, and hereafter say
A madman's mercy bid thee run away.

PARIS

I do defy thy conjuration
And apprehend thee for a felon here.

ROMEO

70   Wilt thou provoke me? Then have at thee, boy!
        They fight

PAGE

O Lord, they fight! I will go call the Watch. *Exit Page*
        Paris falls

PARIS

O, I am slain! If thou be merciful,
Open the tomb, lay me with Juliet.   *Paris dies*

ROMEO

In faith, I will. Let me peruse this face.
Mercutio's kinsman, noble County Paris!
What said my man when my betossèd soul
Did not attend him as we rode? I think
He told me Paris should have married Juliet.
Said he not so? Or did I dream it so?
80   Or am I mad, hearing him talk of Juliet,

To think it was so? O, give me thy hand,
One writ with me in sour misfortune's book.
I'll bury thee in a triumphant grave.
A grave? O, no, a lantern, slaughtered youth.
   He opens the tomb
For here lies Juliet, and her beauty makes
This vault a feasting presence full of light.
Death, lie thou there, by a dead man interred.
   He lays him in the tomb
How oft when men are at the point of death
Have they been merry! which their keepers call
A lightning before death. O how may I   90
Call this a lightning? O my love, my wife!
Death, that hath sucked the honey of thy breath,
Hath had no power yet upon thy beauty.
Thou art not conquered. Beauty's ensign yet
Is crimson in thy lips and in thy cheeks,
And death's pale flag is not advancèd there.
Tybalt, liest thou there in thy bloody sheet?
O, what more favour can I do to thee
Than with that hand that cut thy youth in twain
To sunder his that was thine enemy?   100
Forgive me, cousin! Ah, dear Juliet,
Why art thou yet so fair? Shall I believe
That unsubstantial death is amorous,
And that the lean abhorrèd monster keeps
Thee here in dark to be his paramour?
For fear of that I still will stay with thee
And never from this palace of dim night
Depart again. Here, here will I remain
With worms that are thy chambermaids. O here
Will I set up my everlasting rest   110
And shake the yoke of inauspicious stars
From this world-wearied flesh. Eyes, look your last!

Arms, take your last embrace! and, lips, O you
The doors of breath, seal with a righteous kiss
A dateless bargain to engrossing death!
Come, bitter conduct, come, unsavoury guide!
Thou desperate pilot, now at once run on
The dashing rocks thy seasick weary bark!
Here's to my love! (*He drinks*) O true Apothecary!
Thy drugs are quick. Thus with a kiss I die.   *He falls*
        Enter Friar Laurence, with lantern, crow, and spade

FRIAR

Saint Francis be my speed! How oft tonight
Have my old feet stumbled at graves! Who's there?

BALTHASAR

Here's one, a friend, and one that knows you well.

FRIAR

Bliss be upon you! Tell me, good my friend,
What torch is yond that vainly lends his light
To grubs and eyeless skulls? As I discern,
It burneth in the Capels' monument.

BALTHASAR

It doth so, holy sir; and there's my master,
One that you love.

FRIAR   Who is it?

BALTHASAR   Romeo.

FRIAR

How long hath he been there?

BALTHASAR   Full half an hour.

FRIAR

Go with me to the vault.

BALTHASAR   I dare not, sir.
My master knows not but I am gone hence,
And fearfully did menace me with death
If I did stay to look on his intents.

FRIAR

  Stay then; I'll go alone. Fear comes upon me.
  O much I fear some ill unthrifty thing.

BALTHASAR

  As I did sleep under this yew tree here,
  I dreamt my master and another fought,
  And that my master slew him.

FRIAR   Romeo!
    He stoops and looks on the blood and weapons
  Alack, alack, what blood is this which stains   140
  The stony entrance of this sepulchre?
  What mean these masterless and gory swords
  To lie discoloured by this place of peace?
    He enters the tomb
  Romeo! O, pale! Who else? What, Paris too?
  And steeped in blood? Ah, what an unkind hour
  Is guilty of this lamentable chance!
  The lady stirs.
    Juliet rises

JULIET

  O comfortable Friar! Where is my lord?
  I do remember well where I should be,
  And there I am. Where is my Romeo?   150

FRIAR

  I hear some noise. Lady, come from that nest
  Of death, contagion, and unnatural sleep.
  A greater power than we can contradict
  Hath thwarted our intents. Come, come away.
  Thy husband in thy bosom there lies dead;
  And Paris too. Come, I'll dispose of thee
  Among a sisterhood of holy nuns.
  Stay not to question, for the Watch is coming.
  Come, go, good Juliet. I dare no longer stay.

JULIET

160   Go, get thee hence, for I will not away.   *Exit Friar*
       What's here? A cup, closed in my true love's hand?
       Poison, I see, hath been his timeless end.
       O churl! drunk all, and left no friendly drop
       To help me after? I will kiss thy lips.
       Haply some poison yet doth hang on them
       To make me die with a restorative.
           She kisses him
       Thy lips are warm!

WATCHMAN (*within*)

       Lead, boy. Which way?

JULIET

       Yea, noise? Then I'll be brief. O happy dagger!
           She snatches Romeo's dagger
170   This is thy sheath; there rust, and let me die.
                           She stabs herself and falls
           Enter Paris's Page and the Watch

PAGE

       This is the place. There, where the torch doth burn.

FIRST WATCHMAN

       The ground is bloody. Search about the churchyard.
       Go, some of you. Whoe'er you find attach.
                           Exeunt some of the Watch
       Pitiful sight! Here lies the County slain!
       And Juliet bleeding, warm, and newly dead,
       Who here hath lain this two days burièd.
       Go, tell the Prince. Run to the Capulets.
       Raise up the Montagues. Some others search.
                           Exeunt others of the Watch
       We see the ground whereon these woes do lie,
180   But the true ground of all these piteous woes
       We cannot without circumstance descry.
           Enter some of the Watch, with Balthasar

SECOND WATCHMAN

Here's Romeo's man. We found him in the churchyard.

FIRST WATCHMAN

Hold him in safety till the Prince come hither.

Enter Friar Laurence and another of the Watch

THIRD WATCHMAN

Here is a Friar that trembles, sighs, and weeps.
We took this mattock and this spade from him
As he was coming from this churchyard's side.

FIRST WATCHMAN

A great suspicion! Stay the Friar too.

Enter the Prince and attendants

PRINCE

What misadventure is so early up,
That calls our person from our morning rest?

Enter Capulet and his wife with others

CAPULET

What should it be, that is so shrieked abroad?   190

LADY CAPULET

O the people in the street cry 'Romeo,'
Some 'Juliet,' and some 'Paris'; and all run
With open outcry toward our monument.

PRINCE

What fear is this which startles in your ears?

FIRST WATCHMAN

Sovereign, here lies the County Paris slain;
And Romeo dead; and Juliet, dead before,
Warm and new killed.

PRINCE

Search, seek, and know, how this foul murder comes.

FIRST WATCHMAN

Here is a Friar, and slaughtered Romeo's man,

200   With instruments upon them fit to open
        These dead men's tombs.

CAPULET
        O heavens! O wife, look how our daughter bleeds!
        This dagger hath mista'en, for, lo, his house
        Is empty on the back of Montague,
        And it mis-sheathèd in my daughter's bosom!

LADY CAPULET
        O me! This sight of death is as a bell
        That warns my old age to a sepulchre.

        Enter Montague and others

PRINCE
        Come, Montague. For thou art early up
        To see thy son and heir now early down.

MONTAGUE
210   Alas, my liege, my wife is dead tonight!
        Grief of my son's exile hath stopped her breath.
        What further woe conspires against mine age?

PRINCE
        Look, and thou shalt see.

MONTAGUE
        O thou untaught! what manners is in this,
        To press before thy father to a grave?

PRINCE
        Seal up the mouth of outrage for a while,
        Till we can clear these ambiguities
        And know their spring, their head, their true descent.
        And then will I be general of your woes
220   And lead you, even to death. Meantime forbear,
        And let mischance be slave to patience.
        Bring forth the parties of suspicion.

FRIAR
        I am the greatest, able to do least,
        Yet most suspected, as the time and place

Doth make against me, of this direful murder.
And here I stand, both to impeach and purge
Myself condemnèd and myself excused.

PRINCE

Then say at once what thou dost know in this.

FRIAR

I will be brief, for my short date of breath
Is not so long as is a tedious tale.   230
Romeo, there dead, was husband to that Juliet;
And she, there dead, that Romeo's faithful wife.
I married them; and their stolen marriage day
Was Tybalt's doomsday, whose untimely death
Banished the new-made bridegroom from this city;
For whom, and not for Tybalt, Juliet pined.
You, to remove that siege of grief from her,
Betrothed and would have married her perforce
To County Paris. Then comes she to me
And with wild looks bid me devise some mean   240
To rid her from this second marriage,
Or in my cell there would she kill herself.
Then gave I her — so tutored by my art —
A sleeping potion; which so took effect
As I intended, for it wrought on her
The form of death. Meantime I writ to Romeo
That he should hither come as this dire night
To help to take her from her borrowed grave,
Being the time the potion's force should cease.
But he which bore my letter, Friar John,   250
Was stayed by accident and yesternight
Returned my letter back. Then all alone
At the prefixèd hour of her waking
Came I to take her from her kindred's vault;
Meaning to keep her closely at my cell
Till I conveniently could send to Romeo.

But when I came, some minute ere the time
Of her awakening, here untimely lay
The noble Paris and true Romeo dead.
260   She wakes; and I entreated her come forth
And bear this work of heaven with patience.
But then a noise did scare me from the tomb,
And she, too desperate, would not go with me,
But, as it seems, did violence on herself.
All this I know; and to the marriage
Her nurse is privy; and if aught in this
Miscarried by my fault, let my old life
Be sacrificed, some hour before his time,
Unto the rigour of severest law.

PRINCE

270   We still have known thee for a holy man.
Where's Romeo's man? What can he say to this?

BALTHASAR

I brought my master news of Juliet's death;
And then in post he came from Mantua
To this same place, to this same monument.
This letter he early bid me give his father,
And threatened me with death, going in the vault,
If I departed not and left him there.

PRINCE

Give me the letter. I will look on it.
Where is the County's page that raised the Watch?
280   Sirrah, what made your master in this place?

PAGE

He came with flowers to strew his lady's grave,
And bid me stand aloof, and so I did.
Anon comes one with light to ope the tomb,
And by and by my master drew on him.
And then I ran away to call the Watch.

PRINCE

This letter doth make good the Friar's words,
Their course of love, the tidings of her death.
And here he writes that he did buy a poison
Of a poor pothecary, and therewithal
Came to this vault to die, and lie with Juliet.   290
Where be these enemies? Capulet, Montague,
See what a scourge is laid upon your hate,
That heaven finds means to kill your joys with love.
And I, for winking at your discords too,
Have lost a brace of kinsmen. All are punished.

CAPULET

O brother Montague, give me thy hand.
This is my daughter's jointure, for no more
Can I demand.

MONTAGUE   But I can give thee more.
For I will raise her statue in pure gold,
That whiles Verona by that name is known,   300
There shall no figure at such rate be set
As that of true and faithful Juliet.

CAPULET

As rich shall Romeo's by his lady's lie,
Poor sacrifices of our enmity!

PRINCE

A glooming peace this morning with it brings.
    The sun for sorrow will not show his head.
Go hence, to have more talk of these sad things.
    Some shall be pardoned, and some punishèd.
For never was a story of more woe
Than this of Juliet and her Romeo.   *Exeunt*   310

An Account of the Text

When John Heminge and Henry Condell presented the first collected edition of Shakespeare's plays in 1623 they said in their prefatory address 'To the great variety of readers' that 'It had been a thing, we confess, worthy to have been wished that the Author himself had lived to have set forth and overseen his own writings . . .'. Every editor of Shakespeare, and every reader and producer who cares about the words that Shakespeare used, must echo this wish. For, of all the world's great authors since the invention of printing, Shakespeare is the most unlucky in the way his works have come down to us.

The plays were printed without his supervision and without anything of what would be regarded by a modern author or printer as proof-correction. Yet it would seem that Shakespeare himself set his printers high standards of accuracy. We can judge this from the first editions of his poems *Venus and Adonis* and *The Rape of Lucrece* (1593 and 1594). These were issued by a fellow Stratfordian, Richard Field, who, like Shakespeare, had come to London to make his name. They were distinctly *literary* works; they were graced by dedications to Shakespeare's young patron, the Earl of Southampton; and they were accorded due care by the printer. Scarcely a misprint sullies their pages.

With the plays the situation is quite different. Until Ben Jonson issued his *Works* in 1616 a stage-play in English does not seem to have been regarded as a literary work. One or two dramatists may have given the printing of their plays a little cursory attention. But most of them left printing entirely to the printer, and in many cases they seem to have had no say at all in the publication of their plays; for it was usual for a play to belong, not to its author, but to the theatre company which performed it. Many of Shakespeare's plays were issued in his own lifetime in what, from their size, are termed 'quarto' editions. Some of these plays were printed from good, reliable copy, obtained honestly from the theatrical companies. Some were printed from bad copy, surreptitiously acquired from disloyal actors in the plays, who had memorized their own parts and tried to remember the speeches of the other characters. In none of the quartos is the quality of printing high; for play-books were merely 'popular' literature.

These quartos – and even the collected edition, issued some seven years after Shakespeare's death, in the larger, folio, size (hence the term, the first Folio) – contain hundreds of observable printing errors that no intelligent reader, and certainly not the author, would have passed in proof. Furthermore, where plays were issued in quartos and in the Folio, they often show remarkable differences in content. *Hamlet*, indeed, is available to us in a thoroughly bad quarto, a good quarto, and a good, but often differing, Folio version. To make matters even worse, it is probable that Shakespeare himself, like some modern writers, was responsible for different versions existing concurrently. (T. S. Eliot has 'Northolt' in the English version of *The Family Reunion* but 'airport' in the American version.) Sometimes a cancelled version of a line or two, or a 'false start' imperfectly deleted, accidentally gets printed from Shakespeare's manuscript (or a transcription of it), as well as the lines Shakespeare wrote in substitution; so we are confused by having awkward repetitions of words and ideas (see notes on I.2.15, IV.1.110, V.3.102–3 and 106–10 in *Romeo and Juliet*).

Although some changes were made in proof and some in the course of printing, an Elizabethan printer of plays did not stop his presses working in order to read proofs; pages were printed in 'incorrect' versions until proofs had been read and the 'corrections' were made. Unfortunately, these 'corrections' lack authorial support. The proofreader *may* have consulted his manuscript copy; but often it is evident he was only concerned to smooth out nonsense and to make the page look tidy typographically.

Many of the differences between the Folio and preceding texts, and many of the words and passages for which no alternative version exists, are clearly corrupt. Often the correction is obvious (as *theu* may need to be changed to *then*). But far too frequently we cannot be sure exactly what from the correction should take. Many of the awkward readings may be defended by an appeal to topical allusions, different verbal and grammatical practices and the linguistic fantasies so beloved of Elizabethan and Jacobean writers. Furthermore, professional scribes, keepers of prompt books in the theatre, compositors and proofreaders have often so much smoothed out lines that puzzled them that we cannot now be sure that passages seemingly sound are, in reality, what Shakespeare wrote. We do not know how accurately printers could set Shakespeare's manuscript. But we *do* know that they were capable of introducing dozens of alterations into what they reset from a printed book; some are errors due to mere care-lessness, some are deliberate falsifications. What is so discon-certing is to realize that, had we not a copy of such an earlier version, we should not have been able to detect these errors and changes. So, there must be hundreds of printers' errors and alter-ations in Shakespeare's plays which we cannot discover because the false word or words make a kind of sense, though not the sense the author intended.

The situation is familiar to anyone who has had a typist tran-scribing handwritten drafts. Most of the errors can be put into categories. There are mechanical ones; inversions (*mna* for *man*) and errors due to the proximity of keys (*hot* for *jot*). There are certain recurring errors which derive from difficulties in the handwriting: a similarity in the forming of *n/r/u* in a particular handwriting may lead to errors of the kind *land/lard/laud*. Normally, the sense helps the typist to choose the right alterna-tive. But especially inconvenient, and easily missed, is the error made when an intelligent typist produces a word which makes good sense in the sentence but is not the word intended.

Just so, a compositor may, inadvertently, reverse letters. He may, like a typist striking an adjacent key, select a piece of type from a box adjacent to the correct one, or pick up a piece that has fallen into the wrong box. Some letters, too, are easily confused in Elizabethan handwriting: the way of writing *e* and *d* could be very similar and thus a word like *turn* (regularly spelt with an *e* at the end) could appear in the past tense, *turnd*, instead of the present, *turne* (and both are 'normal' Elizabethan spellings). Usually a compositor (like a modern typist) would 'make sense' of what was put before him, but it may not be the sense required and the results may be absurd or feeble or obscure: in any case, destructive of Shakespeare's meaning. Conditions for the Elizabethan printer were much worse than for a modern printer or typist. Writing and spelling were highly idiosyncratic, equipment less regular, hours much longer, and heating and lighting not up to modern standards. Though we regret the poor quality of the texts of Shakespeare's plays, and their variability, we do well to bear in mind the conditions under which they were produced. Indeed, it is by a knowledge of these conditions that we may be helped to restore a lost reading, or make an intelligent supposition.

Thus the preparation of the text of a play by Shakespeare may require a great deal of informed and carefully controlled guessing. Decisions often have to be made on a delicate balance of probabilities, and the balance may be so fine that a decision will have to be reached without much confidence. An editor may be helped by a knowledge of Elizabethan handwriting, theatre documents, printing-house practices and the language (especially the idiomatic usage) of Shakespeare's time. In many instances, literary taste ultimately has to decide; and what one editor or reader finds admirable another may think intolerable or absurd.

To take an example: *Romeo and Juliet*, IV.1.98–101 in the Quarto of 1599 reads as follows (the Friar is describing to Juliet what will happen after she has taken the potion):

98   No warmth, no breast shall testifie thou liuest,
99   The roses in thy lips and cheekes shall fade:
100   Too many ashes, thy eyes windowes fall:
101   Like death when he shuts vp the day of life.

We can begin by amending the punctuation to accord with modern logical indications: the second half of line 100 goes with line 101; so we can remove the colon. Lines 98 and 99 are independent sentences and so we can perhaps put a heavier stop than a comma between them. We can confidently amend *breast* (98) as being a misprint for *breath*. In line 100 *Too many ashes* cannot be right: the words are ungrammatical and meaningless in this position.

We can remove the colon at the end of line 99, and for *Too* read *To* (this is only a spelling change). Presumably *many* is an error for some other adjective. A knowledge of Elizabethan hand-writing suggests that a compositor (or a scribe writing a 'fair copy' of Shakespeare's play from his manuscript) might have misread *many* for *wany* (that is, *wanny*); or he might have set up *many*, thinking he saw *manie* (for *y* and *ie* could both be used in this fashion). But the *manie* he thought he saw could as easily have been *wanie* or (because of the possibility of confusing *e* and *d*) even *waned*. Thus an editor relying on evidence of confusion caused by similarities in handwriting might choose *wanny* or *waned*, believing not only that this word was appropriate to the sense but that his argument showed how such an error had arisen – even though we do not know exactly what the handwriting of the manuscript looked like. (We get no help from the 'bad Quarto' of 1597 here, for the four lines are represented by only one line, corrupted: 'No signe of breath shall testifie thou liust.')

But there is another fact to consider. When *Romeo and Juliet* was printed for the fourth time (in 1622), we find that the phrase has been replaced by *paly ashes*. Where has *paly* come from? We cannot assume it has Shakespeare's approval. It may be without any authority. But we observe that the person who made the change has at least been reading the text carefully and noticed something was wrong (though, alas! there were many new errors introduced elsewhere into this reprinting). The correction makes good sense; but is it merely a guess on the part of the printer, of no more or less value than yours or mine? In answering that question we have to bear in mind two things. First, whoever made the change spoke the idiom of the time of Shakespeare and might be in a better position to judge the appropriateness of an epithet than we are. Secondly, *Romeo and Juliet* was a very popular play on the stage and the change to *paly* might have been made by someone who had heard what Friar Laurence said – and it can hardly have been the nonsensical *Too many ashes*. We cannot know what phrase he used. But it is possible that the sudden appearance of *paly* here reflects stage practice, and that stage tradition preserved Shakespeare's word or, at least, a word used in a production by Shakespeare's company. In seeing *wanny* behind the erroneous *many* we may be relying too much on the clue of handwriting; *many* may be due to the picking up of the wrong sort of type being followed by unintelligent 'correcting' – or even to absent-minded substitution.

A study of all the instances where Shakespeare uses the words *ashes*, *wan(n)y*, *wane(d)*, *pale*, *paly* does not seem to help us much in determining literary probabilities here. On balance, a modern editor will probably choose, but without much confidence, to print *wanny*. And so in our text the passage appears as:

No warmth, no breath, shall testify thou livest.
The roses in thy lips and cheeks shall fade
To wanny ashes, thy eyes' windows fall
Like death when he shuts up the day of life.

A version of Shakespeare's play of *Romeo and Juliet* was first published in 1597. (We refer to this as Q1.) The title page describes it as 'An excellent conceited tragedy of Romeo and Juliet, as it hath been often, with great applause, played publicly by the right honourable the Lord of Hunsdon his servants'. Like similar 'pirated' texts – editions printed without the permission of the author or the acting company – it is a detestable text, probably a reconstruction of the play from the imperfect memories of one or two of the actors. It is short (2232 lines, in comparison with the 3003 lines of the present edition), for it has been heavily cut. It is confused, often ungrammatical; much of the poetry has gone or been spoilt by the corrupting of the lines. The following is an average specimen, in modernized spelling, of this text (Juliet's soliloquy before taking the sleeping-potion, IV.3.14–59, is reduced from forty-six lines to eighteen):

Farewell; God knows when we shall meet again.
Ah, I do take a fearful thing in hand.
What if this potion should not work at all?
Must I of force be married to the county?
This shall forbid it. Knife, lie thou there.
What if the friar should give me this drink
To poison me, for fear I should disclose
Our former marriage? Ah, I wrong him much.
He is a holy and religious man.

I will not entertain so bad a thought.
What if I should be stifled in the tomb?
Awake an hour before the appointed time?
Ah, then I fear I shall be lunatic,
And, playing with my dead forefather's bones,
Dash out my frantic brains. Methinks I see
My cousin Tybalt, weltering in his blood,
Seeking for Romeo. Stay, Tybalt, stay!
Romeo, I come! This do I drink to thee.

Two years later (1599) another version of the play appeared (issued by a different and more respectable printer), described on the title page as: 'The most excellent and lamentable tragedy of Romeo and Juliet, newly corrected, augmented, and amended, as it hath been sundry times publicly acted by the right honourable the Lord Chamberlain his servants.' (This text we call Q2.) It is essentially the play we know. Much of it was set up from Shakespeare's manuscript or (at least) from a transcription fairly close to Shakespeare's manuscript. The 1599 printing (Q2) is, by comparison with Q1, a good text. Yet we soon discover, from a careful study of it, that in this play, as in most of Shakespeare's plays, we are dealing with a work of art that has not been finally 'polished', not prepared for the press by the tidying up of details and petty inconsistencies. This, the only authoritative text we have, has been subjected by scholars to careful analysis, and the disquieting situation (in all probability) is this:

1. The beginning of the play, up to about I.2.52, seems to have been set up by the printer from a fair copy of Shakespeare's manuscript;

2. From I.2.53 to about I.3.35 was printed directly from the imperfect and corrupted form of the play which had been issued two years before (Q1);

3. I.3.36 to III.4 was from the fair copy again;

4. From III.5 onwards the printer seems to have been working from Shakespeare's 'foul papers': that is, from his rough working manuscript which had not been copied out fair.

The heterogeneous nature of the printer's copy is reflected in many ways: for example, in the differing names given to some of the speakers. Juliet's mother is variously *Lady of the House*,

Old Lady, *Lady*, *Wife*, and *Mother*. A modern editor has to tidy
this up and use 'Lady Capulet' throughout.

The 1599 text of the play (Q2) was reprinted in 1609 (Q3)
and again (though the title page was undated) in 1622 (Q4) and
in 1637 (Q5). The text in the Folio edition of 1623 (F) derives
from Q3. Later Folios appeared in 1632 (F2), 1663–4 (F3), and
1685 (F4). The reprints after Q2 contain many alterations and
corrections, though these cannot be assumed to have any
authority. They also contain many new errors.

The main problem of the text of *Romeo and Juliet* depends
on the nature of the 'bad Quarto' of 1597 (Q1). It would be
convenient if we could reject the whole thing as a garbled version
of the play, and depend entirely on the authoritative Q2.
Unfortunately no editor can do this, for three reasons:

1. Q2 itself is corrupt in many places and in some fifty of these
instances the reading in Q1 has the appearance of being the correct
(or at least a probable or reasonable) one. A list of the readings
from Q1 accepted in this edition is given in section 1 of the
Collations below.

2. The printer of Q2, though apparently fairly conscientious,
unquestionably had a copy of Q1 beside him and used it. As
already mentioned above, he used a leaf of it for one long passage
of his text (I.2.53 to I.3.35), perhaps because a piece was missing
from the manuscript copy he had been given. There is, moreover, evidence that he consulted the 'bad Quarto' at various other
places in the play where the 'bad Quarto' text seemed fairly accurate and where therefore it was possible – and much quicker and
easier – to work from printed rather than manuscript copy.

3. Whatever the circumstances of the compilation of the text
of the 'bad Quarto' may have been, it clearly derives from a
performance of the play. The reporters remember and record a
good deal of what was seen on the stage. The stage directions
are, in fact, remarkably full and interesting, and they help us to
visualize an early performance (though we cannot be sure that
it was a performance by Shakespeare's own company, the Lord
Chamberlain's Men). A list of these stage directions is given in
the fourth list of collations. Several of them have been taken over
into the present text, where they add something to the stage business not explicit in the words of the characters.

COLLATIONS

The following lists are *selective*. They include the more important and interesting variants. Minor changes which are not
disputed, small variations in word order, obvious misprints and
grammatical corrections not affecting the sense are not usually
included here.

1

The following readings in the present text of *Romeo and Juliet*
derive from Q1, and not from Q2. The reading (which generally represents the Q1 form in, of course, modernized spelling)
is followed by the Q2 form, unmodernized.

I.1
      177 create] created
      179 well-seeming] welseeing (Q1: best seeming)
      192 lovers'] louing (Q1: a louers)
      202 Bid a sick man in sadness make] A sicke man in
          sadnesse makes
I.2
      29 female] fennell
      68 *Rosaline and Livia*] Rosaline, Liuia
      76 thee] you
I.3
  67, 68 honour] houre
     100 make it fly] make flie
I.4
     7–8 Nor no without-book prologue, faintly spoke |
        After the prompter, for our entrance] *not in* Q2
     39 done] dum
     42 Of] Or
     45 like lamps] lights lights
     69 maid] man
     72 O'er] On
     90 elf-locks] Elklocks
    113 sail] sute

I.5

    95 ready stand] did readie stand

   142 What's this, what's this] Whats tis? whats tis
        (Q1: Whats this? whats that)

II.1

     6 MERCUTIO] *continued to* BENVOLIO *in* Q2

    10 Pronounce but 'love' and 'dove'] prouaunt, but loue
       and day

    13 trim] true

II.2

    41 nor any other part] *not in* Q2

    99 'haviour] behavior

   101 more cunning] coying

   162 mine] *not in* Q2

II.3

    18 sometime's] sometime

II.4

    19 I can tell you] *not in* Q2

    28 fantasticoes] phantacies

   112 for himself] himself

III.1

     2 Capels are abroad] Capels abroad

   122 Alive] He gan

   124 fire-eyed] fier end

   166 agile] aged

   188 hate's] hearts

   192 I will] It will

III.2

    56 swounded] sounded

    72 NURSE] *continued to* JULIET *in* Q2

    73 JULIET] NURSE

III.3

    15 Hence] Here

    53 Thou] Then

   117 lives] lies (Q1: too, that liues in thee; Q2: that in thy
       life lies)

   144 upon] vp (Q1: frownst vpon; Q2: puts vp)

III.5

   181 trained] liand

IV.1

7 talked] talke
45 cure] care

IV.5

41 long] loue
81 In all] And in
126 And doleful dumps the mind oppress,] *not in* Q2
132, 135 Pretty] Prates

V.1

24 defy] denie
76 pay] pray

V.3

3, 137 yew] young, yong
68 conjuration] commiration (Q1: coniurations)

2

The following readings in the present text of *Romeo and Juliet* are emendations of the words found in Q2 (which are placed afterwards, in the original spelling except that the 'long s' (ʃ) has been replaced by 's', with where appropriate the forms found in other early texts). A few of these alterations were made in the printing of Q3 (1609), Q4 (1622), or the Folios F (1623), F2 (1632), F3 (1663–4). Most of the other emendations were made by the eighteenth-century editors; a few are gratefully attributed to recent editors (see Further Reading).

I.1

72 CITIZENS] *Offi.*
153 sun] same
197 left] lost

I.2

32 Which, on more] Which one more

I.4

47 our five wits] our fine wits
57 atomies] Q3; ottamie Q2; Atomi Q1
59–61 Her chariot . . . coachmakers] *placed after line 69 in* Q2

I.5

    18 a bout] about

II.1

    38 open-arse and thou] J. S. Farmer and W. E. Henley,
       Slang and its Analogues (1903), vol. I, p. 68, and J.
       Dover Wilson; open, or thou Q2; open *Etcætera*,
       thou Q1

II.2

   167 nyas] J. Dover Wilson, 1955; Neece Q2; Madame
       Q1; Deere Q4; sweete F2

III.1

    89 A FOLLOWER Away, Tybalt!] W. W. Greg; *Away
       Tybalt (as stage direction)*
   184 MONTAGUE] Q4; *Capu.*

III.2

    9 By] Q4; And by
    49 shut] shot
    76 Dove-feathered raven] Rauenous douefeatherd rauë
    79 damnèd] Q4; dimme

III.3

   144 pouts] Q4; puts

IV.1

    85 tomb] *not in* Q2; shroud Q4; graue F
   100 To wanny] Too many Q2; Too paly Q4
   110 *Q2 adds a superfluous, probably rewritten, line:* Be
       borne to buriall in thy kindreds graue. *See
       Commentary*

IV.3

    49 wake] Q4; walke

IV.5

    65 cure] care
    82 fond] F2; some
   122 Then have at you with my wit] *attributed to Second
       Musician in* Q2

V.3

   102 *Q2 adds superfluous words:* I will beleeue. *See
       Commentary*
   107 palace] Q3; pallat

108 Q2 *adds four superfluous, probably rewritten, lines. See*
    Commentary
299 raise] Q4; raie

3

The following are some of the more interesting and important
variant readings and proposed emendations *not* accepted in the
present text of *Romeo and Juliet*. Many of these rejected readings will be found in older editions (especially nineteenth-century
ones).

The reading of this edition (which derives from Q2 unless
otherwise stated) is given first, followed by the rejected variants.
If a source of the variant is not given, the reading is an emendation by an editor (most of such emendations are of the eighteenth century).

I.I

21 civil] cruell Q4
62 washing] swashing Q4
120 drive] drave Q3
127 Which then most sought where most might not be
    found] That most are busied when th'are most alone
    Q1
190 made] raisde Q1
211 uncharmed] vnharmd Q1

I.2

65 Utruvio] Vitruvio F3

I.3

66 dispositions] disposition F
99 endart] engage Q1

I.4

1 ROMEO] BENVOLIO
3 BENVOLIO] MERCUTIO
45 like lamps] Q1; light lights, light lamps, like lights
53 Q1 *adds* BENVOLIO Queene Mab whats she?
57 atomies] Q3 Atomi Q1
58 Over] A thwart Q1
81 he dreams] dreames he Q1

91 untangled] entangled F3
103 side] face Q1

I.5

41 Q1 *adds* Good youths, I faith. Oh youth's a iolly
     thing
45 It seems she] Her Beauty F2
94 sin] fine
132 here] there Q1

II.1

13 Abraham Cupid] Adam Cupid

II.2

31 lazy, puffing] lasie pacing Q1; lazy-passing
44 word] name Q1
69 stop] let Q1
84 should] would Q1
107 vow] sweare Q1
152 strife] sute (= suit) Q4
163 'My Romeo!'] my Romeos name Q1
167 What o'clock] At what a clocke Q1
168 By the hour] At the houre Q1
180 silken thread plucks] silke thred puls Q1
188–91 *attributed to* ROMEO] *attributed to* FRIAR *as opening*
     lines of II.3 *in* Q1; *printed twice in* Q2
192 Friar's close cell] fathers Cell Q1; sire's close cell

II.3

1   *see under* II.2.188–91 *above*
19 weak flower] small flower Q1
22 stays] slaies Q1
36 with] by Q1
81 chide me not. Her I love] chide not, she whom I
     loue Q1

II.4

14 run] shot Q1
22 He rests his minim rests] rests me his minum rest
     Q1
33 pardon-me's] pardonnez-moi's, perdona-mi's
60 Sure wit] Well said Q1
105 fairer face] fairer of the two Q1

142 Q1 *adds* Marry farewell *at beginning of Nurse's speech*

160, 161 bid . . . bid] bad . . . bad Q1

211 Before] Peter, take my fanne, and goe before Q1

II.6

34 sum of half my wealth] half my sum of wealth

III.1

59 love] hate Q1

91 a'both houses] a both your houses

113 cousin] kinsman Q1

122 Alive] again

147 O Prince! O cousin! Husband] cousin *omitted*

III.2

15 grow] grown

21 when I shall die] when hee shall die Q4

66 dearest] deare loude Q1

III.3

10 vanished] issued *or* 'banished'

53 hear me a little speak] heare me but speake a word Q1

86–7 O woeful sympathy! | Piteous predicament] *attributed to Friar, not Nurse*

III.5

43 love-lord, aye husband-friend] my Lord, my Loue, my Frend Q1

55 so low] below Q1

126 earth] Ayre Q4

145 bride] Bridegroome Q3

181 trained] Q1; allied Q3; lien'd

IV.1

78 any] yonder Q1

81 hide] shut Q1

94 distilling] distilled Q1

IV.3

29 Q1 *adds* I will not entertaine so bad a thought

58–9 Romeo, Romeo, Romeo. | Here's drink. I drink to thee] Romeo I come, this doe I drinke to thee Q1

IV.4

21 Good Father] good faith Q4; God Father

IV.5

    36 There she lies] see there she lies F2

  103–4 'My heart is full'] my hart is full of woe Q4

V.1

    15 How doth my lady Juliet] How fares my Juliet Q1

V.3

    68 conjuration] Q1 (conjurations); commination

  136 unthrifty] vnluckie Q3

  170 rust] Rest Q1

  194 your ears] our ears

  209 now early] more early Q1

  210 Q1 *adds* And yong *Benuolio* is deceased too

4

The following are the more interesting of the stage directions in
Q1, probably indicating impressions drawn from a contemporary performance of the play. (The line references are to the
present edition.)

I.1

    0 *Enter 2 Seruing-men of the Capolets*

    31 *Enter two Seruingmen of the Mountagues*

  58–81 *They draw, to them enters Tybalt, they fight, to
        them the Prince, old Mountague, and his wife, old
        Capulet and his wife, and other Citizens and part
        them*

I.4

    0 *Enter Maskers with Romeo and a Page*

I.5

    16 *Enter old Capulet with the Ladies*

  122 *They whisper in his eare*

II.4

    98 *Enter Nurse and her man*

  130 *He walkes by them, and sings*

  151 *She turnes to Peter her man*

II.6

    15 *Enter Iuliet somewhat fast, and embraceth Romeo*

III.1

    88 *Tibalt vnder Romeos arme thrusts Mercutio, in and flyes*

  131 *Fight, Tibalt falles*

III.2

   31 *Enter Nurse wringing her hands, with the ladder of cordes in her lap*

III.3

   71 *Nurse knockes*

   78 *Shee knockes againe*

   91 *He rises*

  108 *He offers to stab himselfe, and Nurse snatches the dagger away*

  162 *Nurse offers to goe in and turnes againe*

III.4

   11 *Paris offers to goe in, and Capolet calles him againe*

III.5

    0 *Enter Romeo and Iuliet at the window*

   36 *Enter Nurse hastely*

   42 *He goeth downe*

   64 *She goeth downe from the window*

  159 *She kneeles downe*

  235 *She lookes after Nurse*

IV.2

   22 *She kneeles downe*

IV.3

   59 *She fals vpon her bed within the Curtaines*

IV.4

    0 *Enter Nurse with hearbs, Mother*

   13 *Enter Seruingman with Logs & Coales*

IV.5

   42 *All at once cry out and wring their hands*

   95 *They all but the Nurse goe foorth, casting Rosemary on her and shutting the Curtens*

V.1

   11 *Enter Balthasar his man booted*

V.3

    0 *Enter Countie Paris and his Page with flowers and sweete water*

12 *Paris strewes the Tomb with flowers*
21 *Enter Romeo and Balthasar, with a torch, a mattocke,*
   and a crow of yron
48 *Romeo opens the tombe*
70 *They fight*
120 *Enter Fryer with a Lanthorne*
139 *Fryer stoops and lookes on the blood and weapons*
147 *Juliet rises*
170 *She stabs herselfe and falles*
181 *Enter one with Romeos Man*
183 *Enter one with the Fryer*
187 *Enter Prince with others*

Commentary

In these notes the early editions of *Romeo and Juliet* are referred to as follows:

Q1 the first edition (1597), commonly called the 'bad Quarto';

Q2 the second edition (1599), the 'good Quarto', which is our principal text for the play;

Q3 the reprint of 1609;

Q4 the undated reprint (now known to have appeared in 1622);

F the Folio edition of Shakespeare's plays (1623).

Only the more substantial variants are discussed here, and the readings of the early editions are usually given in *modern spelling*. For further details and lists of variants in the original spelling see An Account of the Text above. Biblical references are to the Bishops' Bible (1568, etc.), the official English translation of Elizabeth's reign.

THE PROLOGUE

The first Chorus (a sonnet) has generally been used in the theatre, often spoken by the actor who plays the role of the Prince of Verona. It contains fine phrases which effectively set the tone of the play: *fair Verona, star-crossed lovers, misadventured piteous overthrows, death-marked love*; and even if it is inadequate as a

summary of the plot, it gives the right emphasis. The first four
lines describe the family feud. The second four introduce the two
lovers whose deaths, though not clearly attributed to the feud,
bring about its end. The next three lines summarize in different
words the previous eight. Line 12 says that the above is a plot
summary of the play about to be performed, and the final couplet
humbly asks for the patience and favour of the audience. The
Prologue confines itself strictly to the tragic theme of the play;
there is no hint of the comic element (the Nurse and Mercutio)
or of the efforts at reconciliation by the Friar.

Between Acts I and II is another Chorus in the form of a
sonnet; see note on p. 173.

Q1 (1597) includes a clumsy version of Chorus 1 (but not
Chorus 2), which suggests that this prologue was spoken in early
performances (see An Account of the Text). Both choruses appear
in Q2 (1599). Curiously this text omits Q1's jeer at a *without-
book prologue, faintly spoke* (see note on I.4.7–8). The F text
(1623) is a direct reprint of Q3 (1609); but whereas Q3 (following
Q2) gives both choruses, F omits the first. There is no evidence
to explain this. It may have been left out accidentally, owing to
some defect in the copy of Q3 used by the printer of F. But
possibly it was omitted by a deliberate decision; if so, its exclu-
sion by his trustworthy friends suggests that it was not written
by Shakespeare (and in that case the inclusion of Chorus 2, also
unauthentic, was simply overlooked by those who excluded
Chorus 1).

2 *Verona*: This famous Italian city had already appeared
in Shakespeare's plays. *The Two Gentlemen of Verona*
has its early scenes set there. Petruchio in *The Taming
of the Shrew* is a gentleman of Verona and comes thence
to Padua. The whole of *Romeo and Juliet* (apart from
V.1, which is in Mantua) is set in Verona: in the streets
(I.1, 2, and 4, II.4, III.1), in the Capulet house and
garden (I.3 and 5, II.1, 2, and 5, III.2, 4, and 5, IV.2,
3, 4, and 5), in Friar Laurence's cell (II.3 and 6, III.3,
IV.1, V.2), or in the churchyard by the Capulet monument (V.3). The changes of scene are indicated to the

audience by the words of the speakers, by simple
changes of costume (such as cloaks for outdoor scenes),
or by simple properties (such as chairs for indoor
scenes).

3 *ancient grudge*: The origin of the feud between the
two families is not explained. The sympathies of the
audience are not therefore engaged on one side or
the other.

mutiny: Outburst of violence.

4 *civil blood makes civil hands*: In the first instance *civil*
does not merely mean (as in the second) 'belonging
to citizens' but has behind it such phrases as 'civil war',
'civil strife'.

6 *star-crossed*: Destined by the stars to be thwarted. There
are numerous references to the fateful influence of the
stars in this play.

8 *Doth*: Plural.

9 *passage*: Course.

12 *two hours' traffic*: An Elizabethan play seems to have
been regarded as lasting approximately two hours.
Many of the surviving texts of plays are clearly longer
than that, and the phrase *two hours* is perhaps to be
interpreted vaguely, and as emphasizing that the enter-
tainment is free from tediousness. See The Play in
Performance.

traffic: Business.

14 *What here shall miss*: What may seem to you to be
inadequate in this performance.

our toil: The actors' efforts.

THE PLAY

I.1

0 *Sampson and Gregory*: Sampson is a boaster and, Capulet-
wise, makes a virtue of quarrelling; Gregory is more of
a tactician. Although Gregory is twice addressed (1, 61),
the audience is never told Sampson's name.

0 *with swords and bucklers*: The servants are armed and ready for trouble. But the play begins like a comedy.

1 *carry coals*: Perform menial tasks, be humiliated.

2 *colliers*: Term of abuse. The puns on *colliers*, *choler*, *collar* (hangman's noose) continue.

3 *draw*: Swords.

5, 6 *moved*: Aroused (similarly *move(s)* in 7 and 10). But in 9 Gregory interprets *To move* as 'to run away'.

11 *take the wall*: Keep to the clean side of the path, nearest the wall.

15 *weaker vessels*: 1 Peter 3:7: 'ye husbands, dwell with them . . . giving honour unto the wife, as unto the weaker vessel . . .'
thrust to the wall: In amorous assault.

21 *civil*: Sampson is using the word ironically or obscenely. In Q4 it was changed to *cruel*, which is followed by many editors.

25 *sense*: Meaning. But in 26 Gregory quibbles on *sense* as 'feeling'.

27 *to stand*: With a bawdy quibble.

30 *poor-John*: Dried salted hake (probably with a bawdy quibble, as not being *flesh* that would *stand*).

30–31 *Here comes of the house*: Here come (some) of the house.

31 The second servingman is not named in the quartos. Some editors identify him with Balthasar, Romeo's servant, who appears in V.1 and 3. But, in any case, the audience never learns the name of Abram, who is so called only in the speech-prefixes.

40 *list*: Please.

41 *bite my thumb at*: This was an insulting gesture, made by inserting the thumbnail into the mouth and jerking it from the upper teeth, making a click.

57–8 *one of my master's kinsmen*: Presumably this is Tybalt (who comes in abruptly at 64); but Benvolio, a Montague, enters first.

62 *washing*: Swashing, slashing.

63–8 *Part, fools! . . . part these men with me*: Benvolio is characterized as a peace-maker (see III.1.1–4, 49–52 and notes). His name ('well-wishing') suggests his role.

65 *What, art thou drawn...*: By the introduction of Tybalt,
with his unmotivated quarrelsomeness, thus early in
the play Shakespeare prepares us for the fatal conflict
between him and Romeo which is to be the turning
point of the action.

heartless hinds: Cowardly yokels or menials (presumably punning on female deer without their harts).

72–4 *Clubs, bills, and partisans! ... Down with the Montagues*:
Attributed to *Offi.* in Q2, but the words appear to be
uttered by various members of the crowd, rather than
by one officer.

72 *bills, and partisans*: Kinds of pikes used by guards, the
bill having a curved blade and the partisan a broad
head with (sometimes) a side projection.

74 *gown*: Night-gown (the modern 'dressing-gown'). This
indicates that the time is early morning and Capulet
is not yet properly dressed for going outside his house.

75 *long sword*: Old-fashioned weapon in Shakespeare's
time.

76 *A crutch, a crutch*: Capulet is at once established as an
old man and his younger wife (see note on 1.3.73–4)
as having a tart tongue. The Prince emphasizes the
point by calling him *old Capulet* at 90. Lady Montague's
determined words (80) contrast with Lady Capulet's
sarcasm.

78 *in spite of me*: To scorn me.

80 *Escalus*: The name is given as *Eskales* in Q2. Otherwise
in entries (III.1.140 and V.3.187) and in dialogue he is
the Prince. Brooke called him 'Escalus' and Painter 'the
Lord Bartholomew of Escala'. This represents the
name of the famous rulers of Verona, the family della
Scala. It was in the times of Bartolommeo della Scala
(early fourteenth century) that Luigi da Porto, and
following him Bandello, had placed the story of Romeo
and Julietta. (See Further Reading.)

81–103 *Rebellious subjects, enemies to peace . . . all men depart*:
The grave sonorous language of the Prince, with its
excess of adjectives and its elaborate imagery (*purple
fountains issuing from your veins*), reminds us of many

passages in the historical plays on themes of civil
dissension which Shakespeare was writing in these
years.

82 *Profaners of this neighbour-stainèd steel*: Misusers of
your swords by staining them with the blood of your
neighbours.

85 *purple*: This adjective, meaning 'dark red' rather than
a mixture of blue and red, was commonly used of
blood.

87 *mistempered*: A pun. They are tempered (on the anvil)
with evil intent and intemperately used.

89, 91 *Three . . . thrice*: See second note on 104 below.

95 *Cankered with peace*: Grown rusty through disuse (in
the same way as hate has malignantly affected the hearts
of the two families).

97 *Your lives shall pay the forfeit of the peace*: You will be
executed as a penalty for your having broken the peace
(a compressed expression).

102 *Free-town*: Shakespeare found this name in Brooke's
Romeus and Juliet, where it translates the Italian 'Villa
Franca', the name of Capulet's castle.

104 *set . . . new abroach*: Caused to be stirring once again
(*abroach* is used of a cask of liquor pierced and left
running).

ancient quarrel: Like the *ancient grudge* of the Prologue
and the Prince's *Three . . . thrice* (89, 91), this gives
an extension of time. Montague's words at 104–5 show,
perhaps, that his heart is not really in the quarrel.

109–12 *The fiery Tybalt . . .*: Benvolio's description of Tybalt's
way of fighting (which already has a touch of sarcasm
in it: *hissed him in scorn*) prepares for Mercutio's more
derisive account in II.4.19–26.

114 *on part and part*: Some on each side.

116–17 *O where is Romeo? . . .*: Romeo is engagingly introduced into the play by these eager inquiries by his
mother.

118–30 *Madam, an hour before the worshipped sun . . .*: Benvolio's
poetical manner here is a striking change from his
preceding account of the fight, and contrasts equally

with his subsequent conversations with Romeo and Mercutio.

120 *drive*: Pronounced 'driv', is past tense (similarly 'write' has past tense 'writ' as well as 'wrote'); in Q3 it was changed to the commoner form *drave*.

121 *sycamore*: This tree was traditionally dedicated to melancholy lovers; cf. the song Desdemona borrows from 'poor Barbary' in *Othello*, IV.3.38 ('The poor soul sat sighing by a sycamore tree').

122 *westward rooteth from this city side*: Grows to the west from this side of the city.

126–7 *my own, | Which then most sought where most might not be found*: My own (affections or inclinations) which, at that time, particularly sought (prompted me to seek) places where the least number of people might be found.

129 *humour*: Mood.

130 *who*: Him who.

136 *Aurora*: Goddess of the dawn, married to Tithonus, whose 'bed' she was imagined to leave in the morning.

137 *heavy son*: Quibbling on *light* in this line and on *sun* in 134.

145 *importuned*: Three syllables, with accent on the second.

153 *sun*: This is an emendation of Q2 *same*.

156 *So please you*: If you please.

159 *To hear true shrift*: As to hear a true confession from Romeo.

160 *Is the day so young*: Romeo is surprised to be addressed with a 'good morning', for he thought the day was much further advanced.

161 *new struck nine*: Indications of the time of day are numerous in the play.

171 *whose view is muffled*: Cupid is often shown as having light bandages over his eyes.

172 *Should without eyes see pathways to his will*: Should, though blind, see clearly the ways to bring about what he wants.

173 *Where shall we dine*: An unloverlike question, especially at nine o'clock in the morning – unless it indicates

Romeo's distracted state of mind. But perhaps he
wishes to divert Benvolio's curiosity about his love.

175 *much to-do with hate, but more with love*: Much turmoil
in the streets over the feud, but a greater turmoil within
me because of love. The noun *to-do* (bustle, turmoil)
was an Elizabethan usage as well as a modern colloquial one.

176–82 *Why then, O brawling love, O loving hate . . . no love
in this*: Romeo speaks in the commonplace antithetical
language of contemporary love poetry. This gives a
feeling of artificiality to his passion.

177 *O anything, of nothing first create*: This is a paradox-
ical treatment of the old saying that 'nothing can come
of nothing' ('*nil posse creari de nihilo*').

183 *coz*: Short form of 'cousin', used in familiar speech
when addressing a kinsman.

187–8 *Which thou wilt propagate, to have it pressed | With
more of thine*: *pressed* connects with *oppression* in 184
and develops the image of sexual embrace leading to
'propagation'.

190 *made*: Q1 has *raised*, which is often adopted by editors.

191 *purged*: Purified, the smoke becoming less thick.

193–4 *A madness most discreet, | A choking gall and a preserving
sweet*: Many of Romeo's fanciful statements about love
bear no relation to his subsequent experience with Juliet.

195 *Soft*: Wait a moment!

199 *in sadness*: Seriously. Apparently Benvolio does not
know whether to take Romeo's love-expostulations
seriously.

209 *Dian's wit*: The wisdom of the goddess Diana (who
guarded herself from love and remained chaste).

210 *in strong proof*: With strong armour.

211 *uncharmed*: This is the reading from Q2. Q1 has
unharmed, which is easier but probably mistaken.

214 *ope her lap to saint-seducing gold*: It is curious that
Romeo, for all his idealistic protestations, should have
entertained the idea of buying Rosaline's chastity. The
image is that of Danaë, who was taken by Jupiter in
a shower of gold.

216 *when she dies, with beauty dies her store*: This is the theme of the first seventeen of Shakespeare's *Sonnets*.

218 *sparing*: Economy of love.

221 *too*: Excessively.

222 *To merit bliss by making me despair*: In deserving heavenly bliss by her continence, while involving me in the deadly sin of despair.

224 *I live dead*: I go on living, but in a half-dead condition.

229 *To call hers, exquisite, in question more*: To bring her exquisite beauty into my thoughts even more.

234–6 *Show me a mistress that is passing fair, | What doth her beauty serve but as a note | Where I may read who passed that passing fair*: When I see a surpassingly beautiful woman, it only serves to remind me of her who surpasses that surpassing beauty.

238 *I'll pay that doctrine*: I'll teach you that lesson as a debt of friendship.

I.2

At the entry of Capulet and Paris we break in on their conversation. As we have last seen Capulet being taken off by the Prince (I.1.99), the discussion with Paris is naturally about the injunction against the quarrel.

0 *Paris*: He is named at 16. He is usually called a *Count* or *County*, but he is *Sir Paris* at III.4.12 and *this noble earl* at III.4.21 (perhaps because Brooke says 'County Paris cleped he was; an earl he had to sire', l. 1883). It is stated that, as well as being the Prince's kinsman (V.3.295), he is Mercutio's (V.3.75).

1–5 *But Montague is bound as well as I . . . at odds so long*: This sensible attitude to the family feud shows that the time is ripe for reconciliation, if only the young men and servants stop giving provocation.

1 *bound*: To keep the peace.

3 *men so old*: Cf. note on I.1.76.

4 *honourable reckoning*: Public esteem. Paris is adding the notion of rank and position to the years Capulet mentioned.

5 *so long*: See note on I.1.104 (*ancient quarrel, ancient grudge*, and so on).

6 *my lord*: Paris addresses Juliet's father in an ingrati-
   ating manner. Cf. III.4.18.

8 *My child*: We are not told Juliet's name until I.3.4;
   and since we are not told Rosaline's name until 68
   and 82 below, an audience which does not know the
   story would suppose that the object of Romeo's love-
   longings in the previous scene and of Paris's suit here
   is the heroine of the play.

   a stranger in the world: Juliet has led the secluded life
   of a girl growing up (and therefore, incidentally, she
   has no acquaintance with Romeo and the rest).

9 *change*: Of the seasons.

   fourteen years: There is much emphasis on Juliet's age.
   Cf. I.3.13–23. Marina in *Pericles* is fourteen. Miranda
   in *The Tempest* is fifteen.

10 *two more summers*: It is amusing to remember this later
   when Capulet is impatient for her marriage within a
   few days.

   summers: Implies that the season is now summer. At
   I.3.16 we are told it is mid July (a fortnight before
   Lammastide). See note on I.5.29.

12 *Younger than she are happy mothers made*: Lady Capulet
   says much the same thing at I.3.70–72.

13 *marred*: Spoilt by bearing children (and perhaps he
   is also thinking of her being brought to death by
   bearing children too early. The loss of his other children (14) makes him anxious for his only-surviving
   daughter).

   made: Made mothers.

14–15 *Earth hath swallowed all my hopes but she; | She's the
   hopeful lady of my earth*: Juliet's position as the Capulet
   heiress is made clear, and repeated at various points
   in the play (I.5.117, III.5.164–6, IV.5.46).

14 *hopes*: Children, which were his hope for posterity.

15 *earth*: His body or (perhaps) the inheritance. The repetition of *Earth* from 14, with a different meaning, is
   awkward when read; but perhaps it can be spoken
   effectively. It has been plausibly suggested that 14 or
   15 (and perhaps both of them) should be omitted, as

being one of Shakespeare's 'false starts', imperfectly deleted in his manuscript and so accidentally printed. The touch of sentiment in Capulet's words is, however, very much in character.

16–19 *But woo her . . . fair according voice*: This indulgent attitude towards Juliet is not borne out by his subsequent dealings with her (especially III.5.141–96).

24 *my poor house*: It is characteristic of the hospitable Capulet to belittle, rather ostentatiously, his own possessions and activities. He disparages Juliet's merits (32–3 below); he offers a *trifling foolish banquet* (I.5.122); and he says *We'll keep no great ado* for Juliet's marriage feast (III.4.23), which nevertheless needs *twenty cunning cooks* (IV.2.2).

25 *Earth-treading stars that make dark heaven light*: The ladies will be like stars walking on (or dancing on) the earth and reflecting light up into the sky, which would otherwise be dark.

26 *lusty young men*: Capulet's fancy is retrospective, full of memories of youth (cf. I.5.22–5 and 31–41).

27 *well-apparelled April*: Because in April the earth is newly clothed with leaves and plants and flowers.

28 *limping winter*: Because winter only slowly departs to give place to spring.

29 *female buds*: So Q1. The reading of Q2 is *fennel buds*, which has been defended as referring to a herb which played a part in wedding ritual. But the connection seems to be too remote.

31 *And like her most whose merit most shall be*: Capulet is giving to Paris the same sort of advice as Benvolio gives to Romeo at 81–98.

32–3 *Which, on more view of many, mine, being one, May stand in number, though in reckoning none*: And when you have had a more thorough view of many of the girls, my daughter, who will be one of those there, may be one of the number you will consider for first place – except, of course, for the old saying, that one isn't a number. (Capulet is, as usual, rather obviously undervaluing his own property.)

39 *meddle with*: Busy himself about (with a bawdy quibble; see II.1.34–6 and note).

40 *yard*: Yard measure (with a bawdy quibble).
    last: Perhaps quibbling on 'the last thing I have mentioned'; that is, his yard, too.
    pencil: Paint brush (probably continuing the quibble).

44 *In good time*: Here come some people to help me.
    Enter Benvolio and Romeo: Continuing the conversation where we left them at the end of I.1.

45–50 *Tut, man, one fire burns out another's burning . . .' And the rank poison of the old will die*: Benvolio speaks the sestet of a sonnet, with characteristic paradoxes. He recommends Romeo to fall in love a second time, for this will cure him of his first love; and events prove him to be right.

46 *another's anguish*: The anguish of a second pain.

47 *holp*: Helped (old past participle).
    backward turning: Turning in a reverse direction.

48 *cures with another's languish*: Is cured by the languishment that comes from a second grief.

51, 52 *your*: Here a kind of indefinite article, meaning 'the kind of thing you know well'.

51 *plantain leaf*: It was apparently used to tie over small cuts and grazes, to prevent the part becoming infected. Romeo brushes aside Benvolio's advice by taking *infection* (49) literally, and mocking at everyday remedies for such a serious case as his is.

53 *Why, Romeo, art thou mad*: From about here until about I.3.35 the text of the second (or 'good') Quarto was merely a reprint of the earlier 'bad Quarto' and we can have little confidence in its accuracy in representing Shakespeare's words. (See An Account of the Text.)

54–6 *Not mad, but bound more than a madman is . . .*: This describes the usual treatment of the insane in Shakespeare's time.

56 *Good-e'en*: Good evening (but the phrase could be used at any time after noon).

57 *God gi' good-e'en*: May God grant you good evening.

62 *Rest you merry*: The servant says goodbye, supposing

from Romeo's cryptic answers that he has said he cannot read.

65 *Utruvio*: The editions at the end of the seventeenth century changed this to 'Vitruvio' (a more common name). But there is some evidence for the existence of Utruvio as a name.

66 *Mercutio*: Whom we are to meet as Romeo's friend in I.4, is invited to the Capulet party.

68 *My fair niece Rosaline*: We do not yet know that this is Romeo's beloved, but obviously the actor playing Romeo can reveal the impression the name makes on him. Capulet's niece is soon to be replaced by Capulet's daughter as Romeo's love.

69 *Tybalt*: Whom we met as the fire-eater in I.1.65, will reappear ominously at the party (I.5.54–92).

72 *To supper*: The phrase is awkward and should perhaps be transferred to the next speech of the servant.

78 *the great rich Capulet*: The servants have a just idea of their master's position; compare the Nurse on *the chinks* at I.5.117, and Romeo's *rich Capulet* at II.3.54.

79 *crush*: Drink down.

81 *this same ancient feast*: At 20 Capulet calls it *an old accustomed feast*.

82 *Rosaline*: This is the first mention that Romeo's love is Rosaline. For all the audience knows, the love-language hitherto might be directed towards the lady whose name appears in the title of the play.

84 *unattainted*: Unprejudiced.

87–90 *When the devout religion of mine eye . . .*: Romeo is presumptuous in his use of religious language for his love-situation.

89 *these, who, often drowned, could never die*: These eyes of mine, which I often drowned with tears but which didn't die (go blind) in spite of the drownings. Romeo seems to be referring to the testing of those suspected of being in league with the devil, by means of trying to drown them: if they kept afloat they obviously had supernatural assistance and were *Transparent heretics*.

90 *Transparent heretics*: His eyes are 'transparent' and the heretics are 'easily discovered'.

91–2 *One fairer than my love?* . . .: Again Romeo's hyperbolical language courts disaster.

93–8 *Tut, you saw her fair, none else being by* . . .: Precisely what Benvolio here proposes, and Romeo rejects, takes place when Romeo sees Juliet – as he himself admits (I.5.52–3).

94 *poised*: Weighed.

95 *scales*: Singular. Benvolio fantastically imagines Romeo's eyes as a pair of scales which ought to weigh the merits of two different ladies, one in each.

96 *Your lady's love against some other maid*: The love you feel for Rosaline against the love you would feel at seeing the beauty of some other girl.

98 *scant*: Scarcely.

99 *I'll go along*: It is amusing to note that Romeo goes to the party to see Rosaline, and Juliet to see Paris (I.3.98).

I.3

1–35 *Nurse, where's my daughter?* . . . *bid me trudge*: These lines (like the ones in the preceding scene from about I.2.53) are reprinted in Q2 from Q1 and are therefore not to be taken as accurately representing Shakespeare's writing. From 36 onwards, where the printer returned to a manuscript which was either Shakespeare's or a transcription of Shakespeare's, the verse becomes regular and the writing better organized.

2 *Now, by my maidenhead at twelve year old*: The Nurse's first words are characterful.

3 *ladybird*: This was probably already in Shakespeare's time a word for a light o'love. The Nurse remembers this after she has spoken and so adds an apology: *God forbid!* (Cf. her *God forgive me! Marry, and amen!* at IV.5.7–8.) Or perhaps she merely means 'I hope nothing has happened to her'. The uncertain quality of the text here makes it impossible to be sure of the meaning of what Shakespeare originally wrote.

4 *Juliet*: About one-sixth of the play has passed before we are allowed to receive an impression of Juliet herself.

8 *give leave*: Leave us alone.

10 *thou's*: Thou shalt.

12 *an hour*: Q1, on which the text must be based here,
reads *a houre*; this may indicate the Nurse's pronunciation with initial aspirate, but we can infer nothing
confidently from a 'bad Quarto'. The printer of Q2
changed it to *an houre*.

13 *She's not fourteen*: The Nurse apparently retained her
virginity at twelve (2 above), but we are not told how
much longer.

14 *teen*: Grief (she quibbles on 'four' 'teen').

16 *Lammastide*: First of August (originally a harvest
festival when the first loaves from the new corn were
consecrated). The time of the year (high summer) and
Juliet's age (she will be fourteen on 31 July, about a
fortnight's time) are strongly impressed on the audience by these repetitions. Presumably Shakespeare deliberately gives a heroine named Juliet a birthday in July.

17 *Even or odd*: By *odd days* Lady Capulet meant 'a few
more days', but the Nurse misunderstands this and
says it doesn't matter whether the days are even or
odd in number.

19–20 *Susan and she . . . | Were of an age*: Shakespeare thinks
of the Nurse as one who had a daughter nearly fourteen years ago and who had suckled Juliet, for three
years, until about eleven years ago.

19 *God rest all Christian souls*: A pious ejaculation when
the dead are mentioned.

23 *marry*: By Mary!

24 *since the earthquake now eleven years*: Some editors
hoped that this would turn out to be a topical allusion
and that the writing of the play could be dated eleven
years after an earthquake – presumably in England,
rather than in Italy. But it seems likely that the precise-
ness of the Nurse's memory and her associations of
events are due to Shakespeare's dramatic artistry rather
than to real events. (There was a serious earthquake
felt in England on 6 April 1580, and lesser ones in 1583
and 1585.)

29 *Mantua*: See note on III.3.149.

30 *Nay, I do bear a brain*: I have a good memory still perhaps.

33 *tetchy*: Fretful.

34 *Shake, quoth the dovehouse*: Presumably this refers to the earthquake which occurred that day. The movement of the personified building is expressed in words – a common practice of unsophisticated story-telling. But the text may be sketchy and abbreviated here (see first note on this scene).

    trow: Assure you (pronunciation rhymes with 'slow').

35 *To bid me trudge*: 'To send me packing', to get me out of the way (because of the earthquake and because Juliet didn't want me as a wet-nurse any more).

37 *stand high-lone*: Stand upright by herself (presumably).
   by th'rood: By the Cross on which Christ died.

39 *broke her brow*: Cut the skin of her forehead.

41 *'A*: He.

43 *fall backward*: Ready for making love.
   wit: Understanding.

44 *holidam*: 'Halidom', holiness.

46 *come about*: Come true eventually (Juliet is now ready for marriage and so for love-making).

49 *stinted*: Ceased.

53 *it brow*: Its brow. ('Its' was not much in use in Shakespeare's time; it does not appear to occur in the texts of his plays printed during his life, nor in the Authorized Version of the Bible (1611). The usual form was 'his' or occasionally 'it'.)

54 *stone*: Testicle.

55 *perilous*: Probably to be pronounced 'parlous'.

59 *say I*: Juliet puns on the Nurse's *said 'Ay.'* in the previous line.

60 *God mark thee to his grace*: May God make you one of his elect!

62 *once*: Some day.

66 *dispositions*: Changed in F to *disposition*, but the plural form also was used in the seventeenth century and is probably correct here.

67, 68 *honour*: The reading of Q1. Q2 has *hour*, which could be defended in 67, but it does not suit the Nurse's reply in 68–9.

68 *An honour*: The Nurse approves of Juliet's view of marriage and says she is a wise girl. But the *honour* of a woman was a word used in bawdy senses, and there may be an unwitting jest here.

69 *thy teat*: The teat you sucked (the Nurse's own teat).

70–72 *Younger than you . . . | Are made already mothers*: This is exactly what Paris had said at I.2.12.

73–4 *I was your mother much upon these years | That you are now a maid*: This gives an indication that Lady Capulet is about twenty-eight. Capulet is clearly much older (cf. I.1.76 and 90; I.2.3; I.5.22–5 and 31–41). But Lady Capulet's words could be spoken so that the audience interpreted them as untruthful: she is a lady still pretending to be 'nearly thirty' in spite of her having a marriageable daughter. At V.3.206–7 she says (perhaps more truthfully): *This sight of death is as a bell | That warns my old age to a sepulchre*.

77 *a man of wax*: 'A perfect picture of a man' (but, as usual, the Nurse slips, wittingly or unwittingly, into a bawdy quibble).

79 *Nay*: A kind of affirmative, introducing a stronger opinion than the one just stated.

81 *This night you shall behold him at our feast*: The episode is not represented in I.5, in spite of this promise.

82–93 *Read o'er the volume . . .*: Lady Capulet begins an elaborate comparison of Paris with a manuscript book (*volume, writ, pen, content, margent, book, unbound, cover, clasps, story*). The contrast between these fancies and real passion is very effective.

84 *married*: Joined in harmony.

85 *content*: (1) The 'contents' of the book; and (2) satisfaction accent on second syllable.

87 *written in the margent*: In sixteenth-century books annotations and interpretations of obscurities (the equivalent of modern footnotes) were generally printed in the margins.

88 *unbound lover*: Even Lady Capulet puns: Paris is like a book without its binding, and he is also not yet bound by the ties of marriage.

89 *cover*: Cover of a book and the embraces of a wife.

90–91 *The fish lives in the sea, and 'tis much pride* | *For fair without the fair within to hide*: She imagines Juliet as the cover of the book which 'binds' Paris. It is a fine and natural thing to give to a book with very good contents (Paris) a binding (Juliet) worthy of them. Such a book in a good binding is in its natural element as is a fish in the sea.

92–3 *That book in many's eyes doth share the glory.* | *That in gold clasps locks in the golden story*: This carries on the imagery of 90–91. There is a kind of book which is esteemed, by many people, both because of its good contents (*golden story*) and because of its rich binding (*gold clasps*). As the binding and the contents share equally in the *glory* (the admiration in which the book is held), so will you and Paris share equally in honour when you are united in marriage.

But by her allusions to *gold* and *golden* and *all that he doth possess*, Lady Capulet also seems to be suggesting that the marriage is one that is financially advantageous.

93 *clasps*: Fastenings of the book covers and the embraces of love.

96 *bigger! Women grow by men*: By becoming pregnant.

98 *I'll look to like*: I shall expect to like (she quibbles with *looking* 'the act of seeing'). See note on I.2.99.

99–100 *But no more deep will I endart mine eye . . .*: These words contain unwitting irony. For within a few hours Juliet will have fallen in love and plighted her troth, regardless of her parents' *consent*, and next day her marriage will be solemnized and consummated. In this scene Juliet is an unawakened girl, submissive to her mother.

99 *endart*: Bury as if it were an arrow (presumably).

101–4 *Madam, the guests are come, supper served up . . . follow*

103 *cursed*: Because she is not about her household duties; see note on IV.4.5.

104 *straight*: The sudden intrusion of vigorous prose for the domestic anxieties is a lively contrast to the artificialities of Lady Capulet's discourse to her daughter. Cf. similarly the comic servant's prose at I.2.38–44.

105 *County*: This two-syllabled form for 'Count' seems to be due to the Italian '*Conte*'.

106 *happy nights*: The Nurse's usual thoughts are on sexual matters.

I.4

0 *Mercutio*: He was mentioned in Capulet's letter (I.2.66), but he is not named to the audience until 95 below. The name, which Shakespeare took from Brooke's poem, suggests that he is a 'mercurial' type, that is, sprightly, quick-witted, and volatile. Although a close friend of the Montagues, Romeo and Benvolio, he is invited to the Capulet party. His kinship with the Prince is alluded to at III.1.145 and 188–9, and V.3.295.

1–10 *What, shall this speech be spoke for our excuse? . . .*: The attribution of these two speeches to Romeo and Benvolio is surprising. 1–2 are in Benvolio's manner and 3–10 very much in Mercutio's; and 10 seems contrary to Benvolio's words at 104–5.

The text of Q2 follows Q1 closely here (with the omission of lines 7–8) and may have been corrupted by it. Q1 makes errors in speech-prefixes: at 53 it omits the prefix Mercutio and so attributes the Queen Mab speech to Benvolio; wrongly, as is clear from 95.

A director could perhaps be bolder than an editor and transfer the two speeches to Benvolio and Mercutio respectively.

1 *this speech*: Presumably Romeo and his friends have a formal speech ready to speak as an excuse for the intrusion of the maskers into Capulet's party. Examples in Shakespeare's plays are: *Love's Labour's Lost*, V.2.157 (by Mote), *Timon of Athens*, I.2.120 (by Cupid), *Henry VIII*, I.4.65 (by the Chamberlain).

3 *The date is out of such prolixity*: It is nowadays unfashionable to give these tedious speeches of apology on arriving uninvited at a masqueradeo.

4 *Cupid*: Commonly the 'presenter' of maskers (as in *Timon of Athens*; see note on 1 above).

hoodwinked: Blind-folded.

5 *Tartar's painted bow*: Name usually given to the short bow shaped like the outline of the upper lip – the traditional shape of Cupid's bow).

lath: Thin wood (that is, it was an imitation sword).

6 *crowkeeper*: Boy acting as a scarecrow.

7–8 *Nor no without-book prologue, faintly spoke | After the prompter, for our entrance*: These two lines are only found in Q1. Perhaps they were cut at some time as being rather insulting to the speaker of the Prologue to *this* play. Benvolio describes the kind of prologue spoken (*without-book*, not read from a script) but so ill-learned that it is delivered without energy and only with the help of the prompter. Shakespeare generally speaks with a kind of mocking self-consciousness about the stage practices of his time.

8 *entrance*: Three syllables.

9 *let them measure us by what they will*: Let the Capulets at the party judge us by whatever standard they like.

10 *measure them a measure*: Mete out for them a dance (with quibbles on *measure* in the previous line).

12 *Being but heavy, I will bear the light*: Romeo continues his quibbles on *heavy* and *light*; cf. I.1.178.

15 *soles . . . soul*: The pun on 'sole' and 'soul' occurs elsewhere in Shakespeare.

16 *So stakes me to the ground*: Like a bull or a bear.

18–22 *And soar with them above a common bound . . . do I sink*: They get all the possible puns from *soar*, *sore* and *bound* ('limit', 'leap', and 'chained').

21 *pitch*: The height a falcon soars.

23 *to sink in it, should you burden love*: Mercutio perverts Romeo's words, characteristically, into sexual quibbles: in order to make love you would have to be a burden on the woman you love. cf. *the mire | Of – save your reverence – love, wherein thou stickest* (41–2).

24 *oppression*: Cf. I.1.184.

26 *it pricks like thorn*: The nightingale was supposed to

sing its love-songs while pricking its breast against a
thorn.

28 *Prick love for pricking, and you beat love down*: Give
vent to love and satisfy it, and so will love be brought
down (with sexual quibbles).

29 *case*: Mask.

30 *visor*: Mask, and so also an ugly face.

31 *quote*: Observe.

32 *the beetle brows shall blush for me*: It seems that
Mercutio's mask has large overhanging eyebrows and
ruddy cheeks.

36 *rushes*: They were strewn on the floors of Elizabethan
houses. It is probable that they were sometimes also
used on the stage.

37–8 *I am proverbed with a grandsire phrase* . . .: I have my
worldly wisdom from a good old-fashioned proverb:
the onlooker (or candle-holder) sees the best of the
game.

39 *The game was ne'er so fair* . . .: The proverb recom-
mended one to leave the gambling-table when the game
was at its best; *game* seems to be a quibble on 'quarry'
(his Rosaline) and 'gambling'.
done: This is the reading of Q1. Q2 has *dum* (which
cannot be right), amended in later Quartos to *dun*
('dusky', and so 'gloomy'). The *done/dun* pun is also
a quibble on *fair*.

40 *dun's the mouse*: Keep quiet! (apparently; a proverbial
phrase).
the constable's own word: What the constable says when
he is on the alert to arrest someone.

41 *Dun*: The allusion is to an ancient Christmas game of
pulling Dun the horse (represented by a log of wood)
out of the (imaginary) mire.

41–2 *the mire | Of – save your reverence – love*: Mercutio makes
a mock apology for seeming to be about to utter an indecent word, though he continues his bawdy quibbles.

44 *Nay, that's not so*: Romeo, himself a chronic quibbler,
pretends to be literal-minded, saying that it is now
dark, not daytime; and Mercutio has to explain what

he meant by *we burn daylight* (we waste time by delay). This part of the conversation and the stage direction of the carried torches make the audience feel that the scene is taking place at night.

45 *like lamps*: Q2 reads *lights lights*. By omitting the final 's' on the first word, this could make sense punctuated thus: *We waste our lights, in vain* [we] *light lights by day*. The reading *like lamps* comes from Q1. Some editors take a word from each reading and prefer 'light lamps' or 'like lights'.

46 *Take our good meaning*: Accept the meaning intended by what we say (not a false meaning due to a misleadingly literal interpretation of the words).

46–7 *our judgement sits* | *Five times in that ere once in our five wits*: Our good sense is to be found in the intended meaning far more often than in the mere words which relate literally to what we experience through our *five wits* (the five senses).

48–9 *And we mean well in going to this masque,* | *But 'tis no wit to go*: Romeo continues to express his reluctance, picking up *meaning* (46) and *wits* (47): 'We may have good intentions in going to the Capulet party, but it is an unwise thing to do.'

50 *I dreamt a dream tonight*: Romeo does not get a chance to relate this dream, but presumably its nature is indicated by his speech at the end of the scene (106–11). (Cf. V.1.6–9, where he similarly has a foreboding dream, in that case related.)
   tonight: Last night.

52 *In bed asleep*: Romeo takes Mercutio's *lie*, 'tell untruth', as 'be prone on one's bed'.

53 *Queen Mab*: Apparently she is Shakespeare's invention, or, if she is not, this at any rate is his introduction of a country belief into literature.

54 *fairies' midwife*: Probably not the midwife who helps fairies to give birth to other fairies, but rather the one among the fairies who performs the duties of midwife, in 'delivering' the fancies of men, *the children of an idle brain* (97).

55 *agate stone*: Commonly used for seal-rings; probably the reference is to the engraved figure in such an agate ring.

57 *atomies*: Little atoms (tiny creatures). Q1 reads *Atomi*, which may be correct (Latin plural of '*atomus*') and is supported by Q2 *ottamie* (with first letter misprinted). The Q2 reading was amended to *atomies* in the printing of Q3.

59–61 *Her chariot is an empty hazelnut . . . the fairies' coach-makers*: These three lines are printed after 69 in Q2. But the sense of the passage seems to demand their transference here; otherwise the parts of the *chariot* are described before the chariot itself is mentioned.

60 *joiner squirrel or old grub*: The squirrel gnaws nuts and the grub bores holes in them.

62 *spinners*: Spiders.

65 *moonshine's watery beams*: The moon was associated both with the tides and with dew.

66 *film*: Gossamer (curiously spelt *philome* in Q2).

68 *round little worm*: There was a proverbial expression that the idle hands of maidens breed maggots.

70 *state*: Stately progress.

77 *courtier's*: The repetition of the instance of the courtiers (72) is a little awkward and perhaps indicates that some rewriting of this speech took place. Q1 reads *lawyer's*, which also does not seem right, as the lawyers had already appeared in 73.

78 *suit*: Court-petition, for presenting which the courtier would expect a fee from the petitioner.

79 *tithe-pig*: The legal due of the parson was the tenth of a litter of pigs.

84 *ambuscados*: Ambushes.
   Spanish blades: The swords of Toledo were famous throughout Europe.

85 *healths five fathom deep*: Deep drinking.

90 *bakes*: Makes them hard and matted.
   elf-locks: Horses' hair so treated, it was supposed, by elves.

91 *untangled*: Tangled up.

92–4 *This is the hag, when maids lie on their backs,* | *That presses them . . . good carriage*: Love dreams were formerly attributed to evil spirits who took the form of a sexual partner.

92 *hag*: Fairy, generally an evil one, producing nightmares.

94 *carriage*: Three syllables. He puns on 'bearing children', 'deportment' and 'bearing a lover's weight'.

100–103 *And more inconstant than the wind . . . dew-dropping South*: The variable wind is imagined as a fickle lover who woos the North, but, having a cold reception there, in pique turns towards the more responsive South (which is *dew-dropping*, in contrast to the *frozen bosom* of the North).

104 *from ourselves*: From what we intended to do (go to the Capulets' party).

106–13 *I fear, too early . . .* | *Direct my sail*: This is probably to be spoken as a soliloquy.

107–11 *Some consequence . . .* | *Shall bitterly begin his . . . date* | *. . . and expire the term . . .*: The metaphor is legal. Romeo imagines that he has mortgaged his life from a date beginning that evening. The mortgage will be forfeit, and so he will lose his life.

108 *fearful date*: Period of time full of fear.

109–10 *expire the term* | *Of*: Bring to an end.

112 *He*: God as Providence.

1.5

Editors have marked a new scene here (and it is convenient to keep the numbering for reference purposes); but Mercutio and the others do not go out (*They march about the stage*), and they are met by the Capulet party, who enter at 16 (*Enter . . . to the maskers*).

1–5 *Where's Potpan, that he helps not . . . 'tis a foul thing*: Apparently the two Servingmen are trained house-servants and they speak sarcastically about inferior (perhaps hired) servants (Anthony and Potpan) who are shirking their work; *one or two* perhaps implies that the extra 'hands' are too few.

The part of the First Servingman is doubtless to be taken by the actor of the Clown in I.2.38–80 and

the Servingman in I.3.101–4, Gregory or Sampson in
I.1, and perhaps Peter.

2 *trencher*: Wooden dish.

6 *joint-stools*: Stools made of parts fitted together by
joiner's work.

7 *court-cupboard*: Sideboard.
plate: Table utensils (generally of pewter or silver).

8 *marchpane*: Marzipan.

9 *Susan Grindstone and Nell*: Girls coming to the servants'
party to be held after the great folks have finished.

11, 14 THIRD SERVINGMAN, FOURTH SERVINGMAN: Presumably the Potpan and Anthony called at 10.

13 *Great Chamber*: Hall of a great house, used for social
occasions.

15–16 *the longer liver take all*: Proverbial expression, originally meaning, of course, that the survivor takes the
whole property (as of a group of joint-tenants), but
becoming a vaguely cheery saying that it doesn't matter
what happens when you're dead.

16 *Enter Capulet . . . to the maskers*: There is no sign of
Paris in this scene, in spite of Capulet's invitation at
I.2.20–34 and Lady Capulet's statement to Juliet at
I.3.81 (*This night you shall behold him at our feast*).
Only Tybalt, not the gentle Paris, appears as the repre-
sentative of opposition to Romeo.

17, 22 *Welcome, gentlemen*: Capulet addresses the maskers
(Mercutio and his friends in disguise); and as usual he
is hospitable.

18 *walk a bout*: Have a dance.

20 *makes dainty*: Fastidiously hesitates to accept the invitation.

21 *Am I come near ye now*: Have I not said something that
strikes home?

27 *A hall, a hall*: Clear a space for dancing!

28 *you knaves*: To his servants.
turn the tables up: Probably they would be boards and
trestles, easily packed up.

29 *quench the fire*: At I.3.16 we have been told that it is
the middle of July – and in Italy. At IV.4.16 logs for

the fire are being fetched. Shakespeare is perhaps
thinking of a summer evening in England, not in Italy;
or he may have been unwittingly influenced by his
source: in Brooke's poem the Capulet party takes place
at Christmas. But cf. III.1.2 (*The day is hot*).

30 *sirrah*: It is not clear whom he addresses: perhaps *cousin
Capulet* of the next line; perhaps himself.
unlooked-for sport: The arrival of Mercutio and friends,
uninvited guests, which made the dance possible.

31 *good cousin Capulet*: He is *Mine uncle Capulet* in the letter
of invitation at I.2.67. But 'cousin' can be used in
addressing any kinsman with familiarity or affection.

34 *Were in a mask*: Wore a mask.
thirty years: We remember that at I.3.73–4 his wife had
informed us that she was about twenty-eight; again,
the old age of Capulet is emphasized.

41 *ward*: Minor (a male ward ceased to be under guardian-
ship at twenty-one).

43 *I know not, sir*: A surprising remark: the servant does
not know who is the daughter of the house. Or perhaps
it is a bit of stage business: the servant is too busy or
too supercilious to trouble to answer such a foolish
(and absurdly phrased) question.

44 *she doth teach the torches to burn bright*: The onset of
love does not deprive Romeo of his power of exaggerated language.
teach: Because she is brighter than they are.

46 *Ethiop*: Common Elizabethan word for a black African.

47 *Beauty too rich for use, for earth too dear*: Her beauty is
too splendid for ordinary life, for 'the uses of this
world'. Romeo's verbal quibbles are foreboding; we
remember that at I.2.14 Capulet had said: *Earth hath
swallowed all my hopes but she*.

48, 49 *shows*: Appears.

48 *a snowy dove trooping with crows*: At I.2.86 Benvolio
had said that, if Romeo will accompany him to the
Capulet party, *I will make thee think thy swan a crow*.

49 *her fellows*: The ladies who are her companions.

50 *The measure done*: When the dance is finished.

51 *touching hers*: Romeo is already forming the image of
   Juliet as a statue of a saint, the touching of which will
   bless (93–6 below).

52–3 *Did my heart love till now? Forswear it, sight! | For I
   ne'er saw true beauty till this night*: What Benvolio had
   foretold at I.2.81–98 has happened.

52 *Forswear it*: Deny the previous oath.

54 *This, by his voice, should be a Montague*: Tybalt is
   allowed to overhear part of Romeo's soliloquy. It is
   not clear how he should recognize a Montague by his
   voice. But the theatrical convention is sufficient. We
   have seen Tybalt only for a few moments (speaking
   I.1.65–71), but it established him as the principal adversary Romeo would have to face. And while Romeo
   watches Juliet dancing, entranced by her beauty, Tybalt
   is threatening *To strike him dead*.

56 *covered with an antic face*: Masked. Such carnival masks
   were often comic or grotesque in appearance.

57 *fleer*: Sneer.

57, 63 *solemnity*: Festive occasion.

65 *Content thee*: Take it calmly.
   gentle coz: Capulet begins courteously to Tybalt.

66–70 *'A bears him like a portly gentleman . . . disparagement*:
   This striking testimonial from Capulet in favour of
   Romeo is evidence that, as Friar Laurence is to suggest,
   the family quarrel is not insoluble if only fire-eaters
   like Tybalt can be kept under control.

66 *portly*: Well-mannered (at this party).

70 *disparagement*: Indignity.

74 *semblance*: Expression on the face.

76–88 *He shall be endured . . . I'll make you quiet, what*: Capulet
   preserves the peace at his party. But, when provoked
   by Tybalt's *I'll not endure him*, he displays the same
   quick temper as Tybalt himself, and so we are prepared
   for his later display of angry harshness towards Juliet.

77 *goodman boy*: This is a double insult: a yeoman (not a
   gentleman) and a youngster; the second insult is passed
   on by Tybalt to Romeo at III.1.65 and 130.

77, 78, 82 *Go to*: An expression of impatience.

79 *God shall mend my soul*: An impatient oath.

80 *mutiny*: Disturbance.

81 *set cock-a-hoop*: The phrase is of obscure origin. In the earlier uses it seems to mean 'to drink recklessly', and so, generally, 'to abandon all restraint'.

You'll be the man: You'll play the big fellow! (derisively).

83 *saucy*: Insolent (stronger than the modern meaning of the word: cf. II.4.142).

Is't so, indeed: Referring to Tybalt's *Why, uncle, 'tis a shame* or perhaps it is the first of Capulet's interruptions to speak to a guest; see note on 86 below.

84 *This trick may chance to scathe you*: Presumably Capulet is threatening Tybalt with some such punishment as a reduction of his money expectations. But, ironically, his *trick* of quarrelling leads to his death at Romeo's hands.

scathe: Injure.

I know what: I know what I am doing.

85 *contrary*: Accent on second syllable.

'tis time: It is not clear whether he is still addressing Tybalt or has turned to the company at large; probably the former. Perhaps it suggests some piece of stage business: Tybalt may bow with constrained respect to his uncle-in-law's commands.

86 *Well said, my hearts*: Capulet interrupts his reprimanding of Tybalt with words to his guests generally and to the servants. The exact division of these remarks is not always clear.

86, 88 *my hearts*: My friends (the company).

86 *princox*: Pert young fellow.

87 *For shame*: This might go with *More light, more light!*, but it seems more likely to be addressed to Tybalt.

89–92 *Patience perforce . . . bitterest gall*: Tybalt's rhyming couplets are the ominous prelude to the meeting of the two lovers. His menaces are fulfilled in III.1.59–60.

89–90 *Patience perforce with wilful choler meeting | Makes my flesh tremble*: My having to restrain myself, since I have come up against Capulet's angry determination, causes my body to quiver.

90 *in their different greeting*: At the meeting of these opposite mental states (patience and anger).

92 *Now seeming sweet*: The punctuation of this text indicates that it is an adjectival phrase qualifying *intrusion*. Some editors prefer to omit the commas before
and after the phrase and treat it as the object of
convert.

93–106 *If I profane with my unworthiest hand . . .*: In this duet
Romeo and Juliet speak a sonnet, which is concluded
by their kissing. They begin another sonnet (107–10),
but Juliet half-breaks it with *You kiss by th'book*, and
then they are interrupted by the Nurse (111).

The artificial rhymed verse here provides a kind of
music to accompany the meeting. It has a somewhat
indefinite seriousness of metaphor which is perfectly
appropriate, for the audience can give their full attention to the lovers, without having too much concern
with what they say. The religious phraseology (*holy
shrina, sin, pilgrims, devotion, saint, holy palmers, prayer,
faith, trespass*) gives a strong elevation to the dialogue.
But although on one level it is artificial in tone, yet at
the same time the whole thing is delicious verbal
fencing, in which Romeo smoothly makes his mascu-
line audacity acceptable and Juliet gives feminine
replies which restrain him without stopping him.

It is clear that Juliet has already been observing
Romeo while she was dancing and he was standing
aside. See note on 132 below.

94 *holy shrine*: Her hand.
sin: The meaning of this, the unanimous reading of
the early editions, is rather difficult; perhaps *the gentle
sin is this* means 'this is only a mild and unimportant
sin'. Some editors accept an emendation to 'fine'
(penalty, forfeit). Another attractive emendation is
'pain' (suffering due as a penance). But *sin* seems to
anticipate 107–10 below, and at III.3.39 (in a passage
with reminiscences of their words at this meeting)
Romeo says that Juliet's lips *Still blush, as thinking
their own kisses sin*.

95 *pilgrims*: Because his lips intend to visit her hand, which he has just described as a *holy shrine*.

97 *pilgrim*: The emphasis on this word has led to the suggestion that Romeo is wearing the conventional pilgrim's garb (large hat, cloak, staff, scallop shell) as a fancy-dress disguise at the party. Mercutio and his friends are 'maskers', but there seems to be no evidence that they are wearing masquerade costumes. It is probable that there is a further quibble and that Shakespeare knew that the Italian '*romeo*' meant 'a pilgrim to Rome'. In the Italian dictionary of Shakespeare's contemporary Florio, the word '*romeo*' is defined as 'a roamer, a wanderer, a palmer'.

you do wrong your hand too much: Your hand is not so rough as you say it is (and so there is no need of a kiss to smooth my hand).

98 *mannerly*: Proper.

99 *For saints have hands that pilgrims' hands do touch*: For the images of saints (and you seem to be addressing me as if I were a saint) have hands (as I have) which are touched by the hands of pilgrims (and so a hand-clasp, instead of a kiss, is sufficient for us).

100 *And palm to palm is holy palmers' kiss*: She quibbles on palm (of the hand) and palmer (pilgrim, originally one who on return from the Holy Land bore a palm-branch or palm-leaf).

102 *prayer*: The emphasized word. Juliet has enticingly ambiguous answers in the fencing of their love-conversation. Here she seems to refute Romeo's argument by reapplying his imagery, but at the same time, perhaps, urges him to further *prayer* for her favour if he wants a kiss from her. She is learning quickly.

103 *let lips do what hands do*: Let our lips, like our hands, press each other's (in a kiss)!

104 *They pray: grant thou, lest faith turn to despair*: My lips are indeed praying. You must grant their prayer. Otherwise my faith (my love for you) will turn to despair (which is an irreligious state of mind).

105 *Saints do not move, though grant for prayers' sake*: The

statue of a saint (such as you call me) does not move (and take the initiative). But a saint may respond to prayers and grant what is asked for.

106 *Then move not while my prayer's effect I take*: Then keep still as a statue (don't resist) while I kiss you (and so *take* the answer to my prayer).

109 *urged*: Mentioned as an argument.

110 *by th'book*: Expertly, as if by instructions in a book of etiquette. Shakespeare generally mocks at the books of instructions; cf. Mercutio's scorn of Tybalt as one who *fights by the book of arithmetic* (III.1.101–2).

111 *Madam, your mother craves a word with you*: This may perhaps be played as merely a chaperon's wary intrusion; the Nurse has obviously been watching them (115).

112 *Marry, bachelor*: Good gracious, young man.

115, 143 *withal*: With.

117 *Shall have the chinks*: The Nurse, as well as being garrulous to a stranger, shows her mercenary interests. There is the usual emphasis on Juliet's position as an heiress (see note on I.2.14–15).

118 *O dear account*: Terrible reckoning to pay!
       My life is my foe's debt: My life (since I love her so much) is now owing to (dependent upon) my family foe.

119 *The sport is at the best*: For the proverbial expression cf. I.4.39.

120 *Ay, so I fear*: Yes, for I fear that worse things are to come.
       unrest: Uneasiness.

121 *gentlemen*: Capulet addresses the maskers.

122 *banquet*: Light refreshments (a dessert of, usually, sweetmeats, fruit and wine).
       towards: 'On the way', 'just coming'.
       They whisper in his ear: This comes from Q1 and seems to represent an appropriate piece of stage business by which the maskers excuse themselves. The audience can imagine their saying that they are going to visit some other ladies, or something of the sort – to give a meaning to Capulet's *Is it e'en so*.

124 *honest*: Honourable.

125 *More torches here*: To show his guests the way out or
     their way home.

126 *sirrah*: Speaking to himself, or perhaps to 'cousin
     Capulet' – cf. 30.

     fay: Faith.

128–32 *Come hither, Nurse. What is yond gentleman? . . . would
     not dance*: Juliet does not ask about Romeo at once, but
     leads up to the question by her inquiries about two
     other men. She is rapidly learning love's pretty little
     deceits.

129, 131 *The son and heir of old Tiberio . . . young Petruchio*:
     Neither of these are mentioned in the letter of invita-
     tion at I.2.64–9. Petruchio is a Capulet (cf. note on
     the III.1.33 stage direction) and so cannot be a masker.
     (The name 'Petruchio' is pronounced with a soft 'ch'
     sound, not a 'k' sound. The Elizabethan spelling
     'Petruchio' represents the Italian *Petruccio*; and so to
     pronounce the name as 'Petrookio' because one knows
     that in Italian the symbol 'ch' represents the 'k' sound
     is misapplied knowledge.)

132 *that would not dance*: Romeo had said (I.4.11–22 and
     35–9) he had no intention of dancing. Juliet's words
     indicate that she had seen Romeo watching her while
     she was dancing with one of the guests (from 42 to
     about 86, which sounds like the end of the *measure*,
     for which Romeo is waiting).

134 *If he be marrièd . . .*: Juliet now at once thinks of
     marriage, though at I.3.67 she had said that *It is an
     honour that I dream not of.*

135 *My grave is like to be my wedding bed*: This is the intro-
     duction of the theme of death as Juliet's lover. At
     III.2.137 she says: *death, not Romeo, take my maiden-
     head!* cf. IV.5.35–9 and V.3.102–5.

138 *My only love, sprung from my only hate*: The one man
     I love is the son of the one household I, as a Capulet,
     hate.

139 *Too early seen unknown, and known too late*: I saw him
     too soon without knowing who he was, and fell in love
     with him; and, now that I have found out who he is,

it is too late to do anything about it, for I am already
in love.

140 *Prodigious*: Monstrous and so ill-omened. Juliet, too,
has her premonitions of disaster, at discovering with
whom she has fallen in love.

142 *What's this*: Q2 reads *Whats tis?*, which may indicate a
vulgar or dialectal form of the demonstrative pronoun.

143 *one I danced withal*: She cannot be referring to Romeo
since she clearly did not dance with him (132), and the
Nurse had seen her *talking* with Romeo (115). She is
giving an evasive reply.

  Anon: At once.

II.*Chorus*

See note on the Chorus-prologue to Act I (pp. 141–2).
Dr Johnson justly commented: 'The use of this chorus
is not easily discovered, it conduces nothing to the
progress of the play, but relates what is already known,
or what the next scenes will shew; and relates it without
adding the improvement of any moral sentiment.'
Although the Chorus-prologue is often spoken, the
second Chorus has usually been abandoned by stage
tradition. This may have already been so in
Shakespeare's time, for in Q1 (which seems to derive
from a theatre production) the Chorus-prologue
appears, but the second Chorus does not.

1 *old desire*: Romeo's former love for Rosaline.

2 *young affection*: His new love for Juliet.

  gapes: Longs eagerly, as with open mouth.

3 *That fair*: Rosaline.

  love: The lover (Romeo).

6 *Alike bewitchèd*: Both he and she equally are enchanted
by love.

7 *his foe supposed*: Juliet, who is of the family of the
Capulets and so supposed to be an enemy.

  complaint: Make his lover's lamentations.

8 *fearful*: Causing fear. Juliet is playing a risky game;
she is like a fish trying to take the bait off the hook
without being caught.

9 *access*: Accent on second syllable.

10 *use*: Are accustomed.

13 *time means*: Time lends them means.

14 *Tempering extremities with extreme sweet*: Mitigating the hardship of their situation by means of the great sweetness of their meetings.

extreme: Accent on first syllable.

II.I

1 *forward*: Away from Juliet.

2 *dull earth*: His body.

thy centre: Juliet is now the centre of his world, since his heart is where she is.

6 *conjure*: Summon spirits by magical incantation. Mercutio begins a parody of the formulas of practical magic, including a list of names (7) by which a spirit is summoned.

7 *Humours*: Moods and affectations.

10 *Ay me*: This phrase had almost been Romeo's first words on entering the play (I.1.161).

11 *my gossip Venus*: My friend, the goddess of love.

12 *purblind*: Dim-sighted.

13 *Abraham Cupid*: This phrase is difficult. 'Abraham men' were beggars, and perhaps Cupid is imagined in the guise of a hypocritical beggar. The emendation to *Adam Cupid* has often been accepted, on the grounds of similarity with the sentence in *Much Ado About Nothing*: 'shoot at me, and he that hits me let him be clapped on the shoulder, and called Adam' (I.1.247–9). It has been suggested that *Young Abraham* is a paradox, as Abraham was the biblical patriarch: Cupid, too, is both a young boy and the oldest of the gods.

trim: Q2 reads *true*. But the correctness of *trim* (from Q1) seems confirmed by the line in the old ballad on the subject of King Cophetua and the beggar maid: 'The blinded boy, that shoots so trim . . .'

14 *When King Cophetua loved the beggar maid*: The old ballad which told this story has been preserved in a printed text of 1612.

16 *The ape is dead*: The poor creature is pretending to be lifeless.

17–21 *I conjure thee . . . appear to us*: Mercutio continues his parody of the formulas of magical incantation.

20 *demesnes*: Domains.

24 *raise a spirit*: By magical power compel a spirit to appear (with a bawdy quibble).

   circle: Magical circle (with bawdy quibble).

25 *strange*: Belonging to another person (not Romeo).

26 *laid it*: By magical power appeased a spirit and compelled it to cease to appear (with bawdy quibble).

   conjured: Two syllables; with accent on second syllable, unlike 6, 16, 17, 29.

27 *were some spite*: Would be doing him some wrong.

   invocation: Five syllables.

29 *to raise up him*: Make him, like a conjured spirit, appear to us (with a bawdy quibble).

31 *be consorted with*: Be associated with.

   humorous: Humid, but punning on the meaning of 'humorous' as 'full of humour' (as in 7 above).

34, 36 *medlar tree . . . medlars*: As 'to meddle' was a common word for sexual activity, the word 'medlar' was an obvious opportunity for bawdy puns about the sex-organs.

38 *open-arse*: Country-name for the medlar-fruit.

   poppering pear: Kind of pear named after the Flemish town of Poperinghe with bawdy quibble.

39 *truckle-bed*: Small bed on wheels ('truckles') which could be pushed under another bed.

40 *field-bed*: Bed on the ground (but punning on 'camp bed').

II.2

0 (*coming forward*): Presumably Romeo had moved to the back of the stage or retired behind a pillar (*he hath hid himself among these trees*, II.1.30), where he would be assumed to be unseen by Mercutio and Benvolio but visible to the audience. He now comes forward.

1 *He jests at scars that never felt a wound*: Romeo completes the couplet of which Benvolio had spoken the first line.

   He: A man like Mercutio.

2 *But soft! What light through yonder window breaks*: It is

remarkable that Shakespeare provides no transition, beyond Romeo's single sentence at 1, between Mercutio's ribaldries and the appearance of Juliet at her window.

7 *Be not her maid*: Do not be a follower of the virgin goddess Diana, cold to love and averse to marriage.

8 *vestal*: Virgin.

sick and green: Suggestive of the pallor of moonlight.

9 *none but fools do wear it*: It is foolish to remain cold to love and the *pale* and *green* of such maidens remind one of the motley of court jesters.

11 *O that she knew she were*: 'My love' is understood.

15 *stars*: Planets (as is shown by the *spheres* of 17).

16 *Having some business*: Having something to do away from home.

17 *spheres*: The concentric spheres in which (in the astronomy before Copernicus) the planets were supposed to move.

18 *there*: In the spheres left by the two stars.

they: The stars.

21 *region*: Of the sky.

28 *wingèd messenger*: Angel.

29 *white-upturnèd . . . eyes*: Eyes with the whites turned upwards.

31 *lazy, puffing*: Q1 has the pleasant reading *lazy-pacing*. But *puffing* (Q2) makes good sense (swollen in bulk, 'puffed out').

33 *wherefore*: Why.

34 *refuse*: Abjure.

39 *though not a Montague*: Whatever you call yourself; even though you *do* take some name other than Montague. Some editors punctuate: 'Thou art thyself though, not a Montague.'

40–42 *What's Montague? It is nor hand nor foot . . . Belonging to a man*: Romeo remembers this at III.3.106–7.

44 *word*: The Q1 reading *name* was included in many of the older editions of Shakespeare, and so became usual in the proverbial saying.

46 *owes*: Owns.

48 *for thy name*: In exchange for thy name.

53 *counsel*: Self-communings.

53–4 *By a name | I know not how to tell thee who I am*: I do not know by means of what name I am to tell you who I am.

55 *dear saint*: Romeo subtly refers to their earlier meeting. He had addressed her as *dear saint* at I.5.103.

61 *thee dislike*: Is unpleasing to you.

62–5, 74, 79 *How camest thou hither, tell me, and wherefore*: Juliet's questions and comments are all direct and practical. Romeo's answers are all vague and fantastic.

62 *wherefore*: Accent on second syllable.

66 *o'erperch*: Fly over.

68 *can*: Emphasized.

76 *but*: Unless.

78 *proroguèd*: Deferred.

83 *vast*: Large and empty.

84 *adventure*: Venture (the word was especially used for mercantile enterprise overseas).

85–7 *Thou knowest the mask . . . speak tonight*: Juliet is conscious of her tendency to blush. Cf. III.2.14 (*Hood my unmanned blood, bating in my cheeks*). The Nurse notices it (*Now comes the wanton blood up in your cheeks*, II.5.70). Charles Darwin in his book *The Expression of the Emotions in Man and Animals* (1872) has some interesting remarks about Juliet's blushing. Since blushes may be excited in absolute solitude, the darkness would not prevent Juliet's blushing; Darwin concludes that Shakespeare may have erred or may have meant that the blush was unseen, not that it was absent.

88 *Fain*: Gladly.

dwell on form: Preserve my formal behaviour.

89 *farewell compliment*: Shakespeare's young women in love thus overcome their conventional restraints and female arts. Likewise Miranda in *The Tempest* exclaims 'Hence, bashful cunning!' (III.1.81), when declaring herself to Ferdinand.

compliment: Polite conventions.

92–3 *At lovers' perjuries, | They say, Jove laughs*: A proverbial

expression, which comes from the *Art of Love* of Ovid:
'*Juppiter ex alto perjuria ridet amantum*' (i. 633).

97 *So thou wilt woo*: If only you will woo me.

98 *fond*: Somewhat foolishly in love.

99 *'haviour*: Behaviour.

101 *cunning*: See the quotation from *The Tempest* in note
   on 89 above.
   strange: Distant, reserved.

106 *Which*: Yielding.

107 *Lady, by yonder blessèd moon I vow*: Romeo is about to
   slip into the characteristic phrases of the affected lover,
   but Juliet promptly cuts short these protestations (109).

110 *circled orb*: Sphere in which the moon moves (cf. note
   on 17 above)

111 *variable*: Four syllables, with secondary accent on the
   third syllable and a light fourth syllable.

117 *contract*: Exchange of lovers' vows (accent on second
   syllable).

118 *unadvised*: Without careful consideration.

124 *as that*: As to that heart which is.

129 *I would it were to give again*: I wish I had it so that I
   could give it a second time.

141 *substantial*: Four syllables.

143 *thy bent of love*: Inclination of your love.

144 *Thy purpose marriage*: As at 1.5.134, her thoughts are
   immediately on marriage.

145 *By one that I'll procure to come to thee*: In a character-
   istically practical spirit Juliet arranges the means of
   communication.

145 *procure*: Arrange.

150 *anon*: Very soon.

151 *By and by*: Immediately.

152 *strife*: Striving. The reading *suit* (which is found in Q4)
   is adopted, by many editors; but the Q2 *strife* is acceptable, meaning 'endeavour to woo me'.

153 *So thrive my soul*: As my immortal soul may be saved
   from damnation.

155 *to want thy light*: Lacking the light of your presence
   (see 2–4 above).

159 *tassel-gentle*: Male falcon.

160 *Bondage is hoarse*: Because she is in bondage in her father's house, she has to whisper Romeo's name.

161 *tear the cave*: Rend the hollow vault of air.

162 *airy tongue*: Echo has no real tongue but merely reverberates the air.

167 *nyas*: Young hawk, still in its nest. Romeo carries on the reference to falconry, from *tassel-gentle* in 159. In Q2 the word is spelt *Neece*; this was obscure to the printers of later quartos and folios and it was amended to *my dear* (Q4) or *my sweet* (F2). But the brilliant explanation of the word by J. Dover Wilson (1955) can hardly be doubted.

168 *By the hour of nine*: It is in fact noon (II.4.109–10) when the Nurse meets Romeo the following morning.

170–85 *I have forgot why I did call thee back . . . till it be morrow*: Granville-Barker writes: 'This is the commonplace made marvellous. What is it, indeed, but the well-worn comic theme of the lovers that cannot once for all say good-bye and part, turned to pure beauty by the alchemy of the poet?'

177 *wanton*: Young mischievous person.

179 *gyves*: Shackles (now pronounced with a soft 'g', as in 'gypsy').

180 *And with a silken thread plucks it back again*: The metrical irregularity is expressive.

188–91 *The grey-eyed morn smiles on the frowning night . . . From forth day's pathway made by Titan's wheels*: In Q2 these four lines are printed twice; once here and then again (with small changes) as the opening of the Friar's speech in the next scene. Many editors leave them with the Friar. But the wild imagery of the lines is more characteristic of Romeo.

188 *grey-eyed*: Probably this means 'with blue eyes'. See note on II.4.42.

190 *fleckled*: Dappled (with spots of light).

191 *From forth*: Out of the way of.

Titan's wheels: The sun god, according to classical

mythology, was Hyperion, one of the Titans, and he drove across the sky in his chariot (cf. III.2.1–4).

192 *Hence*: From here.

ghostly: Spiritual.

close: Narrow.

193 *dear hap*: Precious piece of good fortune.

II.3

1–26 *Now, ere the sun advance his burning eye . . . eats up that plant*: This long rhyming soliloquy given to the Friar enables him to impress himself upon the audience. He is shown to be simple, good-humoured, and well-meaning, but also willing (as he shows later, 87–8) to suppose himself a manipulator of the fates of others. The discussion of the power of herbs prepares us for his offer of the potion that Juliet drinks; also for the Apothecary's poison that slays Romeo. For the four lines often printed at the opening of this scene (*The grey-eyed morn smiles . . . Titan's fiery wheels*), see note on II.2.188–91 above.

1 *advance*: Raise.

2 *The day to cheer and night's dank dew to dry*: The pace of this line seems at once to indicate the Friar's manner of speech.

3 *osier cage*: Willow basket.

5 *nature's mother*: The mother of all natural things (including the *plants, herbs, stones* of 12).

6 *her burying grave*: The grave which buries all natural things.

that: Stressed.

7 *her womb*: The place where natural things are begotten.

children: That is, plants.

divers: Various.

8 *We sucking . . . find*: We find sucking.

10 *None but for some*: There are no plants which are not useful for *some* purpose.

11 *mickle*: Great.

grace: Divine power and effectiveness.

12 *true qualities*: Inherent powers.

13 *For naught so vile*: For there is nothing so vile.

14 *to the earth*: To the inhabitants of the earth.

15 *strained*: Perverted.

that fair use: That proper and virtuous use intended by
nature.

16 *Revolts from true birth*: Denies the power for which it
was created (emphasis on *true*).

stumbling on abuse: If it chances to be mistakenly abused.

17–18 *Virtue itself turns vice, being misapplied, | And vice
sometime's by action dignified*: This is a somewhat casu-
istical demonstration that good qualities can be applied
in the wrong spirit to have ill effects, and that bad qualities rightly used can have good effects.

17 *turns*: Turns into.

18 *vice sometime's by action dignified*: An evil quality may,
occasionally, have our approval because it results, in
certain circumstances, in a good action.

19 *Within the infant rind of this weak flower . . .*: Q2 indicates the entry of Romeo here, and some editors retain
it at this place so that he overhears the Friar's medita-
tion on poison, grace, and will (19–26), with some
ironical effect. But the marking of entries of characters earlier than their first words is not unusual; and
in production the Friar is generally allowed to complete
his piece before the attention of the audience is diverted
by Romeo's entrance.

20 *Poison hath residence, and medicine power*: Both poison
and curative power are contained.

21 *with that part*: By means of smelling it.

cheers each part: Revives each portion of the body.

22 *stays*: Q1 reads *slays*, and this has been adopted by
many editors on the grounds that the Friar is here
talking about death (26), and so the anticipation of
Juliet's suspended animation (see his words at
IV.1.93–106) does not seem admissible. But *stays* need
not refer to suspended animation: rather, 'to bring the
heart to a standstill, and with it all the senses'.

23 *still*: Always.

24 *grace and rude will*: On the one hand, the capacity to

receive divine grace; on the other, the impulse to give
way to one's fleshly desires.

25 *the worser*: Rude will.

26 *canker*: Cankerworm.

27 *Benedicite*: May God bless you! (five syllables, with
accent on third syllable, which is pronounced to rhyme
with 'nice', and final vowel as short 'i').

29 *argues*: Proves.
   distempered: Disturbed by an unhealthy mixture (or
   tempering) of the bodily humours.

30 *good morrow*: Farewell (unlike the *Good morrow* of 27,
   which is a greeting at meeting).

31 *keeps his watch*: Keeps awake.

33 *unbruisèd*: Undamaged by the world.
   unstuffed: Not clogged up with troubles (like one's
   nose when 'stuffy').

36 *distemperature*: See note on *distempered*, 29 above.

40, 41, 62, 66, 74, 77 *Rosaline*: The audience, in spite of the
   enchantments of the last scene, is not allowed to forget
   Rosaline, though Romeo has *forgot that name and that
   name's woe* – as Benvolio had prophesied in I.1.225–38.
   See again at II.4.4.

41 *ghostly*: Spiritual.

42 *that name's woe*: The woe that that name caused me.

45 *mine enemy*: Capulet.

46 *one*: Juliet.

46, 47 *wounded*: With Cupid's arrows, but Romeo is quibbling on *enemy* and *foe*.

47 *That's*: (Juliet) who is.
   Both our remedies: The remedy, for both of us.

48 *holy physic*: His powers not as a physician but as a
   priest, who will heal them by the sacrament of marriage.
   lies: A plural form in Shakespeare's usage.

49 *I bear no hatred*: At having been wounded by my foe,
   Juliet.

50 *intercession*: Petition (the word usually had a religious
   suggestion in Elizabethan usage).
   steads: Benefits.

51 *homely*: Straightforward.

52 *shrift*: Absolution.

54 *rich Capulet*: Cf. I.2.78, and the Nurse's words to
    Romeo at I.5.116–17: *he that can lay hold of her | Shall
    have the chinks.*

56 *all combined*: Altogether united in heart.

59 *as we pass*: As you and I go along (as usual, Romeo is
    in a hurry: cf. 89 below).

61 *Holy Saint Francis*: Laurence is, of course, a Franciscan.

68 *To season love, that of it doth not taste*: (You have tried)
    to 'preserve' love (by salting it down in your tears), but
    (in spite of the salting, your) love still has no flavour.

75 *sentence*: General maxim, proverbial saying.

77 *chidst*: Past tense, short vowel.

81–2 *Her I love now | Doth . . .*: She whom I love now
    does . . .

82 *grace for grace*: A mutual exchange of love's favours.

84 *Thy love did read by rote, that could not spell*: Your
    notions of love were like those of someone who could
    recite words of a text learnt by heart without actually
    being able to read the words.

85 *waverer*: Three syllables.

86 *In one respect*: On account of one thing.

87–8 *this alliance may so happy prove | To turn your house-
    holds' rancour to pure love*: For the audience this is an
    ironical hope – the alliance *will*, but only by the death
    of the two lovers (see V.3.296–304).

89 *stand on*: Insist upon.

II.4

2   *tonight*: Last night.

4   *that same pale hard-hearted wench, that Rosaline*: See
    note on II.3.40.

6   *Tybalt*: The first shadow falls. We are now reminded
    of Tybalt's ominous threats at I.5.89–92 and again feel
    the irony of the Friar's hopefulness at II.3.87–8.

9, 11 *answer*: Appear in person in response to a challenge.
    But in 10 Mercutio with a quibble takes the word merely
    as 'reply to a letter'.

11 *how*: As.

12 *dared*: Challenged.

15 *the very pin of his heart*: The 'bull's eye'.

16 *blind bow-boy*: Cupid.

butt-shaft: Blunt-headed arrow for practising archery.

18 *Why, what is Tybalt*: This is not a question, asking for information, but a derisive comment on Tybalt's abilities. At I.1.108–12 Benvolio had already described with some sarcasm Tybalt's manner of fighting (*the winds . . . hissed him in scorn*).

19 *Prince of Cats*: Tybalt is his name in the medieval stories of Reynard the Fox. Similarly, in III.1.74–7 Mercutio calls him *King of Cats* and *ratcatcher* and mocks at his alleged *nine lives*.

20 *compliments*: Formalities of the duel.

20–21 *as you sing pricksong*: As orderly as one follows the printed music (not extempore) in singing.

21 *proportion*: Rhythm.

23 *butcher of a silk button*: A skilful fencer could, allegedly, touch any particular button on his opponent's garment.

24 *duellist*: This was apparently a novel term in Shakespeare's time; Mercutio mocks at the new-fangled word.

first house: Best school of instruction.

25 *first and second cause*: These are the steps by which a quarrel developed, ending in a duel. In *As You Like It* (V.4.48–100) Touchstone gives a satirical account of the seven 'causes': 'we quarrel in print, by the book, as you have books for good manners'.

passado: Lunging thrust (from the Italian '*passata*').

26 *punto reverso*: Backhanded thrust (from the Italian, literally 'point reversed').

hay: Thrust through (from Italian '*hai*', 'thou hast [it]').

28 *The pox of*: The plague upon.

antic: Grotesque.

fantasticoes: Fops.

29 *new tuners of accent*: Those who introduce novel kinds of language.

30 *tall*: Brave.

31 *grandsire*: Benvolio (mockingly perhaps because he is rather serious and peace-loving).

32 *flies*: Parasites.

33 *pardon-me's*: Q2 reads *pardons mess* and Q1 *pardonmees*.
Some editors 'improve' the joke by giving the phrase
an Italianate or Frenchified form: '*perdona-mi's*' or
'*pardonne\?-moi's*'; but it seems that it is the affected
English phrase that Mercutio is jeering at.
stand: Insist.

34 *form*: Code of manners.
bench: He quibbles on the previous *form*, as he does on
stand and *sit*.

35 *their bones*: Their fastidious or sensitive bodies (presumably; with a quibble on French '*bons*'), which are
uncomfortable on the old kind of furniture (*bench*).

37 *roe*: Punning on the first syllable of Romeo, so that he
is only 'half himself', as well as on 'roe', deer.

38 *flesh, how art thou fishified*: Continuing the quibble on
roe – a man is being compared to a herring.
for the numbers: Inclined to the composition of
(metrical) poetry.

38–9 *the numbers that Petrarch flowed in*: The sonnets that
Petrarch (1304–74) wrote to his chaste love Laura de
Noves were a model for love-poetry throughout
Europe. The poet celebrates her beauty and virtue,
and laments somewhat tearfully (hence *flowed*) the
pangs of his unfulfilled love. Shakespeare often
mentions critically or satirically the conventions of
Petrarchan love-poetry, notably in Sonnet 130 (in praise
of the lady's beauty).

39 *to his lady*: In comparison with his lady.

39–40 *Laura, to his lady, was a kitchen wench – marry, she had
a better love to berhyme her*: It was only because Laura
had a lover better at making poetry than Romeo is
that, in spite of her being a kitchen-wench in comparison with Rosaline, she is so famous.

41 *Dido a dowdy*: Perhaps because Dido, the queen of
Carthage and Aeneas's love, was a widow. There are
jests about 'widow Dido' in *The Tempest*, II.1.71–96.
The alliteration here (and in *Helen and Hero hildings
and harlots*) is part of the jest at poetry.

Cleopatra a gypsy: She is twice called a 'gypsy' in a derogatory way in *Antony and Cleopatra* (I.1.10 and IV.12.28). The Elizabethans seem to have imagined Cleopatra as, vaguely, a dark-complexioned Egyptian (in Shakespeare's play she has a 'tawny front' and is 'with Phoebus' amorous pinches black') though she was, of course, of pure Macedonian blood. When the gypsies first appeared in England about the beginning of the sixteenth century they were commonly believed to be Egyptians in origin.

41 *Helen*: Of Sparta, whose abduction by Paris was the cause of the Trojan war.

   Hero: Of Sestos, the beloved of Leander, who swam the Hellespont from Abydos to visit her and was drowned.

42 *hildings*: Good-for-nothings.

   Thisbe: The beloved of Pyramus, familiar to us from the playlet of the rude mechanicals in *A Midsummer Night's Dream*, which was probably written soon after *Romeo and Juliet*.

   grey eye: Both grey and what we now call 'blue' eyes were, it seems, described as 'grey' in Shakespeare's time. Cf. *grey-eyed morn* in II.2.188. The phrase 'blue-eyed' was used of a person with dark shadows around the eyes due to weeping, sickness and so on.

42–3 *not to the purpose*: That is of no importance.

44 *to your French slop*: Appropriate to your loose trousers. Presumably this indicates Romeo's costume.

48 *slip*: Counterfeit coin. Mercutio puns on the other meaning of *slip*, 'an evasive action'.

   Can you not conceive: Can you not use your imagination?

52 *to bow in the hams*: Mercutio (as Romeo explains in the next line) puns on *courtesy* and *curtsy*, which apparently had the same pronunciation.

53–85 *Meaning, to curtsy . . . a broad goose*: Romeo is now in high spirits and is the equal of Mercutio in making verbal jests. There is a series of associations: (1) *courtesy, curtsy, courteous*, leads to *pink of courtesy*; (2) *pink* is not only 'highest degree' but also the *flower* and

perforated ornaments on a *pump* (shoe); (3) *pump* leads
to *sole* and thence to *solely* (singularly) and perhaps
'soul', since 'single-souled', mean or contemptible, is
a phrase like 'narrow-souled'.

54 *kindly*: Naturally.

59 *pump well-flowered*: If *pink* is a flower, then the 'pink-
ings' (perforations of a decorative kind) of his shoes
are 'flowerings'.

64 *single-soled*: Thin.
singleness: Simplicity, silliness.

68 *Swits and spurs . . .*: Urge your horse faster with switches
and spurs . . .!

68–9 *cry a match*: Claim the victory.

70 *wild-goose chase*: Erratic cross-country horse-race in
which whoever takes the lead has to be followed by
the others. Mercutio picks up the metaphor in Romeo's
swits and spurs, and a series of jests on *goose* now begins,
mostly sexual quibbles.

72–3 *Was I with you . . .*: Did I manage to keep even with
you . . .?

73 *goose*: Whore (probably).

75 *for the goose*: As the 'silly goose' of the company.
(Romeo's jibe that Mercutio is the jester in any company
he is with strikes home, as Mercutio's reply shows.)

76 *bite thee by the ear*: To show affection, but Mercutio
speaks ironically.

78 *sweeting*: Sweet apple.

80–81 *well served in to a sweet goose*: Because a goose needs
a sharp apple-sauce.

82 *cheverel*: Kid, easily stretched.

83 *ell*: Forty-five inches.

85 *broad goose*: With bawdy quibble.

87–8 *art . . . art . . . art*: Quibbling on *thou art* and the *art*
which is opposed to nature.

89 *natural*: Idiot (by nature; quibbling on the *nature* in the
previous sentence).
lolling: With the tongue (or *bauble*) hanging out.

90 *bauble*: decorated stick carried by a professional fool
(with a bawdy quibble).

92–3 *against the hair*: Against the grain. Mercutio puns in-
         decently on *there* (91).

  94 *thy tale large*: With a bawdy pun.

  97 *occupy*: This was an indecent word in Shakespeare's
         time. Cf. Doll Tearsheet in *Henry IV, Part II*
         (II.4.143–6): 'God's light, these villains will make the
         word as odious as the word "occupy", which was an
         excellent good word before it was ill-sorted.'

  98 *goodly gear*: Matter for mockery (referring to what has
         gone before).

  99 *A sail, a sail*: This perhaps indicates that the Nurse is
         rather overdressed. It has not been explained why she
         has taken three hours to come to meet Romeo.

 100 *A shirt and a smock*: A man and a woman.

104–5 *the fairer face*: This is the Q2 reading. Q1 has *the fairer
         of the two*, adopted by some editors.

 107 *God ye good-e'en*: (God give you) good evening (or
         afternoon).

 108 *Is it good-e'en*: Is it evening?

 111 *Out upon you*: Expressing indignation. The Nurse reacts
         promptly to Mercutio's way of saying that the clock
         shows it is now midday.

112–13 *for himself to mar*: Q2 omits *for* (which is found in Q1),
         but as the Nurse repeats the phrase in line 114, its inser-
         tion is probably justified here.

115–16 *can any of you tell me where I may find the young Romeo*:
         Presumably Shakespeare has forgotten that the Nurse,
         having already spoken to the masked Romeo at the
         party, had been later sent by Juliet to identify him
         (I.5.112–17 and 132–7).

 119 *for fault of*: In default of.

 124 *confidence*: Presumably she blunders for 'conference'.

 126 *endite*: Invite (perhaps a deliberately blundering word,
         following the Nurse's misuse of *confidence*).

 127 *So ho*: Huntsman's cry when the game (such as a hare)
         is sighted. Romeo therefore replies with *What hast
         thou found?* and Mercutio continues with jokes about
         hare (whore).

 129 *lenten pie*: One without meat, served in Lent.

130 *stale and hoar*: Both quibbles on 'whore'.
    spent: Used up.

141 *Lady, lady, lady*: The refrain of an old ballad.

142 *I pray you, sir*: Some editors insert, before this, *Marry, farewell!* from Q1.
    saucy merchant: Insolent fellow (*saucy* had a strong meaning).

143 *ropery*: Rascality.

145–6 *stand to*: Abide by.

147–8 *take him down*: Humble him (with unwitting bawdy quibble).

149 *Jacks*: Low fellows (cf. III.1.11 and IV.5.143).

150 *flirt-gills*: Fast girls.

151 *skains-mates*: Knives-mates; that is, cut-throat fellows.

152–5 *and suffer every knave to use me at his pleasure! . . . weapon should quickly have been out*: As usual, the Nurse lapses into unintentional bawdry and Peter continues in the same vein.

157 *the law on my side*: Cf. the anxiety of Sampson and Gregory in the quarrel in the opening scene (I.1.37 and 46).

160 *as I told you*: Apparently Romeo and the Nurse have been conversing apart during Mercutio's singing (131–6).

160, 161 *bid*: Past tense.

162 *lead her in a fool's paradise*: Seduce her.

165 *deal double*: Deceive.

167 *weak*: Contemptible.

168, 189, 208 *commend me*: Give my best regards.

169, 174 *protest*: Romeo begins to say 'I swear . . .', but the Nurse takes *protest* in its colloquial sense of 'I make a declaration of love.'

177 *shrift*: Absolution.

178 *Friar*: The word is sometimes two syllables, sometimes one syllable, in Shakespeare's verse.

179 *shrived*: Absolved.

180 *No, truly, sir. Not a penny*: After a show of protest, the Nurse takes the money.

185 *tackled stair*: Rope ladder.

186 *high topgallant*: Summit (literally, the highest platform or sails on a ship, to which Romeo imagines himself climbing by means of his rope ladder).

187 *convoy*: Conveyance.

188 *quit*: Requite (with payment).

189 *mistress*: Three syllables.

193 *Two may keep counsel, putting one away*: Two, but not three, can keep a secret (a proverbial expression).

197–8 *lay knife aboard*: make his claim for her (at table a diner brought his own knife).

199 *I anger her sometimes*: Shakespeare here ignores the time-scheme of the play; the Nurse could only have heard about Romeo a few hours ago, but she talks as if the affair had been going on for some time. Cf. Juliet's words at III.5.238–40 (and note).

201 *versal*: Universal (in the Nurse's language).

202 *rosemary and Romeo*: Cf. the rosemary in IV.5.79 and 95 (stage direction).
    a letter: the same letter. The Nurse cannot read or write.

204 *the dog's name*: 'R' was commonly called the dog's letter as its sound resembled a dog's growling. Probably the r-sound was more strongly sounded in Shakespeare's pronunciation than it is at the present time in standard (southern) English.

206 *sententious*: A blunder for 'sentences' (presumably).

208 *Commend me to thy lady*: Romeo departs, apparently not much interested in *the prettiest sententious* that the Nurse wants to relate.

211 *Before, and apace*: Some editors insert, in front of this, from Q1: *Peter, take my fan, and go*; but this is probably a repetition from 103 above.

II.5

1 *The clock struck nine*: As she and Romeo had agreed at II.2.168; but it was noon when the Nurse met him, II.4.110 and 10 below.

5 *glides*: Plural form.

6 *louring*: Looking dark and threatening (rhymes with 'flowering').

7 *pinioned*: Winged.

draw: In her chariot.

love: The goddess of love, Venus.

9 *highmost*: Highest. It is midday and the sun is at its
zenith.

11 *hours*: Two syllables.

14 *bandy*: Toss back (as in tennis, carrying on the
metaphor of *ball* in the previous line).

15 *And his to me*: And his words would bandy her back
to me.

16 *old folks, many feign as they were dead*: Many old people
act as if they were only half alive. In *feign as they
were dead* we have a curious anticipation of Juliet's
later ordeal. But the awkward lines could perhaps
mean 'many people talk about old folks, in a fanciful
way, as being dead . . .' There may, however, be something wrong with the text here: among the emendations proposed, 'marry, fare' for *many feign* gives good
sense.

25 *Give me leave*: Let me alone.

26 *jaunce*: Jaunt (literally, prance).

29 *stay*: Wait.

34 *excuse*: Thyself from telling.

36 *stay the circumstance*: Wait for details.

38 *simple*: Foolish.

41 *body*: Q1 prints this as *baudie*, and some editors have
seen this as evidence that a suggestive pun is intended,
especially as the Nurse continues: *though they be not to
be talked on* (which could, however, mean 'though they
are not worth talking about').

44 *Go thy ways, wench. Serve God*: Conversational phrases
meaning 'enough of that'.

50 *a't'other*: On the other. The usual stage business here
is that Juliet rubs the Nurse's back.

51 *Beshrew*: Confound.

52 *jauncing*: Jaunting (cf. 26 above).

55 *honest*: Honourable.

62 *Marry come up, I trow*: Expressions of impatience or
wounded dignity here affected by the Nurse.

65 *coil*: Trouble.

68, 72, 77, 78 *hie*: Hasten.

    70 *Now comes the wanton blood*: For Juliet's blushing, see note on II.2.85–7.

    71 *They'll be in scarlet straight*: Your cheeks are always inclined to flush suddenly.

72–3 *I must another way,* | *To fetch a ladder . . .*: As instructed by Romeo at II.4.183–7.

    76 *bear the burden*: She quibbles on the meanings: 'carry the responsibility of work' and 'bear the weight of your lover'.

    78 *Hie to high fortune*: Juliet quibbles, in her excited state of mind, but her height of fortune is ominous; the wheel will soon begin to turn.

II.6

    1 *So smile the heavens*: So may the heavens smile.

    3 *But come what sorrow can*: But let whatever sorrow come that possibly may come.

    4 *It cannot countervail the exchange of joy*: The sorrow will not be able to outweigh the joy for which it must be taken in exchange.

    7 *do*: May do.

9–15 *These violent delights have violent ends . . . as too slow*: The Friar gives his brief marriage-sermon on the theme of *Love moderately. Long love doth so.*

11–12 *The sweetest honey* | *Is loathsome in his own deliciousness*: Honey is sweet; but merely because the sweetness is so strongly delicious it has the possibility of becoming loathsome.

    13 *confounds*: Destroys.

    19 *idles*: Plural form.

    20 *vanity*: The empty delights of this transitory world (the Friar speaks from the point of view of religion).

    21 *confessor*: Accent on first syllable.

    23 *As much to him, else is his thanks too much*: If Romeo is to give thanks on behalf of both of you, I must give him a greeting too, the same one as I gave to you.

24–9 *if the measure of the joy . . . by this dear encounter*: If you are filled with joy as I am, and if you have greater skill than I have in describing it appropriately, then let

your sweet and musical voice be heard, revealing the
happiness which we receive from each other by our
thus coming together.

26 *blazon*: To set out in appropriate colours (a heraldic
term).

30–31 *Conceit, more rich in matter than in words, | Brags of
his substance, not of ornament*: Imagination, when it is
richer in substance than in mere words, makes a display
of the reality (of feeling), not of the appearances.

34 *I cannot sum up sum of half my wealth*: In order to make
the line simpler, some editors rearrange the words as:
'I cannot sum up half my sum of wealth.'

III.I

The contrast between the quiet close of the previous
scene and the impending violence at the opening of
this scene is theatrically striking.

0 *Enter Mercutio, Benvolio, and their men*: The *men*
include Mercutio's page, whom he addresses at 94.

1–4 *I pray thee, good Mercutio, let's retire . . . mad blood stirring*: Benvolio tries to be a peace-maker (as in I.1.63–8).
See also 49–52 below, where he urges prudence.

2 *The day is hot*: See note on I.5.29.
Capels: Capulets (as in V.1.18 and V.3.127). The abbreviated form is found in Brooke's *Romeus and Juliet*.

3 *And if*: Perhaps 'An if': that is, merely a double form
of 'if' (see 15, 30 below, where in the original text 'an'
is spelt *and*).

5 *Thou art like one of these fellows . . .*: Benvolio has been
speaking in simple blank verse, but Mercutio changes
to lively and characterful prose.

5–7 *when he enters the confines of a tavern, claps me his sword
upon the table . . .*: The braggart ostentatiously lays
aside his sword, but he is really issuing a defiance to
all present in the tavern; his apparent prayer for peace
is itself a kind of provocation.

6 *me*: This grammatical usage (an indefinite indirect
object, which in the old grammar books used to be
called the 'ethic dative') gives an air of familiarity and
ease to the dialogue.

8 *operation*: Influence on the brain or body (that is, the second draught of liquor begins to work on him).

8–9 *draws him on the drawer*: Draws his sword on the tavern-servant.

10 *I*: Ironically emphasized by Benvolio, for he regards the description as fitting Mercutio himself. Cf. 20 below.

11 *Jack*: Fellow, chap (somewhat disparaging, as the Nurse uses it in II.4.149 and a Musician in IV.5.143).

12 *moved to be moody*: Inclined to anger.

13 *moody to be moved*: Angry at being provoked.

15 *two*: Mercutio puns on Benvolio's *to*.

20 *What eye but such an eye*: Presumably the second *eye* is a pun on *I* and Mercutio is amusedly accepting the self-description, referring to Benvolio's ironical *I* in 10. He does indeed behave very like this, a few lines later in the scene (38–48), in reacting to Tybalt's provocative *consortest*. He ironically prepares the audience for his losing his life for his petty quarrelsomeness.

22 *meat*: Food.

23 *addle*: Rotten.

27 *doublet*: Close-fitting jacket with short skirt.
before Easter: That is, during Lent, anticipating the Spring fashions.

27–8 *tying his new shoes . . .*: This cause of offence appears to have no point except its triviality; *his new shoes* probably means 'the shoes supplied by him', rather than 'the shoes he wears'.

28 *riband*: Ribbons were used as shoe-laces.

28–9 *tutor me from*: Give me prudent instruction against.

31 *fee simple*: Permanent lease, full possession.

31–2 *for an hour and a quarter*: That is, he would be dead before that time had elapsed.

33 *simple*: Stupid.
Enter Tybalt and others: Q2 reads *Enter Tybalt, Petruchio, and others*. Petruchio (who otherwise does not appear in the play except as one of Capulet's guests named at I.5.131) may be intended to be the friend who speaks the warning *Away, Tybalt!* at 89 below.

Shakespeare occasionally introduces among the entries a named character whom he subsequently does not need to use.

34 *comes*: The colloquial singular form of the verb (*preceding* a plural subject) expresses excitement better than the amended form 'come'. See I.1.30 for another instance.

35 *By my heel*: Expressing both contempt and his intention of not 'taking to his heels'.

37 *good-e'en*: Good evening (it is the same afternoon, nearly an hour after the marriage of the lovers – see 112 below).

38 *And but one*: Only one.

39 *Make it a word and a blow*: Mercutio is not a Montague; but he deliberately provokes and undertakes Tybalt.

41, 42 *occasion*: Excuse. Tybalt tries to preserve the etiquette of duelling, as it has been described by Mercutio in II.4.19–26.

45 *Consort*: Tybalt uses the word *consortest* in the sense of 'are often in the company of', and presumably wants to inquire where Romeo can be found. As Romeo had apparently not been home since the last evening's party, there could not yet have been any answer to the challenge mentioned in II.4.7. Probably Tybalt does not wish to undertake Mercutio – it is Romeo he is after, and he at once turns to him at 55. But Mercutio interprets *Consort* as an offensive musical metaphor and therefore as a challenge.

45, 46 *minstrels*: Apparently a somewhat derogatory word: menial or hired musical entertainers. In IV.5.113 Peter insults the musicians by giving them *the minstrel*.

47 *Here's my fiddlestick*: Pointing to his sword.

48 *Zounds*: By God's wounds (that is, Christ's on the Cross). The word is pronounced to rhyme with 'wounds'.

49–52 *We talk here in the public haunt of men . . . gaze on us*: Benvolio proposes three possible courses of action to avert the public quarrel. Some editors emend *Or* at the beginning of 51 to 'And', giving Benvolio only two proposals. For Benvolio as peace-maker, cf. I.1.63–8 and III.I.1–4. His firm language contrasts with Romeo's somewhat rash efforts in 82–8 below.

51 *reason coldly*: Discuss calmly.

52 *depart*: Go away separately.

55 *my man*: The man I am looking for. Tybalt had been plotting his revenge on Romeo since the previous evening (I.5.91–2 and II.4.6–8).

56 *But I'll be hanged, sir, if he wear your livery*: Mercutio persists in his wilful misinterpreting of Tybalt's words. He takes *my man* as if it meant 'my manservant', and so carries on the jest about *livery* (servant's uniform) and *follower* (attendant, and one who will literally follow him to the duelling-place).

57 *field*: A place for duelling.

58 *Your worship*: With mocking politeness.
   man: A man of honour, and no coward.

59 *love*: The word is surprising, because Tybalt does not elsewhere use irony. Q1 reads the simpler word *hate* and some editors prefer it as more appropriate to Tybalt's direct character.

60 *thou art a villain*: This is the comprehensive insult, in the code of honour, about birth and conduct. The duel must follow. Cf. I.5.62,64.

61–4 *Tybalt, the reason that I have to love thee . . . thou knowest me not*: The confrontation of Romeo and Tybalt is a turning-point in the play. It is the one occasion when, in a crisis, Romeo shows self-restraint and good sense. Only the audience knows the meaning of his riddling speech.

62 *excuse the appertaining rage*: Excuse my not showing the rage which would be appropriate.

65 *Boy*: The insulting word had been applied to Tybalt himself by Capulet at I.5.77 and 83.

67 *injured*: So Q1.Q2 has the old form of the word, *injuried*.

68 *devise*: Imagine.

69 *Till thou shalt know the reason of my love*: When his marriage with Juliet is made public.

70 *tender*: Regard.

71 *. . . be satisfied*: A wonderful moment of suspense

(though it is difficult to be certain, from the words, exactly what is intended to happen on the stage). Tybalt does not reply to Romeo's pacifying remarks. Is he calmed by being called *good Capulet* and so forth, showing by his contemptuous expression that he agrees with Mercutio's words about Romeo's *calm, dishonourable, vile submission?* He says nothing until he is insulted by Mercutio: *Tybalt, you ratcatcher, will you walk?*, and then only replies with unusual mildness: *What wouldst thou have with me?* He had already once rejected Mercutio's challenge (*Well, peace be with you, sir*) in 55. It is Mercutio who, by his second insolent challenge, brings on the disaster.

72 *submission*: Four syllables.

73 *Alla stoccata*: Mercutio continues (from II.4.19–26) his jeers at Tybalt's manner of duelling with the rapier by thus nicknaming him (*stoccata* thrust). He is also contrasting Tybalt's direct insults with Romeo's evasive politeness. He had already mockingly expressed his doubts whether Romeo was a match for Tybalt at the duel (II.4.16–17).

carries it away: 'Gets away with it'.

74 *ratcatcher*: Because he is the *King of Cats* (76). Cf. II.4.19, where Mercutio calls him the *Prince of Cats*. A few lines later (76–8) Mercutio mocks at his alleged *nine lives*.

walk: Withdraw in order to fight a duel.

77–8 *as you shall use me hereafter*: According to your subsequent behaviour to me.

78 *dry-beat*: Cudgel (without drawing blood).

79 *pluck . . . by the ears*: Contemptuous phrasing; *ears* presumably means 'hilt'.

pilcher: Scabbard (probably; 'pilch' means 'leather coat').

83 *passado*: Cf. the *immortal passado* at II.4.25.

88 *Tybalt under Romeo's arm thrusts Mercutio*: This appears in Q1 only. It is a transference of Mercutio's words at 103: *I was hurt under your arm*.

89 *Away, Tybalt*: This is printed as if it were a stage direction in Q2, meaning 'Exit Tybalt'.

91 *A plague a'both houses*: A dying man's curse, thrice
    repeated (99, 106, 108) and certain to be fulfilled. Q2
    omits *your* the first time Mercutio curses; probably
    correctly, as he is there almost talking to himself, rather
    than addressing others.
    sped: Dispatched.

92 *and hath nothing*: Is not wounded.

93 *a scratch, a scratch*: Made by the *King of Cats*.

94 *villain*: The word is used for a person of lowly station
    in life, not necessarily in an insulting sense (as 60, 63
    above).
    surgeon: Physician.

98 *a grave man*: Mercutio jests to the end; he puns about
    his burial, describing himself as becoming (out of char-
    acter) serious-minded.

100 *Zounds*: See note on line 48 above.

100–101 *a cat, to scratch a man*: See note on line 93 above.

102 *book of arithmetic*: Textbook with diagrams of the
    movements. See notes on II.4.19–26, III.1.73.

105 *Help me into some house, Benvolio*: Mercutio does not
    deign to answer Romeo's feeble *I thought all for the
    best*, and turns for support to Benvolio. Romeo is left
    onstage alone.

109–15 *This gentleman, the Prince's near ally . . . softened valour's
    steel*: Romeo is given more serious lines than he has
    spoken hitherto.

109 *ally*: Relative. Mercutio's relationship to the Prince is
    emphasized (III.1.145, 189; V.3.295).

112 *Tybalt's slander*: See 60 and 65–6 above.

113 *cousin*: Kinsman. The word was used to indicate a vague
    kinship, like that of Romeo now that he was married
    to Juliet.

115 *temper*: State of mind, with a pun on the hardening of
    steel by 'tempering'.

117 *aspired*: Soared up to.

118 *scorn the earth*: Alluding to his bold and magnanimous
    character.

119 *depend*: Impend. (Today's ill fortune threatens the days
    to come with similar misery.) The rhymed couplet

seems to indicate the moment of the turning of Fortune's wheel.

122   *Alive*: This is the reading of Q1. Q2 has *He gan*, which does not make sense; but a plausible emendation is 'Again', spelt 'Agen', misread in the manuscript as ''A gan' and printed *He gan*.

123–9   *Away to heaven respective lenity,* | *And fire-eyed fury . . . go with him*: Romeo now becomes a 'revenge hero', of a type found often in Elizabethan plays, and he uses the typical language, which is in striking contrast with his mild responses to Tybalt's insults earlier (61–4, 67–71). Romeo now mentions these insults and avenges them (*Now, Tybalt, take the 'villain' back again* | *That late thou gavest me,* 125–6).

123   *respective lenity*: Gentleness which respects the Prince's edict about street-fighting, or takes into consideration that Tybalt is Juliet's blood-kinsman.

124   *conduct*: Guide. It is no longer Providence (I.4.112–13) that directs his sail. He dispatches mercy to heaven and invokes a *fire-eyed fury* from hell.

125   *villain*: See 60 above.

130   *boy*: Cf. 65 above.
      consort: Cf. 44 above.

131   *This*: His sword.
      They fight. Tybalt falls: Presumably the fight between Romeo and Tybalt, unlike that between Mercutio and Tybalt, is brief. Benvolio later says *to't they go like lightning* (172).

134   *amazed*: Dazed.

135   *Hence, be gone, away*: The remainder of the scene (apart from Benvolio's narrative to the Prince) is mostly written in rhymed couplets, which differentiate it from the excited exchanges that have gone before.

136   *I am fortune's fool*: I am like a household fool for fortune to mock and amuse herself with. Only the audience (not Benvolio) understands Romeo's agonized dilemma here.

139–40   *Up, sir, go with me.* | *I charge thee in the Prince's name obey*: This is attributed to a *Citizen* in the original text, but he seems a person of authority, perhaps an *Officer*.

140 *Enter Prince, Montague, Capulet, their wives, and all*: This is the second symmetrical assembly of the Prince, the two families, and the citizens. It is curious that neither Capulet nor Lady Montague speaks in this scene. Lady Capulet is given the passionate outbursts on behalf of her nephew Tybalt, so that her hatred of Romeo is to make Juliet's position more difficult.

142 *discover*: Uncover, reveal.

145 *thy kinsman*: Benvolio mentions this at once, to influence the Prince against Tybalt.

146–50 *Tybalt, my cousin! O my brother's child!* . . .: Lady Capulet delivers her pleas over the dead body of Tybalt (onstage).

146–7 *O my brother's child!* | *O Prince! O cousin! Husband!* *O, the blood is spilled*: Probably *child*, *spilled* were a rhyme in Shakespeare's pronunciation.

152–75 *Tybalt, here slain, whom Romeo's hand did slay* . . . *or let Benvolio die*: The excited syntax of this speech is noteworthy (the connecting relative pronouns, 160, 167; *Romeo he* . . ., 164; (he) *rushes*, 167).

153–6 *Romeo, that spoke him fair, bid him bethink* . . .: Benvolio's account is a little exaggerated.

154 *nice*: Trifling.

157 *take truce with the unruly spleen*: Come to terms with the outrageous ill-temper.

161–3 *with one hand beats* | *Cold death aside and with the other sends* | *It back to Tybalt*: This probably indicates that Mercutio and Tybalt fought with two weapons, rapiers in their right hands and daggers in their left.

164 *Retorts it*: Turns it back.

167 *rushes*: See note on 152–75.

168 *envious*: Full of enmity.

170 *by and by*: Immediately.

171 *but newly entertained revenge*: Only just admitted the idea of revenge into his thoughts.

177 *Affection*: Partiality.
Affection makes him false. He speaks not true: Benvolio

is, indeed, not quite accurate in his account. He ignores Mercutio's provocation to Tybalt and in particular (158–9) conceals the fact that Mercutio was the deliberate challenger. Benvolio exalts the Prince's kinsman (*brave*, *bold* and *stout* Mercutio, with his *martial scorn*). But Lady Capulet fails to make her point because she goes on to make vague accusations about *Some twenty of them*.

183 *Who now the price of his dear blood doth owe*: Who is now to pay the penalty for shedding Mercutio's (probably, rather than Tybalt's) blood?

185 *His fault concludes but what the law should end*: In killing Tybalt Romeo had anticipated the law, which would, in the end, have condemned Tybalt to death for killing Mercutio.

187 *exile*: Accent on second syllable.

188 *I have an interest in*: I am personally concerned in *hate's*. This is the reading of Q1. Q2 has *hearts*, which is difficult, but could be defended in the light of the Prince's words at I.1.85 (*purple fountains issuing from your veins*).

189 *My blood*: The blood of someone related to me (that is, Mercutio).

190 *amerce*: Punish by a fine.

193 *purchase out abuses*: Buy off the penalty for crimes.

196 *Bear hence this body*: Shakespeare arranges that Mercutio goes offstage to die, but the body of Tybalt remains onstage until the end of the scene, a visual object of great importance emphasizing Romeo's disastrous act. There are now enough persons on stage to carry it off.

     attend our will: Come to be judged and respect my decision.

197 *Mercy but murders, pardoning those that kill*: If the law is merciful to murderers, then it participates itself in the murders and causes more of them. The Prince is now taking a stronger line than he did in I.1.96–7; but he is not implementing the threat he there made, as he recognizes in V.3.294.

III.2

1–31   *Gallop apace, you fiery-footed steeds . . . And may not wear them*: While Juliet speaks her own passionate marriage-hymn, the audience knows that her ecstatic happiness is about to be ruined by the news of the disastrous murder in the previous scene.

1   *fiery-footed steeds*: The horses which draw the chariot of the sun god (Phoebus Apollo) from the east to their night's *lodging* below the western horizon. Cf. *day's pathway made by Titan's wheels* II.2.191.

3   *Phaëton*: Three syllables, with accent on the first vowel; the traditional pronunciation in English is 'fay-i-ton'. His story is found in Ovid's *Metamorphoses* (where doubtless Shakespeare read it, either in the original Latin or in the verse translation by Arthur Golding – who calls Phaeton a 'waggoner'). He was allowed to drive the sun-chariot of his father Apollo for one day, but let the horses get out of hand and drove the chariot too near the earth. In some respects Juliet's comparison is not appropriate, because it was Phaeton's incompetence rather than speed that was important in the story. It is possible that there is some irony in this. But Shakespeare often treats classical mythology in a casual or independent way.

6   *runaway's eyes*: The meaning is uncertain. The *runaway* may be: (a) the sun (the eyes of the sun will close when night falls); (b) Phaeton (who let the horses get out of hand); (c) (*runaways'*) the horses of Phaeton (whom Juliet imagines as driving the day forward); (d) Romeo (who may relax his vigilance in the Capulet house when he is enjoying Juliet's love); (e) (*runaways'*) officious observers of the actions of the lovers. After all, the word may be an error of transcription or printing.
     wink: Close (and, if *runaway* means the sun, cause darkness).

9   *if love be blind*: Cupid, according to the old mythology, was blind.

10   *civil*: Serious.

12 *learn*: Teach.

    lose a winning match: She surrenders herself, but she gains a lover.

13 *a pair of stainless maidenhoods*: The innocent inexperience of the lovers is often emphasized.

14 *Hood my unmanned blood, bating in my cheeks*: A falcon was said to be *unmanned* when it was untrained and unable to be quiet when held by its trainer; it then 'bates', that is, flutters its wings up and down excitedly. One method of training a young falcon in this condition was to cover its head with a hood, so that it grew accustomed to a man without nervousness. Juliet puns, of course, on *unmanned* as she is a virgin awaiting the coming of her husband; night will conceal her blushes. On Juliet's blushing see note on II.2.85–7 and cf. II.5.70.

15 *strange*: Unfamiliar and so causing reserve.

16 *Think true love acted simple modesty*: Regard the physical act of true love as straightforward chastity.

17 *Come, night*: Probably she puns on 'knight' (her Romeo).

21 *when I shall die*: Many editors prefer the change made in the printing of Q4: *he* for *I*. Juliet's fancy is extravagant and we cannot feel sure that the slightly simpler *he* is more appropriate. She may be imagining, a little jealously, the destiny of Romeo after *her* death rather than *his*. On the other hand, it would be very like Shakespeare to let Juliet have a passing premonition of her belief in 40–60 below that Romeo is dead.

30 *impatient child*: The shift from the fantastic imagery of night and sun and sky to this domestic comparison is striking.

34 *cords*: The rope ladder which Romeo was to use to climb into her window that night.

37 *weraday*: Well-a-day, alas!

40 *envious*: Full of enmity.

    Romeo can: She means (though Juliet does not understand her) that Romeo can be so full of enmity as to kill Tybalt.

45–51 *Say thou but 'Ay,'* . . . *determine of my weal or woe*:
Juliet's frenzied punning on *I*, *eye*, *ay* (yes), and the
vowel, was formerly condemned as unnatural. It is,
however, consistent with Shakespeare's dramatic practice of using un-comic puns in tragic situations; of
allowing words to acquire a terrible ambiguity at
moments of great emotion. For the Elizabethan *reader*
the pun was visually a little closer, since 'ay' was
customarily spelt as 'I'.

47 *cockatrice*: The basilisk (a fabulous animal which was
hatched by a serpent from a cock's egg and was able
to kill by a glance of its eyes).

49 *those eyes shut*: If the eyes of Romeo be shut. But *shut*
is an emendation of *shot* in Q2, and some editors
retain *eyes' shot*, giving the meaning: 'the glance of
the Nurse which implies her saying "yes"'. This is
rather strained.

51 *Brief sounds*: That is, 'ay' or 'no'.
determine of: Make a decision about.

52 *I saw the wound. I saw it with mine eyes* . . .: The Nurse
has, in her distraction, heard only the sound of Juliet's
speech, but not taken in the meaning. She carries on
the *I* and the *eyes*.

53 *God save the mark*: As usual the Nurse, in spite of her
earthiness, apologizes for mentioning anything indel-
icate. She presumably points to the place on her own
chest to show where Tybalt received his wound.

54 *corse*: Corpse.

56 *swounded*: Swooned (rhymes with 'sounded'). Her gory
description has a strong effect on Juliet, who takes it
to refer to Romeo; it is an imaginative premonition of
how Juliet *will* see Romeo at V.3.161–7.

57 *break, my heart*: This phrase had a biblical background
which made it stronger than the modern sentimental
usage. Cf. Psalm 34:18: 'The Lord is nigh unto them
that are of a broken heart' (Authorized Version).

57–8 *Poor bankrupt, break at once!* | *To prison, eyes*: As *break*
can mean 'be declared insolvent', perhaps Juliet is
punning, linking *bankrupt* and *to prison*.

59 *Vile earth, to earth resign*: Yield up her body to the grave ('ashes to ashes, dust to dust').

61–3 *O Tybalt, Tybalt, the best friend I had!* . . .: Her exaggerated praise of the dead Tybalt is excellently in character.

66 *dearest*: Some editors adopt *dear-loved* from Q1. But the exaggeration of *dearest* and the slight paradox of the following *dearer* seem right.

67 *dreadful trumpet, sound the General Doom*: See 1 Corinthians 15:52: 'at the last trump: for the trumpet shall blow . . .'

73 *hid with*: Hidden by.
   flowering face: In pictures the Serpent in Paradise was sometimes represented as appearing to Eve with a human face surrounded by flowers.

74 *dragon keep so fair a cave*: A dragon was supposed to keep guard over treasure in a cave.

75 *tyrant*: Because he is usurping qualities not his by right.
   fiend angelical: Cf. 2 Corinthians 11:14: 'Satan himself is transformed into an angel of light.'

76 *Wolvish-ravening lamb*: Another scriptural phrase; cf. Matthew 7:15: 'Beware of false prophets, which come to you in sheep's clothing, but inwardly they are ravening wolves.'

78 *Just*: Exactly (with a play on the *justly* that follows).

81–2 *the spirit of a fiend | In mortal paradise*: Juliet is thinking of the Serpent in Eden.

83–4 *Was ever book containing such vile matter | So fairly bound*: For the imagery of the book-binding compare Lady Capulet at I.3.82–95.

87 *naught*: Wicked.

88 *aqua vitae*: Brandy or other strong spirits.

90 *Blistered be thy tongue*: Juliet is sometimes given passionate language in addressing the Nurse. Cf. *Ancient damnation!* at III.5.236.

98 *what tongue shall smooth thy name*: Who shall speak thy name kindly (but *smooth* also contrasts with *mangled* in the next line).

99 *three-hours wife*: Another indication of time: it is

now later in the afternoon and two hours since the Tybalt–Mercutio–Romeo quarrel.

101 *That villain cousin would have killed my husband*: Juliet begins shrewdly to understand the situation.

103 *tributary drops*: Tears paying a tribute.

105 *that*: Whom.

109 *fain*: Gladly.

112–24 *banishèd*: Juliet repeats the word five times, with increasing agony.

117 *needly will be ranked with*: Will of necessity be accompanied by.

119 *Thy father, or thy mother*: Her own; she is, as it were, addressing herself.

120 *modern*: Ordinary. The deaths of her father and mother would be events that human experience leads us to regard as usual; but the exile of Romeo at such a time is a grief totally unexpected.

121 *rearward*: Rearguard (behind, as it were, the main part of the navy or army causing destruction).

126 *No words can that woe sound*: She probably puns on *sound* as meaning 'give expression to' and 'plumb the depths of'.

130 *spent*: Expended.

137 *death, not Romeo, take my maidenhead*: See notes on I.5.135, III.5.140, IV.5.35–9 and V.3.102–5.

139 *wot*: Know.

III.3

The audience has been told by the Nurse (III.2.141) that Romeo is in hiding at Friar Laurence's cell. Having seen Juliet's reaction to the catastrophic misfortune of the killing of Tybalt and the exile of her husband, we now see Romeo's condition. In the midst of death and calamity the preparations are made by the Friar and the Nurse for the marriage to be consummated.

1 *fearful*: Full of fear (about the consequences of his having killed Tybalt). But the word is ambiguous because in Shakespeare *fearful* also means 'terrible': Romeo is a 'fatal' and so a frightening character.

2–3 *Affliction is enamoured of thy parts, | And thou art*

wedded to calamity: The words of the Friar take the
mind back to the end of II.6; it is misery, rather than
Juliet, who has fallen in love with him and whom he
has married.

2 *parts*: Personal qualities (as in III.5.182).

3 *wedded to calamity*: Romeo had described himself as
fortune's fool (III.1.136).

4, 8, 9 *Prince's doom*: Judgement decreed by the Prince.

6 *familiar*: Four syllables. The Friar says that Romeo's
relation to sorrow is closer than an *acquaintance* (5).

9 *doomsday*: Day of Judgement (that is, death).

10 *vanished*: Presumably this means 'was breathed out and
disappeared into air, so that it cannot be recalled'. But
the sense is strained and some editors have seen a printer's
or transcriber's error here (for 'issued' or 'vantaged' or
– as if quoting the Prince's word – *banishèd*).

17 *without*: Outside.

19 *Hence banishèd*: Banished from here. Romeo repeats
the word *banishèd* many times, as Juliet has done
(III.2.112–24).

20 *world's exile*: Exile from the world.
exile: Accent on the second syllable, as in 41 and 140;
but in 13 the accent is on the first syllable.

24 *deadly sin*: Ingratitude.

25 *Thy fault our law calls death*: Our law demands death
as a punishment for your crime.

26 *rushed aside*: This presumably means 'forcefully over-
ruled'. But the word is strained, and some editors
suspect an error for 'thrust' or 'brushed' or 'pushed'.

28 *dear mercy*: Unusual mercy which should be valued.

29 *Heaven is here*: The emphasis falls on *here*.

32 *Live*: 'Every' may be followed by a plural verb in
Elizabethan English.

33 *validity*: Value.

34 *courtship*: Courtly behaviour. But Romeo puns on the
other meaning of the word, 'wooing a lady'.

36 *the white wonder of dear Juliet's hand*: Romeo remembers her hands; cf. I.5.51 and 93–102.

37 *immortal blessing*: Carries on the idea of *heaven* in 29, 32.

38 *vestal*: Virgin (like the chastity of the Vestal Virgins in ancient Rome).

39 *Still blush, as thinking their own kisses sin*: In Romeo's extravagant language: her lips are red as if blushing at the way one of them touches the other and so 'kisses' it. At I.5.95 he had called his own lips *two blushing pilgrims*.

40–44 *This may flies do . . . I from this must fly*: The text here follows Q2. But the repetitions of phrase and idea have led many editors to suppose that we have here an example of the accidental inclusion, by transcriber or printer, of a line cancelled by Shakespeare in his manuscript; they place 41 after 44, and omit either 40 or 43. In these lines Romeo seems to echo Juliet's playing with *ay*, *eye* and *I* in her lament at III.2.45–50; and his pun on *flies* and *fly* is as harsh.

45–6 *Hadst thou no poison mixed . . . ne'er so mean*: The thoughts of the means of suicide seem to anticipate the tragic catastrophe; and they keep before the audience the Friar's skill with drugs (II.3.1–26).

46 *mean of death*: Means of procuring death. Romeo then puns on *mean* (base).

50 *confessor*: Accent on first syllable.

53 *fond*: Foolish.

58 *Yet 'banishèd'*: Do you still keep saying 'banished'?

63 *when that wise men have no eyes*: When a wise man like you cannot see what is so obvious. Romeo's retort is petulant, but the Friar continues calmly.

64 *dispute with thee of thy estate*: Have a philosophical discussion on the present state of your affairs with you.

65 *Thou canst not speak of that thou dost not feel*: The Friar's vows of celibacy must have kept him ignorant of the passion of love.
that: That which.

66–9 *Wert thou as young as I, Juliet thy love, | An hour but married, Tybalt murderèd, | Doting like me, and like me banishèd, | Then . . .*: Romeo's broken syntax is expressive. 'If you were as young as I am, if Juliet were your love, if you had been only an hour married

and had murdered Tybalt, if you were as much in love
as I am, and if you were banished as I am, then . . .'

69 *tear thy hair*: As often in Shakespeare, the actor's 'business' is indicated within the speech.

71 *Taking the measure of an unmade grave*: He lies on the
ground as if his outstretched body provides the meas-
urement of the grave in which he is to be buried.

74 *Mist-like infold me from the search of eyes*: As happened
to the heroes in epic poetry.

77 *By and by*: Immediately.

78 *simpleness*: Stupidity (in not getting up and concealing
himself, as the Friar had urged from 72 onwards).

86–7 *O woeful sympathy! | Piteous predicament*: Some editors
transfer these words from the Nurse to the Friar, on
the grounds that it would be out of character for the
Nurse to use such long and learned words (in
Shakespeare's time) as *sympathy* and *predicament*. To
this it can be replied that exclamations of woe are unlike
the Friar; and it is best to leave the text unchanged.

86 *woeful sympathy*: Agreement in woefulness.

91 *an O*: An exclamation of sorrow (presumably Romeo
is groaning as he lies on the ground). The Nurse may
be here (though it is hardly the moment for it) falling
into her familiar trick of unwitting bawdry.

94 *old*: Hardened by experience.

98 *concealed*: Not yet acknowledged as his wife (accent
on first syllable and so jingling with *cancelled*).
cancelled: Invalidated.

101 *on Romeo cries*: Cries out against him.

102–7 *As if that name . . . | Did murder her . . . | Doth my
name lodge*: A reminder of Juliet's words at II.2.38–42.

103 *Shot from the deadly level of a gun*: Another example
of the recurring gun-imagery.
level: Line of aim.

106 *anatomy*: A human body for dissection.

107 *sack*: Pillage (like a house in a sacked city).

108 *mansion*: Juliet had used this word of Romeo's body
in III.2.26.
He offers to stab himself, and the Nurse snatches the dagger

away: The stage direction is from Q1 and seems to indicate the business in an early production. We might have expected the Friar, rather than the Nurse, to snatch the dagger away, but it may be that appropriately both the Nurse and the Friar, in their different ways, take steps to prevent Romeo's folly. His rash attempt at suicide here prepares us for his later determination for suicide when he hears bad news without the support and restraint of the two older people.

113 *ill-beseeming*: Unnatural and inappropriate (because apparently both man and woman).

114 *my holy order*: Of St Francis.

115 *tempered*: Mixed so that the ingredients (the four 'humours' of Elizabethan physiology) are well balanced.

116 *Wilt thou slay thyself*: Ironically, what the Friar upbraids him for seeming to want to do, Romeo actually does, later on.

117 *And slay thy lady that in thy life lives . . .*: The emphasis falls on the second *thy*.

118 *damnèd*: Because suicide is a mortal sin.

119 *Why railest thou on thy birth, the heaven, and earth*: Romeo had not, in fact, done this. But it is interesting to note that in Arthur Brooke's poem Romeo does rail bitterly against Nature, the time and place of his birth, and the stars. It seems that Shakespeare was here remembering what he had read in Brooke, not what he had written in his play.

120 *birth and heaven and earth*: His human origin in his family, his immortal soul, his earthly body, all unite in him; he could destroy them all by suicide.

122, 125, 130 *wit*: Intelligence, sense of reason.

123 *Which*: Who.

123–4 *usurer . . . usest . . . use*: He puns on *use* as meaning 'to lend out at interest'.

124 *true use*: Honourable handling of his wealth.

126 *but a form of wax*: Only a waxwork figure (a different meaning from the Nurse's *a man of wax* at I.3.77).

127 *Digressing*: If it deviates.

129 *Killing*: If it kills.

> *vowed to cherish*: In the recent marriage-ceremony.

131 *Misshapen in the conduct*: Going awry in the guidance.

132 *powder*: Gunpowder.

flask: Horn for the gunpowder.

134 *dismembered with thine own defence*: Blown to pieces by your own gunpowder, which should have been the means for your defending yourself (destroyed by your intellect which should have saved you).

136 *dead*: 'Worried to death', or wishing to be dead (as in 71).

137, 138, 140 *There*: In that respect (emphatic).

137, 138, 140 *happy*: Fortunate.

137–8 *Tybalt would kill thee. | But thou slewest Tybalt*: The Friar reasons as did Juliet in III.2.100–107.

139 *The law*: As declared by the Prince at I.1.96–7.

143 *mishavèd*: Misbehaved (which is the form of the word found in Q1).

144 *pouts*: Poutest. In verbs ending in -t, the second person singular often has -ts, instead of -test, in Elizabethan English.

fortune: Good fortune.

146 *decreed*: Arranged beforehand (II.4.183–7, III.2.34–5 and 132–7).

148–9 *But look thou stay not till the Watch be set, | For then thou canst not pass to Mantua*: Romeo must leave Verona before nightfall, for then the city-gates would be closed and a guard posted. But see 167–8 below.

149 *Mantua*: This – already mentioned by the Nurse at I.3.29 – is in fact the nearest considerable town to Verona, twenty-odd miles away, as Shakespeare could have learned from books and travellers of his time. Shakespeare had already set a good deal of *The Two Gentlemen of Verona* in or near Mantua (IV.1; V.3 and 4), and it is mentioned in *The Taming of the Shrew* as a town not far from Padua. The name is sometimes three syllables, sometimes (III.5.88, IV.1.124) two.

151 *blaze*: Proclaim.

your friends: The members of your two families.

154 *lamentation*: Five syllables.

163 *Here, sir, a ring*: Juliet sent the ring at III.2.142.

164 *Exit Nurse*: The Nurse's exit is not marked in Q2. It is put after 166 in Q1. Some editors insert it after the *Good night* in 166.

165 *comfort*: Happiness.

166 *here stands all your state*: Your situation depends on this (what I am going to say now).

167 *the Watch be set*: The Friar's repetition from 148 emphasizes Romeo's danger.

168 *break of day*: At 148–9 the Friar wanted to get Romeo out of the city before nightfall, but now he gives him the alternative of staying with Juliet until just before break of day. The marriage would not, of course, have been valid unless consummated. The Friar's words look forward to the dawn-parting in III.5.

169 *your man*: Balthasar, who appears at V.1 and 3.

171 *good hap*: But it is the (mistaken) ill hap that Balthasar reports to Romeo at V.1.17–23.

173 *But that a joy past joy calls out on me*: Were it not that I am summoned away by the thought of the surpassing joy of going to Juliet.

174 *It were a grief so brief to part*: It would be a grief so hurriedly to part.

III.4

We have not seen Juliet's wooer, the County Paris, since I.2; nor have we heard of him since in I.3.75–95 Juliet was informed of his intended proposal. His arrival now, at the time of the deep distress and hastily snatched joy of the lovers, introduces a new and ominous element into the plot. We are given further insights into the character of father Capulet: his merely proverbial wisdom (*Well, we were born to die* (4); cf. the Nurse at III.3.92) and his concern for appearances (24–8) prepare us for his stubborn insistence in III.5, which hastens on the tragic catastrophe.

1 *fallen out*: Happened.

2 *move*: Persuade by talking.

5–7 *She'll not come down tonight . . . abed an hour ago*: Capulet gives a polite dismissal to his visitor, and the gentlemanly Paris understands and takes it.

6 *promise*: Assure.

8 *These times of woe afford no times to woo*: Paris jingles his words quite like Romeo.

11 *Tonight she's mewed up to her heaviness*: Actually she is meanwhile with her bridegroom Romeo.

mewed up: As a falcon in its cage.

heaviness: Grief.

12–32 *Sir Paris, I will make a desperate tender . . . against this wedding day*: The contrast between the marriage arranged by parents and the marriage now being consummated is striking. Capulet assumes that his daughter *will be ruled | In all respects* by him, and he is indignant at her disobedience and folly in III.5.141–96.

12 *desperate tender*: Bold offer.

15 *Wife, go you to her ere you go to bed*: The time-scheme is a little vague, but dramatically effective. The hour is late (III.3.172, when Romeo leaves the Friar's cell; and III.4.5 and 34–5). It is a moment of tension when Capulet twice tells his wife to visit Juliet before going to bed (15 and 31), because Romeo is already with her. Lady Capulet comes to Juliet at III.5.64, when Juliet wonders at her early call (III.5.66–7).

16 *son Paris*: Capulet clearly intends Paris to be his son-in-law.

17, 19 *Wednesday*: Eventually (IV.2.24) Capulet returns to this first idea for the marriage on Wednesday.

18 *Monday*: The emphasis on the days of the week and the fivefold repetition of *Thursday* makes the audience feel the urgency of the situation.

my lord: See note on I.2.6.

19 *Ha, ha*: This represents a deliberative hum.

21 *She shall be married to this noble earl*: His *desperate tender* (12) has now become an order.

21 *earl*: Nobleman (indefinitely; Paris is usually a Count or County).

22 *Will you be ready*: It is not easy to decide whether he is now talking to Paris or to Lady Capulet. If to Paris,

his tone has changed to one of banter. But it may be
that in 20–28 the whole passage is addressed to Lady
Capulet; and he then turns to Paris: *But what say you
to Thursday?*

23 *a friend or two . . . half a dozen friends*: The *friend or
two* become *half a dozen friends* by 27, and this prepares
us for IV.2.1–2, where his liking for hospitality has
turned what was to be a private wedding into a large
gathering.

25 *held him carelessly*: Had little esteem for him.

32 *against*: In time for.

33 *Light to my chamber, ho*: Summoning a servant.

34 *Afore me*: A mild oath: As God is before me!

35 *by and by*: Immediately (rather than the modern
meaning 'a little later on'; cf. III.1.170).

III.5

0 *Enter Romeo and Juliet aloft, at the window*: This derives
from Q1 and seems to indicate that Romeo and Juliet
appear on the upper stage to speak their farewells. Cf.
He goes down at 42.

1 *It is not yet near day*: In III.2.1–31 Juliet had implored
the sun to hurry across the sky so that night might come.
Now she laments that the fiery-footed steeds of the sun
do indeed gallop apace: *More light and light it grows* (35).

2–5 *It was the nightingale . . .*: Although it is, we have been
told, mid July, the birds still sing. (Nightingale song
is very irregular after mid June; skylark song continues
till early July and may be heard occasionally in any
month of the year.)

3 *fearful*: Full of apprehension.

4 *she sings*: In Shakespeare's traditional bird-lore it is the
female nightingale (not, as in reality, the male) that
sings.

4 *pomegranate*: Three syllables. This fruit tree had been
grown in England since the mid sixteenth century; but
it remained an exotic and so gives a touch of local
colour here.

7 *envious*: Malicious.

9 *Night's candles*: The stars.

11 *and live*: If I am to live.

13 *meteor*: Meteors were believed to be vapours drawn up out of the earth and ignited by the heat of the sun.

17 *ta'en*: Taken (usually pronounced to rhyme with 'lane').

18 *so*: If.

20 *reflex*: Reflection.

   Cynthia: The moon goddess (Diana).

   brow: Forehead (but also the whole face). Romeo is willing to pretend that the eastern light is not the rising sun but the reflected light of the moon.

21 *Nor that is not*: Emphatic double negatives quite often occur in Shakespeare's grammar.

23 *care*: Concern.

29 *sweet division*: The emphasis is on the adjective.

   division: A trilling or run of notes (four syllables).

31 *Some say the lark and loathèd toad change eyes*: This piece of folk-lore is obscurely authenticated. Apparently the toad's remarkable eyes are contrasted with the lark's insignificant eyes.

   change: Exchange.

32 *changed voices*: Then an ugly croaking like the toad's would be more appropriate than a joyful song like the lark's.

33 *arm from arm . . . doth us affray*: Startles us out of each other's arms.

34 *hunt's-up*: A hunting-song for daybreak.

41 *life*: Because Romeo is this to her.

42 *He goes down*: By means of the rope ladder; presumably at some point during the next twenty-two lines Juliet pulls it up and conceals it.

43 *love-lord, aye husband-friend*: Both illicit lover and lawful husband. Apparently *aye* (= ever; pronounced to rhyme with 'play') merely intensifies the meaning. But the reading *my*, from Q1, may be right.

44–7 *I must hear from thee every day in the hour . . . behold my Romeo*: Juliet speaks this not knowing (as the audience knows) of the intended marriage with Paris.

44–5 *every day in the hour, | For in a minute there are many days*: It will seem that in each minute there are many days of waiting – still more in each hour.

46 *count*: Method of counting time.

much in years: Grown much older.

52 *I doubt it not*: Since 'ay' (yes) was spelt 'I', this could be read 'Ay, doubt it not'.

54 *ill-divining*: Having premonitions of ill.

59 *Dry sorrow drinks our blood*: It was commonly supposed that sighing exhausted the blood, so that sorrow made one pale.

64 *She goes down from the window. Enter Juliet's mother*: Presumably Juliet 'goes in' on the upper balcony, and she appears to meet her mother on the main stage.

65–7 *Who is't that calls? . . . procures her hither*: This is apparently an aside. Her question *Who is't that calls?* may seem odd (unless she calls out as a deliberate deception), for at 39 the Nurse had told her *Your lady mother is coming to your chamber*. But as she speaks these three lines to herself Juliet is recovering from her distraction at Romeo's departure, and begins to feel anxiety about the reason for her mother's surprise visit.

66 *down*: In bed. (Is she very late in going to bed, or is she up very early?)

67 *procures*: Brings.

72 *Some*: A certain amount of (in moderation).

73 *still*: Always.

74 *feeling*: Deeply felt. Juliet begins a series of remarks with double-meanings; Lady Capulet supposes that her grief is for the death of Tybalt, but the audience knows it is for the separation from Romeo.

75–6 *So shall you feel the loss, but not the friend | Which you weep for*: If you do so, you will feel your loss; but your grief won't bring him to life so that you can feel *him*.

77 *friend*: For herself and the audience the *friend* means her lover; cf. 43 above.

83 *like he*: As much as he.

88–91 *I'll send to one in Mantua . . . keep Tybalt company*: The talk of *one in Mantua* who will give Romeo an *unaccustomed dram* prepares the audience for the

catastrophe by which Romeo is given such a poison
for himself so that he will *keep Tybalt company*.

89 *runagate*: Fugitive vagabond. Lady Capulet's words
ignore the time-scheme of the play; for Romeo has
only left for Mantua (on the Friar's advice at
III.3.148–9) a few minutes before.

90 *Shall give*: Who shall give.

  dram: Dose.

93–102 *Indeed I never shall be satisfied | With Romeo till I
behold him – dead . . . that hath slaughtered him*: Juliet
continues to speak with double meanings, one of which
is concealed from her mother. But her words, especially 93–4, have a further ironic meaning for the audience: the next time she will see Romeo he will be dead.

97 *temper*: Mix (but with the double meaning 'make more
moderate').

101 *wreak*: Pay.

102 *his body that*: The body of him who.

103 *means*: Of mixing such a poison.

107 *careful*: Provident.

109 *sorted out*: Arranged.

110 *nor I looked not*: For this emphatic double negative, cf.
the note on 21 above.

111 *in happy time*: How fortunate just now! (ironically).

114 *County*: See note on I.3.105.

119 *Ere he that should be husband comes to woo*: Paris is
aware of his backwardness (III.4.8 and IV.1.7).

126 *When the sun sets the earth doth drizzle dew . . .*: Capulet
sees Juliet in tears.

  earth: Q4 reads *air* and this is adopted by some editors.
But the *earth* of Q2 can be supported by sixteenth-
century notions of meteorology.

126–7 *sun . . . sunset . . . son*: Capulet's puns are of the simplest.

127 *my brother's son*: In view of Lady Capulet's strongly
personal words at III.1.146–50, presumably Tybalt is
the son of Capulet's brother-in-law.

129 *conduit*: City-fountain with a spout of flowing water.
Often they were in the form of a human figure; this
gives a jocular effect to Capulet's description of Juliet.

130–37 *In one little body | Thou counterfeitest a bark . . . | Thy
        tempest-tossèd body*: Capulet's elaborate comparison of
        Juliet in tears to a ship in a storm prepares for Romeo's
        seasick weary bark (V.3.118).

136   *Without a sudden calm*: Unless there comes a sudden
       calm.

139   *she will none*: She will have none of it.

140   *I would the fool were married to her grave*: Parental
       curses were considered ominous. Lady Capulet's wish
       will be fulfilled. Compare Capulet's bitterness in lines
       164–7 below, again ominous.

141   *take me with you*: I don't understand you (with
       mounting anger).

145   *bride*: Bridegroom ('bride' could still be used for either
       sex in Shakespeare's time). Texts later than Q2 read
       bridegroom.

148   *meant love*: Meant to be love.

149   *chopped logic*: Bandying argument to and fro.

151   *Mistress*: Three syllables, as in II.4.189.

153   *fettle*: Make ready.

156–7 *Out, you green-sickness carrion! Out, you baggage! |
        You tallow-face*: These descriptions of Juliet give the
        audience information about her appearance. The boy-
        actor could hardly simulate *green-sickness* and *tallow-
        face*, but these words supplement the doleful face he
        could assume here.

157   *Fie, fie! What, are you mad*: Lady Capulet, who was
       petulant enough herself at 140, is driven to protest at
       Capulet's fit of temper. Cf. 175. (An alternative sugges-
       tion – that she is addressing Juliet – seems less prob-
       able.)

164–6 *we scarce thought us blest | That God had lent us but this
        only child . . .*: On Juliet as an only child, cf. I.2.14–15,
        I.5.116–17, IV.5.46–8.

168   *hilding*: the jade!

169   *rate*: Upbraid.

171   *Smatter*: Prattle.

172   *God-i-good-e'en*: God give you good evening (impa-
       tiently).

175 *You are too hot*: Cf. 157.

176 *God's bread*: The bread consecrated in the Communion Service.

177 *tide*: Season.

181 *demesnes*: Estates.

trained: Q2 reads *liand*, which does not make sense. The reading of Q1, here adopted, is acceptable but some editors prefer emendations: 'limbed' or 'liened' (with noble 'liens' or connexions).

182 *parts*: Personal qualities (as in III.3.2).

184 *puling*: Whimpering.

185 *mammet*: Doll, puppet.

in her fortune's tender: When she is offered a good chance of marriage.

188 *I'll pardon you*: (Threateningly) I'll pardon you in another sense – I'll give you leave to go!

190 *I do not use to*: It is not my habit to.

196 *I'll not be forsworn*: I shall not break my word (in fulfilling my threats to you and in promising you in marriage to Paris).

206–9 *My husband is on earth, my faith in heaven* | . . . *By leaving earth*: My husband Romeo is alive on earth and my marriage-vow to him is registered in heaven; therefore I cannot be released from my vow, unless my husband were to die.

210–11 *that heaven should practise stratagems* | *Upon so soft a subject as myself*: Juliet had before attributed her misfortunes to the malice of Providence (*Can heaven be so envious?* III.2.40). But such self-pity is rare in Juliet.

210 *practise stratagems*: Dishonestly contrive traps.

214 *all the world to nothing*: The odds are a million to one.

215 *challenge*: Claim possession of.

222, 228 *Beshrew*: Cursed be.

229 *Amen*: Juliet replies thus to the Nurse's imprecations (*beshrew* her heart and soul).

231 *Well, thou hast comforted me marvellous much*: Juliet has now acquired sufficient strength to be able to treat the Nurse ironically.

235 *Exit Nurse*: Q1 inserts the stage direction: *She looks after Nurse*.

237 *forsworn*: False (to marriage-vows).

239 *above compare*: As being beyond comparison.

240 *many thousand times*: The time-scheme of the play scarcely allows for this unless extreme exaggeration is intended. Cf., similarly, II.4.199 (and note).

241 *bosom*: Sweet thoughts.
    twain: Separated.

242–3 *to know his remedy. | If all else fail, myself have power to die*: Cf. IV.1.52–67.

IV.1

2 *My father Capulet*: Paris is over-confident of his marrying Juliet, and anticipates the relationship, as did Capulet by speaking of his *son Paris'* love at III.4.16.

3 *nothing slow to slack his haste*: Show no reluctance which might cause him to reduce his haste.

5 *Uneven*: Irregular.

7 *have I little talked of love*: Cf. III.4.8, and Juliet's words at III.5.118–19.

11 *marriage*: Three syllables.

13 *too much minded by herself alone*: Too much brooded upon in her solitude.

18–43 *Happily met, my lady and my wife! . . . this holy kiss*: This is the first time the audience has seen Paris and Juliet together, and she arrives to face him unexpectedly a few moments after the crisis with her father, mother and nurse. Paris is amiably possessive (*my lady and my wife*) and Juliet manages to preserve a dignified bearing – cool, but indulging in a little courteous banter with the admirer who is unwittingly causing her such desperate distress.

31 *before their spite*: Before their malice in marring it.

34 *to my face*: Here the phrase means both 'openly' and 'about my face'.

37 *it is not mine own*: Juliet turns away from these rather flippant interchanges with Paris, after her final ambiguity (*it is not mine own* – because it is Romeo's), giving him a polite hint to go.

38 *evening mass*: This seems to have been an occasional practice in the sixteenth century; but presumably Shakespeare uses the word *mass* in a general sense for 'divine service'.

39 *pensive*: Sorrowful.

41 *God shield I should disturb*: God defend me from disturbing.

47 *compass*: Range.

48 *may prorogue*: Can postpone.

52–67 *If in thy wisdom thou canst give no help . . . speak not of remedy*: She amplifies the statement she made in III.5.242–3.

54, 62 *knife*: It was not unusual for Elizabethan ladies to carry knives.

54 *presently*: Immediately.

57 *label to another deed*: Codicil modifying another legal document.

59 *this*: Knife.
both: Hand and heart.

62–5 *this bloody knife | Shall play the umpire, arbitrating that | Which the commission of thy years and art | Could to no issue of true honour bring*: There are legal metaphors here: her dagger will act as a third party arbitrating (between herself and her miseries) where the usual judicial functionaries cannot satisfactorily decide.

65 *Could to no issue of true honour bring*: After this line the Friar is silent.

74 *chide away this shame*: Drive away this disgrace.

75 *That copest with death himself to 'scape from it*: (You) who are prepared to face death itself in order to escape from the shame of marrying Paris.

76 *remedy*: Echoes *remedy* in 67 above.

78 *any tower*: Q1 reads *yonder tower*, which is apparently a more effective reading.

79 *thievish ways*: Places made dangerous by thieves.

81 *charnel house*: Small building adjacent to a church where skulls and bones from graves were deposited. Human remains seem to have been dug up and put in a charnel house after they had been in the ground a number of

years (cf. Hamlet's conversation with the grave-
digger). That Shakespeare disliked the practice is
perhaps suggested by the inscription on his tombstone
in Stratford-upon-Avon church.

81–5 *Or hide me nightly in a charnel house . . . dead man in
his tomb*: This is a striking anticipation of what is to
happen to her and a preparation for her soliloquy
before drinking the potion (IV.3.30–59).

83 *reeky shanks*: Shinbones giving off foul-smelling vapour.
chapless: Without lower jaws.

85 *tomb*: The word is omitted in Q2. The printer of Q4
in 1622 gave *shroud*. The printer of F put *grave*,
repeated from the previous line. Either is possible; but
it has been pointed out that it would be difficult to hide
in the *shroud* already occupied by a dead man.

90 *Wednesday is tomorrow*: But owing to the bringing
forward of the marriage to Paris by one day (IV.2.24)
Juliet has to take the potion the same evening (Tuesday).

94 *distilling*: Penetrating or infusing the body. The reading
of Q1 *distillèd* is easier, looking back to the Friar's
account of his herbs in II.3.1–26.

96 *humour*: Fluid.

97 *native*: Natural.
surcease: Cease.

100 *wanny*: See An Account of the Text.
windows: Shutters (hence *eyes' windows* eyelids).

105 *two-and-forty hours*: This length of time does not seem
to fit the time-scheme of the play precisely. But an
exact figure is appropriate in the context theatrically.

110 *In thy best robes uncovered on the bier*: In Q2 the line
printed after this is *Be borne to burial in thy kindred's
grave*. This seems to be a line rewritten as 111–12 and
accidentally not deleted from the manuscript.
uncovered: With face uncovered.

113 *against thou shalt awake*: In expectation of the time
when you will awake.

119 *toy*: Whim.

122 *prosperous*: Successful.

125 *help afford*: Provide help.

IV.2

1–2 *So many guests invite as here are writ . . . twenty cunning cooks*: It is not, after all, to be a private wedding (as Capulet intended in III.4.23: *We'll keep no great ado — a friend or two*), and the family mourning has been forgotten. Capulet is hospitably inclined (I.2.20–37 and I.5.17–29).

2 *cunning*: Expert.

3 *none ill*: No bad ones.

5 *try*: Test.

6–7 *'tis an ill cook that cannot lick his own fingers*: A proverbial expression: only a bad cook would not want to taste the dishes he has prepared.

10 *We shall be much unfurnished*: The household preparations and provisioning will not be completed. Nevertheless, Capulet promptly brings forward the marriage from Thursday to Wednesday, in spite of Lady Capulet's protest (*We shall be short in our provision*, 38).

14 *harlotry*: Hussy.

15 *shrift*: Confession.

16 *How now, my headstrong! . . .*: Capulet now quite good-humouredly mocks his daughter.

17–22 *Where I have learned me to repent . . . ever ruled by you*: Juliet follows the Friar's instructions at IV.1.89 (*Go home, be merry, give consent | To marry Paris*). But she slightly overacts the part. Her ready compliance prompts Capulet to bring the marriage forward a day, a fatal mischance. Lady Capulet demurs (*No, not till Thursday. There is time enough*); but while fate hangs in the balance, Capulet overrides her. His impetuosity, like Romeo's, hastens the catastrophe.

19 *behests*: Commands.

20 *to fall prostrate*: Juliet here kneels, as is plain from Capulet's *Stand up* at 28, and from the stage direction in Q1: *She kneels down* (cf. III.5.158: *I beseech you on my knees*).

24 *knot*: Of marriage.

   tomorrow morning: Wednesday.

26 *becomèd*: Befitting.

32 *bound*: Indebted.

33 *closet*: Private room.

34 *sort*: Choose.

38 *provision*: Four syllables.

39 *'Tis now near night*: The day has been dramatically shortened.

40 *warrant*: Assure.

44 *They are all forth*: The servants are all out of the house, so that there is no reply to his *What, ho!*

IV.3

Juliet, now that the marriage-day has been brought forward from Thursday to Wednesday, must take the poison twenty-four hours before the Friar had planned (IV.1.89–117).

1–5 *Ay, those attires are best . . . cross and full of sin*: With courageous guile Juliet now addresses the *Ancient damnation* of III.5.236 as her *gentle Nurse*, like the *good Nurse* and *sweet Nurse* of II.5.28 and 54.

2 *leave me to myself tonight*: The Friar had instructed her to remain on her own at IV.1.91–2.

3–5 *For I have need of many orisons . . . full of sin*: This is one of many religious pretences of Juliet.

3 *orisons*: Prayers.

5 *cross*: Perverse.

7–8 *We have culled such necessaries | As are behoveful for our state tomorrow*: Presumably Juliet speaks with a double meaning: her mother thinks she is talking about her clothes, but Juliet's mind is on the vial of poison and on her dagger.

7 *culled*: Picked out.

8 *behoveful*: Appropriately needed.
   state: Public ceremony (of marriage).

12 *business*: Three syllables.

15 *a faint cold fear*: A fear causing faintness and chill.
   thrills: Shivers.

23 *This shall forbid it*: The knife she had shown to the Friar at IV.1.54.

29 *still been tried*: Always been proved by experience to be.

. . . *tried a holy man*: After this, some editors add the
line: *I will not entertain so bad a thought*, which derives
from Q1.

30–54 *How if, when I am laid into the tomb . . . dash out my
desperate brains*: Juliet's imaginings are an expansion
of what she herself had already described with horror
in IV.1.81–6.

30–32 *How if . . . | I wake before the time that Romeo | Come
. . .*: The Friar had promised that he and Romeo would
come to *watch thy waking* (IV.1.116), but the altering
of the time-plan prompts her fear, repeated in 46.

36, 45 *like*: Likely.

37 *conceit*: Fantasy.

39 *receptacle*: Accent on first syllable or third syllable.

42 *green in earth*: Freshly placed in the earth.

43 *festering*: Corrupting (of a dead body).

47 *mandrakes*: Famous plant in medicine (as an opiate)
and in superstition (sometimes known by its Italian
name '*mandragola*' or '*mandragora*'). Its forked root
sometimes gives it a resemblance to the lower part of
a man's body. It was supposed to utter a shriek as it
came out of the ground and to drive mad anyone who
uprooted it; it was therefore customary to tie it to a
dog by a piece of string in order to pull it out of the
ground.

48 *That*: So that.

49 *wake*: This is an emendation (in Q4) of *walk* in Q3.
But *walk* could be defended on the grounds that Juliet
has already spoken of waking (31, 46) and now imagines herself moving about in the vault.

53 *rage*: Madness.
great kinsman's bone: The *kinsman* is great (as in 'great
grandfather'), not the bone.

55–7 *O look! Methinks I see . . .*: She imagines she sees
Tybalt's ghost in some way attacking the intruding
Romeo as he comes to fetch her from the tomb.

57 *Stay*: Stop.

58–9 *Romeo, Romeo, Romeo. | Here's drink. I drink to thee*:
An alternative line *Romeo, I come. This do I drink to*

thee derives from Q1. Although it makes a smooth line and has been accepted by stage tradition, it cannot be said to have authority, because Q1 has a garbled version of Juliet's soliloquy. It can be argued that the Q2 version (here printed) is theatrically more appropriate: Juliet is becoming hysterical, and this is better expressed by her repetition of Romeo's name and the ghastly jest of *Here's drink* than by the ambiguous *Romeo, I come.*

IV.4

0 *with herbs*: From Q1.

2 *pastry*: Part of the kitchen-quarters where the 'paste' (dough or pastry) was made.

Enter Capulet: Presumably he comes back from seeing Paris (IV.2.44–5).

4 *curfew*: Used not only for an evening bell.

5 *baked meats*: Pies.

Angelica: Probably intended to be the name of the Nurse, for she is definitely associated with the *pastry* in 2 above and with the *pantry* in I.3.103, and it is she who replies to the present remark with her banter at 6–8. It is possible, however, that Capulet is addressing his wife or some servant. Angelica does not seem to have been used as a Christian name in Shakespeare's time; later it appears in Molière (Angélique) and in English Restoration comedies. If Capulet is addressing the Nurse, the effect is comic, for Angelica was the pagan princess of exquisite beauty and heartless coquetry who came to sow dissension among the Christian princes in Ariosto's *Orlando Furioso* (1532).

6–8 *Go, you cot-quean . . . this night's watching*: The Nurse speaks with unexpected familiarity or indeed impertinence to the master of the house. But she is a privileged retainer, of many years' service (as we gather from I.3). Cf. her interference at III.5.168–73.

6 *cot-quean*: A man who meddles with a woman's household matters.

8 *watching*: Keeping awake; similarly, *watched* (9) and *watching* (12); but Lady Capulet's *watch you from* in 12

means 'observe you closely' so that you don't have a
chance of 'doing that sort of thing'.

9–10 *I have watched ere now | All night . . .*: He hints at the
amorous exploits of his youth (like Justice Shallow in
Henry IV, Part II, III.2.206–32). Cf. his words at
I.5.22–5.

11–12 *Ay, you have been a mouse-hunt . . . from such watching
now*: Lady Capulet comments sharply or contemptu-
ously; or perhaps (since everyone is in a good mood)
merely jocularly; *in your time* is a characteristic reference to her husband's age.

11 *mouse-hunt*: Pursuer of women; 'mouse' was used as
an amorous word for a young woman. 'Mouse-hunt'
was also a name for a weasel.

13 *a jealous hood*: Jealous woman (as we say 'a bad hat'
or 'a big wig'). Some editors prefer to spell it 'jealous-
hood' (as if it were a word formed like 'womanhood'),
meaning 'jealousy'.

16 *drier logs*: See I.5.29, note.

18 *I have a head, sir, that will find out logs*: My wooden
head has a natural affinity for logs.

20 *Mass*: By the mass!
whoreson: Fellow (literally, bastard).

21 *loggerhead*: 'Fat-head', blockhead. Capulet enjoys his
pun on *logs* (16, 18).
Good Father: Later editions, perhaps correctly, amend
to *Good faith!*, the familiar oath.

22 *straight*: Immediately.

IV.5

1 *Fast*: Asleep.

4 *pennyworths*: Two syllables: penn'orths; small quanti-
ties (of sleep).

5–7 *Sleep for a week . . . rest but little*: The Nurse makes
the same lewd jokes about Juliet's coming experiences
with Paris as she did about those with Romeo
(II.5.75–6).

6 *set up his rest*: Ventured his whole stake (at cards), firmly
resolved (with bawdy double-meaning).

7–8 *God forgive me! | Marry, and amen*: As usual she

apologizes for her naughty jests. There are probably
further jests in *take you in your bed* (10) and *fright you
up* (11).

12 *and down again*: And then lain down on your bed again.

15 *weraday*: Well-a-day, alas!

16 *aqua vitae*: Brandy or other strong spirits (the Nurse's
   characteristic first appeal: cf. III.2.88: *Give me some
   aqua vitae*).

25–7 *she's cold, | Her blood is settled . . . long been separated*:
   These are the signs of apparent death described by the
   Friar in IV.1.95–103.

26 *settled*: Congealed.

28–9 *Death lies on her like an untimely frost | Upon the sweetest
   flower of all the field*: Shakespeare gives Capulet an
   appropriate solemnly trite image.

28 *untimely*: Out of season (like a frost in spring).

32 *Enter Friar Laurence and the County Paris*: The entry
   of the Musicians is not marked in Q2 and some editors
   follow Q4 in bringing them on here. But Q1 puts their
   entry after 95 and this may represent stage practice, at
   any rate at an early date.

35–9 *the night before thy wedding day | Hath death lain with
   thy wife . . .*: Capulet's elaborate imagining of death
   as his daughter's lover links with Juliet's words at I.5.135
   and III.2.137 and with Lady Capulet's curse at
   III.5.140, and prepares for Romeo's fantasy, later, about
   death as amorous of Juliet and as keeping her as his
   paramour (V.3.102–5).

37 *deflowerèd*: Four syllables.

38 *Death is my heir*: Juliet was his heiress-daughter. See
   46 below.

40 *living*: Means of living: that is, property (carrying on
   the idea of *heir* in 38 and *leave* in 40).

41 *long*: This is the Q1 reading. It has scarcely been for
   very long that he has been looking forward to this day,
   but the time-scheme is occasionally ignored for
   theatrical effect (cf. note on II.4.199). Q2 reads *love*
   (as vocative, addressing the body of Juliet); it is
   awkward, but possibly correct.

45 *in lasting labour*: In the unceasing toil.

46 *But one, poor one, one poor and loving child*: Cf. I.2.14–15, I.5.117 and III.5.164–7.

48 *catched*: Snatched.

55–61 *Beguiled, divorcèd, wrongèd, spited, slain!* . . . *murder our solemnity*: Both Paris and Capulet are thinking of the effects of Juliet's death on themselves.

56 *detestable*: Accent on first syllable.

60 *Uncomfortable*: Discomforting, depriving us of our consolation.

61 *To murder, murder our solemnity*: Spoil the festivity. Even in his grief, Capulet remembers that the marriage party to which he had been looking forward is spoilt.

65 *Confusion*: Being confounded by a blow of fate. But *confusions* in 66 means their disorderly behaviour in lamentation.

69 *Your part*: Her mortal body begotten by you her parents.

70 *his part*: Her immortal soul.

71 *promotion*: Advancement to the marriage state either in itself or by her alliance with Paris (four syllables).

72 *your heaven*: Your idea of bliss (as distinct from God's idea).

73 *is*: Emphasized.

76 *she is well*: The characteristic phrase for the dead.

77–8 *She's not well married that lives married long,* | *But she's best married that dies married young*: The Friar's views on marriage here seem to go beyond the usual limits of the pious 'contempt of life'. Probably Shakespeare is deliberately giving him nervous, exaggerated words, out of character, and pointing the dramatic irony. Contrast his advice to Romeo at II.6.14–15.

79 *your rosemary*: They are carrying rosemary for the wedding and are now to use it for the funeral (see stage direction after 95). The Nurse had associated rosemary and Romeo at II.4.202.

80–81 *and, as the custom is,* | *In all her best array bear her to church*: The Friar encourages them to do what he had expected (IV.1.109–12), to fall in with his plan for extricating Juliet.

82 *fond*: Weak and foolish (but there is a hint of the other meaning of *fond*, too affectionate).

83 *nature's tears are reason's merriment*: Common sense makes a mockery of our grief, natural though it is (because Juliet is now happy in heaven). In *Twelfth Night* (I.5.61–8) Feste had been given leave to prove Olivia a fool:

FESTE Good madonna, why mournest thou?
OLIVIA Good fool, for my brother's death.
FESTE I think his soul is in hell, madonna.
OLIVIA I know his soul is in heaven, fool.
FESTE The more fool, madonna, to mourn for your brother's
    soul being in heaven. Take away the fool, gentlemen.

85 *Turn*: Imperative.
  office: Function.
86 *instruments*: Musical instruments.
87 *wedding cheer*: Festive banquet.
88 *sullen*: Mournful.
90 *change them*: Change themselves (imperative).
91–3 *Sir, go you in; and, madam, go with him;* | *... unto her grave*: The Friar begins to take control, and hastens the funeral, to fit in with his own plans for Juliet's escape.
94–5 *The heavens do lour upon you for some ill.* | *Move them no more by crossing their high will*: A trite conclusion to his funeral sermon, which, in the circumstances, can only be regarded as somewhat hypocritical.
94 *lour*: Look angrily (rhymes with 'sour').
  for some ill: On account of some sin.
95 *Move them*: Move them to anger.
  Enter Musicians: For their point of entry see note on IV.5.32 above. The number of musicians and the allocation of their speeches is not clear from Q2. One of them is a Fiddler (see note on 99 below) and from 106 onwards the speech-prefixes show them as *Minstrels*. The Fiddler speaks 99 and 102, and probably 133–4, as this speaker is addressed as *Hugh Rebeck*; so a producer of the play could conveniently give him the

other speeches of the Second Musician (120–21 and 143–4). This would leave 136 for a tongue-tied Third Musician (the singer).

96–144 *Faith, we may put up our pipes and be gone . . . and stay dinner*: The farcical conclusion to this scene helps to keep well before our consciousness that Juliet is not really dead, and we move with greater apprehension into the tragic misunderstanding of the next scene.

96, 97 *put up our pipes*: 'Pack up'. The use of this common phrase does not imply that the musicians are pipers: they are apparently strings, if we are to judge by their names (Catling, Rebeck, Soundpost). See notes on IV.5.129, 132, 135.

99 *Ay, by my troth . . .*: This is attributed to *Fid.* (presumably for *Fiddler*, as in 102) in Q2, and this points to a jest in *the case may be amended*: his instrument case is worn and needs repairing; thus he can quibble on the Nurse's *pitiful case* (state of affairs) in 98.

99 *Exit Nurse*: This is the last we see of the Nurse. She can have no role in the tragic climax of the fifth act.

100–144 *musicians . . . stay dinner*: In Q2 line 99 is followed by the stage direction *Exit omnes* and the fiddler's jest *the case may be amended* sounds like an exit line. But the Musicians clearly remain onstage until the end of the scene. Moreover, *Exit omnes* is followed by the surprising stage direction *Enter Will Kemp*, which preserves the name of the principal comic actor in Shakespeare's company, who took the part of Peter. All this points to 100–144 as being an addition, providing an extra comic scene to take off the edge of lamentation for Juliet's supposed death.

100 *'Heart's ease'*: Popular song of the time. The music is preserved in John Playford's *The English Dancing Master* (1651) and is reprinted in E. W. Naylor, *Shakespeare and Music* (second edition, 1928) and in William Chappell, *Popular Music of the Olden Time* (reprinted 1965). The words of the song are lost.

103–4 *'My heart is full'*: The tune has not certainly been identified. In 1622 Q4 quotes the title of the song as '*My heart is full of woe*'; this is a line in *A Pleasant New Ballad of Two Lovers*, which may be old but is not known to have been printed until some time after the play.

104 *merry dump*: A dump is a sorrowful song or dance.

110 *give it you soundly*: Pay you out thoroughly (with a pun on *soundly*, as they are musicians).

112 *gleek*: Jeer.

112–13 *give you*: Nickname you.

113 *minstrel*: Somewhat derogatory name for musicians, as Mercutio had revealed at III.1.45: *dost thou make us minstrels?*

114–15 *serving-creature*: More contemptuous than 'serving-man'.

117 *carry no crotchets*: Endure none of your caprices (with a pun on the musical sense of *crotchets*: quarter notes).
    I'll re you, I'll fa you: Peter uses the names of the second and fourth notes on the musical scale as insulting verbs, probably punning on 'ray', 'beray' (befoul), and 'fay' (clear away filth).

118, 119 *note*: Punning on the musical sense: set to music.

119 *you note us*: With emphasis on *you* and *us*.

121 *put out*: Display (probably, rather than 'extinguish').

122 *dry-beat*: Cudgel (without drawing blood), as in III.1.78.

125–7, 140–41 *When griping griefs the heart doth wound . . .*: This is the beginning of a poem in praise of music, printed in *The Paradise of Dainty Devices* (1576) and there attributed to Richard Edwards (1523–66), a poet and playwright of the generation before Shakespeare. A contemporary setting has been preserved. The words in Shakespeare's text show small differences from those printed in 1576 ('Where griping grief . . . There music with . . . Is wont with speed to give redress').

129 *Simon Catling*: A catling is a catgut lute-string. Presumably Peter is inventing surnames for the musicians.

132, 135 *Pretty*: This is the Q1 reading. Q2 reads *Prates* (he prattles), which may be correct.

132 *Hugh Rebeck*: A rebeck (pronounced 'ree-beck') was a kind of three-stringed fiddle.

135 *James Soundpost*: The soundpost is the interior peg which supports the belly of a bass viol.

137 *I cry you mercy*: I beg your pardon.

137–8 *You are the singer. I will say for you*: Emphasis on *for*. The Third Musician (although called Soundpost) is a singer, and so not much of a speaker.

139 *for sounding*: As payment for their making music and for jingling (in their purses).

143 *Jack*: Low fellow (cf. II.4.149 and III.1.11).

144 *stay*: Wait for.

V.1

The place now changes to Mantua (see note on III.3.149), where Romeo had gone immediately after leaving Juliet on Tuesday morning (III.3.148–54, 169; III.5.15, 88–9; IV.1.117). Romeo has not appeared in the fourth act. An absence of the principal performer during approximately the third quarter of the play is usual in Shakespeare. It gives the actor a chance of a rest, which is especially needed if he is to give a good display of swordsmanship in the fifth act.

1 *flattering truth of sleep*: We are often inclined to accept premonitory dreams as truthful because they flatter us.

3 *My bosom's lord . . . in his throne*: Cupid in my heart, or (perhaps) my heart in my body.

10 *love itself possessed*: Love enjoyed in reality.

11 *love's shadows*: Dreams of love.
   booted: Indicates that he has just come from riding.

12 *Balthasar*: Accent on third syllable, like Italian 'Baldassare'.

13 *Dost thou not bring me letters from the Friar*: We learn from the next scene that the Friar's letter (which he had promised the audience he would send to Romeo at IV.1.113–14) has miscarried. Balthasar has reached Mantua with his (false) bad news first.

18 *Capel's monument*: Capulet may be abbreviated to Capel (III.1.2) and is usually so abbreviated when applied to the monument (burial vault); see V.3.127.

21 *presently*: Immediately.

23 *did leave it for my office*: Left me the duty of bringing
    you news (as arranged by the Friar, III.3.169–71).

24 *e'en*: Q2 has *in*, which probably represents a spelling
    of *e'en*. Q1 and later editions have *even*.
    I defy you, stars: Q2 reads *I deny you stars* and Q1 *I
    defy my stars*. Although *deny* has been defended by
    some editors and is found in the more authoritative
    text, it can hardly be doubted that *defy* gives the
    required meaning. Romeo is not making a denial of
    astrological influence, but stands in defiance of his
    ill-luck, in a posture which immediately makes his
    servant plead: . . . *have patience.* | *Your looks are pale
    and wild.* . . .

25 *ink and paper*: For the letter mentioned at V.3.23–4,
    275, 278, 286–90).

27 *patience*: Three syllables.

28–9 *import* | *Some misadventure*: Convey some (coming)
    tragic accident.

31 *Hast thou no letters to me from the Friar*: The question
    is repeated from 13 above.

38 *noted*: Noticed.

39 *overwhelming*: Beetling, overhanging.

40 *Culling of simples*: Selecting the ingredients of herbal
    medicines.

42–4 *And in his needy shop a tortoise hung,* | *An alligator
    stuffed, and other skins* | *Of ill-shaped fishes . . .*:
    Surviving pictures of apothecaries' shops show that
    tortoise shells, stuffed alligators, and fishes were among
    the usual furniture.

45 *beggarly account*: Wretched collection.

46 *bladders*: Used for holding liquids.

47 *cakes of roses*: Rose petals compressed into tight packs
    (used as perfume).

51 *Whose sale is present death*: For the sale of which, imme-
    diate death is the penalty. English law in Shakespeare's
    time did not, it seems, include this penalty, though it
    was usual on the Continent.

52 *caitiff wretch*: Wretched creature.
    would: Who would.

53 *forerun my need*: Anticipate my necessity. He puns on *need* and *needy* (next line).

59 *there is*: Here are.

    forty ducats: The ducat was a gold coin, slightly larger than a sixpence (or a dime). Romeo shows him the money in his hand – temptingly, for it is a considerable sum.

63–5 *And that the trunk may be discharged of breath . . . the fatal cannon's womb*: For the imagery, cf. II.6.10 and III.3.132.

64 *powder*: Gunpowder (to which Shakespeare elsewhere compares the poison aconite: *Henry IV, Part II*, IV.4.48).

66 *mortal*: Deadly.

66–7 *Mantua's law | Is death . . .*: Romeo had himself said this in 50–51.

67 *any he that utters them*: Any person who makes them available.

70 *starveth*: Produce the effects of hunger.

71 *Contempt*: By the world.

74 *this*: The money Romeo offers.

77 *Put this in any liquid thing you will*: But apparently Romeo eventually drinks it off neat (V.3.119–20).
    this: A vial of poison.

78–9 *if you had the strength | Of twenty men it would dispatch you straight*: The Apothecary's claim is borne out by Romeo at V.3.119–20.

85 *cordial*: Medicine (originally, for the heart).

V.2

In the previous scene (13 and 31) Romeo had twice specifically asked Balthasar whether he had a letter from Friar Laurence. Now is explained the unlucky chance whereby the expected letter did not reach him.

1 *brother*: Friar.

5–12 *Going to find a bare-foot brother out . . . there was stayed*: The confused syntax of Friar John's story suggests his anxiety.

5 *bare-foot brother*: Franciscan.

6 *associate*: Accompany. It was usual for members of the

religious orders to travel in pairs.

8 *searchers of the town*: 'Health officers', who were appointed to view dead bodies and report causes of death.

11 *Sealed up the doors*: This was the common practice in London during the plague, to enforce quarantine.

12 *stayed*: Stopped.

16 *infection*: Four syllables.

17 *brotherhood*: Franciscan order.

18 *nice*: Trivial.
    charge: Weighty matters.

19 *dear import*: Serious importance.

21 *crow*: Crowbar.

25 *beshrew me much*: Reprove me severely.

26 *accidents*: Happenings.

V.3

0 *sweet water*: Perfumed water (see 14 below).

1–9 *Give me thy torch, boy. Hence, and stand aloof . . .*:
    There seems to be no adequate cause for Paris's anxiety,
    but this speech helps to create the atmosphere of
    suspense.

3 *yew trees*: With *churchyard* (5 and 11) and *graves* (6)
    help to establish the scene.
    lay thee all along: Lie flat on the ground.

6 *Being loose*: Because the soil is loose.

10 *stand*: Stay.

11 *adventure*: Take the risk.

12–17 *Sweet flower, with flowers . . .*: Paris's little rhymed
    poem and flowers to express his sorrow for Juliet are
    in striking contrast with Romeo's despair and poison.

12 *Sweet flower*: Juliet.
    bridal bed: Lady Capulet had said at III.5.140: *I would
    the fool were married to her grave!*

13 *canopy*: Covering (of her bed of death).

14 *sweet water*: See note on stage direction above.

15 *wanting*: Lacking.

16 *obsequies*: Funeral rites.
    keep: Observe regularly.

30–32 *But chiefly to take thence from her dead finger . . . In dear employment*: This is merely Romeo's pretence, to deceive his servant about his real intention, which is suicide.

32 *dear*: Personally important.

33 *jealous*: Suspicious.

36 *hungry churchyard*: Because death has a ravenous appetite; cf. 45–8 below.

41–2 *Take thou that. | Live, and be prosperous*: Again, as with the Mantuan apothecary, Romeo thinks of the welfare of others.

41 *that*: Money (perhaps his purse).

43 *For all this same*: All the same, in spite of all this.

44 *doubt*: Suspect.

45 *detestable*: Accent on first syllable.
  womb: Belly (rather than the female organ).

46 *dearest morsel*: Juliet.

48 *in despite*: Defiantly.
  more food: His own body.

52 *villainous shame*: Such as stealing parts of bodies for purposes of witchcraft.

53, 56, 69 *apprehend*: Arrest.

59 *Good gentle youth*: Romeo does not recognize Paris until 75, after he has killed him.

60 *these gone*: Juliet, Tybalt, and others, buried in the tombed.

65 *armed against myself*: Because he brings the poison for suicide.

67 *bid*: Past tense.

68 *conjuration*: Warning entreaty. Q2 reads *commiration* and Q1 *conjurations*. An interesting conjecture is 'commination', meaning 'threatenings'.

75 *Mercutio's*: The only mention of Mercutio after his death scene in III.1.

80 *him talk of Juliet*: Emphasis on *him*, Paris. See 73 above.

83 *triumphant*: Glorious.

84 *lantern*: (Architectural) superstructure with openings giving light.

86 *feasting presence*: Festival presence-chamber.

87 *Death*: The dead body of Paris.
  a dead man: Himself – by anticipation.

89 *keepers*: Nurses or gaolers.

90, 91 *lightning*: Juliet had spoken of their love as a lightning (II.2.119–20). Perhaps the *lightning* in 90 is a pun on the 'lightening of the spirits'.

92–6 *Death, that hath sucked the honey . . . is not advancèd there*: Seeing Juliet's lifelike appearance in (supposed) death Romeo almost stumbles upon the truth; and again at 101–2. This adds a feeling of suspense, almost a ray of hope, to the agony with which we listen to Romeo's suicide-speech.

101 *cousin*: Tybalt.

102 *Why art thou yet so fair*: See note on 92–6.

102–5 *Shall I believe | That unsubstantial death is amorous . . .*: See note at IV.5.35–9 on death as Juliet's lover.

102–3 *Shall I believe*: Before this Q2 has a superfluous *I shall believe*. This is probably one of Shakespeare's 'false starts', accidentally not deleted in his manuscript. Cf. I.2.15, IV.1.110 and V.3.106–10 (just below).

105 *to be his paramour*: This is a curious hint of the classical legend of Proserpina, who was abducted by Pluto (or Dis) and taken to Hades to be his consort.

106–10 *For fear of that . . . everlasting rest*: In Q2 these lines are printed as follows:

(a) For feare of that I still will staie with thee,
(b) And neuer from this pallat of dym night.
(c) Depart againe, come lye thou in my arme,
(d) Heer's to thy health, where ere thou tumblest in.
(e) O true Appothecarie!
(f) Thy drugs are quicke. Thus with a kisse I die.
(g) Depart againe, here, here, will I remaine,
(h) With wormes that are thy Chamber-maides: O here
(i) Will I set vp my euerlasting rest:

It seems that Shakespeare, having written lines (c) to (f), cancelled them and started again at (g). But the lines were imperfectly deleted in his manuscript, and so *both* versions came to be printed. He transferred parts of (d), (e) and (f) to lines 119–20 in the text.

107 *palace*: Q2 has *pallat* which might represent 'pallet bed'. Although 'pallet of dim night' is a strained phrase, it could be right. The change to *palace* was made in the printing of Q3.

110 *set up my everlasting rest*: Make my resolve to remain here for ever (with a pun on *rest*, as in IV.5.6).

115 *dateless bargain*: Everlasting agreement (one without a terminable date).
engrossing: Monopolizing.

116 *bitter conduct . . . unsavoury guide*: The vial of poison.
conduct: Conductor.

117 *Thou desperate pilot*: Himself; or perhaps his own soul.

118 *bark*: His body.

119 *Here's to my love*: Cf. Juliet's *I drink to thee* at IV.3.59. Presumably the Apothecary's poison had been handed to Romeo in a bottle, corresponding to the *vial* (IV.1.93 and IV.3.20) given by the Friar to Juliet. But at V.3.161 below Juliet finds *A cup, closed in my true love's hand*. This may indicate some stage business by which Romeo pours the poison from a vial into a beaker and so drinks a toast to his love. It is not easy to drink with stage-dignity from a small bottle.

119–20 *O true Apothecary!* | *Thy drugs are quick*: The Apothecary had claimed a speedy effect for his poison in V.1.77–9.

120 *Thy drugs are quick. Thus with a kiss I die*: From the frequency of verbal quibbles in the play, even at the most serious moments, we should expect that the other meaning of *quick* ('alive') would be brought to mind by its opposite idea in Romeo's *die* (which could itself also mean 'to experience the sexual pleasure'). Probably such paradoxes are irrelevant here.

121 *speed*: Protector.

122 *stumbled at graves*: This refers to the superstition about stumbling when taking a decisive step.

125 *vainly*: Uselessly.

136 *unthrifty*: Unlucky.

137–9 *As I did sleep under this yew tree here . . . my master slew him*: Balthasar appears to be prevaricating. He has seen

the death of Paris at Romeo's hands, but pretends it
was a dream.

142 *masterless*: Abandoned by their owners.

145 *unkind*: Unnatural (accent on first syllable).

148 *comfortable*: Bringing fortitude and consolation.

151–7 *I hear some noise. Lady, come from that nest . . . sisterhood of holy nuns*: The Friar's words as he faces the
real disaster are strikingly different from his formal
speech after the supposed death of Juliet (IV.5.65–83).
His humbled admission that *A greater power than we
can contradict | Hath thwarted our intents* (153–4) relates
ironically to his hypocritical couplet at IV.5.94–5.

161–70 *What's here? A cup, closed in my true love's hand? . . .
and let me die*: Juliet has a short dying speech, in
contrast to Romeo's long one. Probably Shakespeare
could not altogether trust his boy-actor to maintain
the tension for long. (In his plays only Cleopatra,
among the women, is allowed to take her time dying.
Cordelia is carried onstage already dead.)

161 *cup*: See note on V.3.119.

162 *timeless*: Untimely.

163 *O churl*: Addressing Romeo.

166 *restorative*: The kiss she gives him.

169 *happy*: Opportunely found.

170 *rust*: Some editors prefer the reading *rest*, which comes
from Q1. But *rust* has better authority and is more vivid.

173 *attach*: Arrest.

176 *two days*: The Friar had spoken of forty-two hours at
IV.1.105.

179–80 *ground . . . ground*: He puns on the meanings 'earth'
and 'reason'.

179 *woes*: Woeful creatures (the three dead bodies).

181 *circumstance*: Detailed surrounding facts.

187 *Enter the Prince and attendants*: This is the third
symmetrical assembly of the two families and the
Prince, this time over the dead bodies of their heirs.
Cf. I.1.80 and III.1.140.

194 *your ears*: Some editors emended to 'our'. This gives
an easier meaning, but *your* makes sense.

203 *mista'en*: Gone away.
   his house: Its sheath.

204 *Montague*: Romeo.

207 *my old age*: On Lady Capulet's age see note on I.3.73–4.

209 *down*: Dead on the ground.

210 *my wife is dead tonight*: Lady Montague is a small part:
   she only speaks three lines in the play. Presumably it
   was doubled with a part required in this last act
   (perhaps the Page) and so Shakespeare makes a virtue
   out of the necessity and gives an extra touch of pathos
   by killing her off. Q1 even adds: *And young Benvolio
   is deceasèd, too*. But who would notice the absence of
   Benvolio, Montague's nephew, at this moment? It is
   possible that Q1 here preserves a line subsequently
   deleted by Shakespeare as an unnecessary explanation,
   even though the actor of Benvolio was required for
   another part in this last scene.

211 *exile*: Accent on second syllable.

214 *O thou untaught*: He chides his son, with affectionate
   pity, for his ill manners.

216 *mouth of outrage*: Utterances of passionate grief.

219 *general of your woes*: Leader in lamentation.

220 *even to death*: Even though sorrow were to kill me.

221 *let mischance be slave to patience*: Let our patience
   control our misfortunes.
   patience: Three syllables.

222 *suspicion*: Four syllables.

223 *the greatest, able to do least*: The most liable to be
   suspected, although actually the weakest.

225 *make against me*: Weigh to my discredit, implicate me.

226 *impeach and purge*: Accuse and exonerate.

229–69 *I will be brief, for my short date of breath . . . severest
   law*: This long narrative by the Friar is often omitted
   in modern productions as being unnecessary. But it is
   needed if there is to be a strong emphasis on the reconciliation of the two families. It is noticeable that the
   one thing the Friar omits in his narrative is his motive
   of reconciling the families (see II.3.87–8).

229 *date of breath*: Period of life allowed.

233 *stolen*: Secret.

234 *doomsday*: Day of death.

236 *For whom, and not for Tybalt, Juliet pined*: Cf. Paris's belief at 50–51 above.

237 *You*: The Capulets.

    siege of grief: Assailing grief.

247 *as*: On.

248 *borrowed*: Temporarily taken, since she was not dead.

253 *prefixèd*: Prearranged.

255 *closely*: Secretly.

260 *She wakes*: A vivid present tense.

261 *patience*: Three syllables.

266 *privy*: Accessory in the secret.

268 *his*: Its.

270 *still*: Always.

273 *in post*: Post haste.

275 *letter*: See 23–4 above.

    early: Early in the morning (see 23 above).

280 *made your master*: Was your master doing.

284 *by and by*: At once.

289 *therewithal*: With the poison.

293 *your joys*: Their children, Juliet and Romeo.

    with love: By means of their love.

294 *winking at*: Turning a blind eye to.

295 *a brace of kinsmen*: Mercutio and Paris.

297 *This is my daughter's jointure*: The hand of Montague he is holding (that is, reconciliation) is the only marriage-settlement which, as the father of Juliet, he expects from the bridegroom's father.

299 *raise her statue*: He does not necessarily mean an upright statue. See 303 below. Q2 reads *raie* (array), which some editors have defended. The change to *raise* was made, apparently independently, in Q4 and in F.

301 *at such rate be set*: Be put at such a high value

303 *As rich shall Romeo's by his lady's lie*: Shakespeare is thinking of the recumbent effigies of man and wife on Renaissance tombs (like those of the Cloptons in Stratford-upon-Avon church).